# GIVE US

# TOMORROW

# NOW

# GIVE US
# TOMORROW
## NOW

### ALAN DURBAN'S
### MISSION IMPOSSIBLE

DAVID SNOWDON

First published by Pitch Publishing, 2018

Pitch Publishing
A2 Yeoman Gate
Yeoman Way
Worthing
Sussex
BN13 3QZ
www.pitchpublishing.co.uk
info@pitchpublishing.co.uk

ISBN 978-1-78531-448-3

Typesetting and origination by Pitch Publishing
Printed in Great Britain by TJ International

# Contents

'This is a top-class club and we need top-class players. I am looking for quality and character. The club is about tomorrow.'

(Alan Durban, 1981)

'He always had a plan, and any team he sent out would usually be hard to beat. With Alan Durban, I was never sitting in the dressing room feeling as if the team could not go out and win. We always had a chance.'

(Gary Rowell, 2017)

'Alan Durban was the best man-manager I've had in my life – by far. We had a good team; it could have become a great one.'

(Leighton James, 2018)

# Acknowledgements

The road to completing this book has been fraught with obstacles, and the many hours of meticulous research, compiling, and writing has been completed through days of both sickness and health; in short, the process involved 'a lot of hard yakka'.

For his cooperation in enabling me to fill research gaps, I am particularly grateful to Neil Watson at the *Sunderland Echo*. His overall helpfulness smoothed the path.

I would also like to acknowledge the assistance of the staff at Sunderland Local Studies Library, and L & L Braines.

Within the text or bibliography, I have endeavoured to cite all quoted sources.

A number of people's memories shaped the narrative into a more complete and rounded entity, and I would like to express appreciation to Colin West, Gary Rowell, Chris Stevens, and Leighton James for taking time to answer questions and convey their 'insider' views of events at Sunderland Football Club in the early 1980s – I believe we all enjoyed reminiscing about the 'good old days'.

I thank Pitch Publishing, Olner Design, and Ivan Butler for their work in producing an elegant finished article, as well as Mirror Pix.

I appreciate the encouragement given by Geoff Nash, and the advice supplied by authors Nick Szczepanik, Graham Denton, and Luke G Williams.

The mixture of moral support, practical suggestions, and prayers supplied by June Talbot and Christine Rodgers was welcome and comforting.

Finally, I thank Alan Durban for giving his blessing for the book at an early stage and for taking the time to respond to the occasional queries I posed.

With this book, I hope that I have managed to accomplish a degree of that fine blend and balance between, what Virginia Woolf termed, the 'granite-like solidity of truth' and 'rainbow-like intangibility of personality'.

## Flashback: Some Like It Hot

It was the summer of 1981, and Alan Durban was enjoying a tour of Barbados with his Stoke City squad, the trip a reward for defying expectations and finishing in the top half of the First Division the previous season. Durban, however, was not a man to rest on past laurels. Rather than luxuriating in a glow of satisfaction at exceeding the modest demands of a chairman and board of directors with whom he enjoyed a first-class working relationship, this was one manager contemplating a fresh challenge.

The mission, should he choose to accept it, was to take charge at Sunderland; to relinquish the relative comfort of working at a club not harbouring unrealistic expectation levels and, in exchange, thrust himself into the white heat of a north-east football hotbed where expectation and realism rarely sauntered along hand-in-hand.

Sunderland had narrowly escaped relegation on the last day of the season with an unlikely 1-0 win at a Liverpool side preoccupied with preparations for an upcoming European Cup final against Real Madrid. Mick Docherty had been the caretaker at the helm at Anfield after Ken Knighton, the man who had guided the Roker Park team back into the First Division in 1980, was dismissed with only four matches remaining.

Knighton had not enjoyed a good working relationship with recently elected chairman Tom Cowie, and eventually the millionaire local businessman oversaw the manager's sacking. Nevertheless, a dismissal at such a pivotal point in the fixture list had been surprising. The team had not dropped into the bottom three but, after another disappointing away defeat (ironically at Durban's Stoke), Knighton was not given the opportunity to preserve the team's top-tier status. The seemingly illogical timing of the sacking would become a recurring feature at the club in future years. As far as Durban's own decision-making was concerned, there was one predominant feature he was abundantly aware of; the passionate intensity of feeling in the Sunderland area and glare of attention that would be focussed on his efforts to revive the fortunes of a club that had often been somewhat complacently labelled as 'sleeping giants' while they yo-yoed between First and Second Divisions.

The challenge was appealing to such a natural sporting competitor as Durban, a man who had been on the county cricket club books at Glamorgan, Derbyshire and Shropshire, as well as playing tennis for Shropshire and being a low-handicap golfer – his energy also allowed him to cram in games of squash.

The Welshman had started his playing career at Cardiff City before making almost 350 appearances for Derby County, scoring 91 goals, starting as an inside-forward before reverting to midfield. At international level, he won 27 caps for Wales between 1966 and 1972 (captaining the team to boot). He finished his playing career at Shrewsbury Town and this would be the club where he would serve his managerial apprenticeship, leading them to promotion, before graduating to take charge at Second Division Stoke City.

Early in 1978, Stoke had been dumped out of the FA Cup by Blyth Spartans and had conspicuously failed to mount a promotion challenge. They were stagnating, but Durban arrived and supplied the required discipline and tactical shrewdness. He also brought a keen eye for spotting talent, and gave a clutch of young prospects the opportunity to establish themselves. Under his three-year tenure, Paul Bracewell, Adrian Heath, and Lee Chapman had matured into first-team regulars. From a fan's perspective, most appreciated that Durban had grabbed the club by the scruff of the neck when they were in the doldrums, and had moulded the team into a disciplined unit containing a blend of seasoned campaigners and youthful energy.

Top-flight status was restored in his first full season but, once the elation had worn off, 'short memory syndrome' kicked into gear. Despite having finished in a creditable 11th position, some fans had grown dissatisfied with mere consolidation. Many regular supporters appreciated that Durban had stabilised the club and that hard-fought results were necessary in order for the club to progress to the manager's next planned stage. His starlets promised future improvement, but much of the Stoke public were tardy in displaying enthusiasm.

Stacking up against the element of local apathy he detected, Durban considered the excellent working set-up he enjoyed with the Stoke hierarchy. He would also need to dispel lingering worries over his two daughters' education as they embarked on their O Level studies. From a purely footballing perspective, could he succeed where so many had either failed or declined to attempt the feat? Dare he? Would the dormant volcano erupt with him at the helm?

Two managerial greats hovered into view. Ipswich Town manager Bobby Robson's comments that the Manchester United vacancy had not interested him but an offer of the Sunderland position had made him waver made a huge impression on Durban. And there was Brian Clough. The significant influence of that idiosyncratic and mercurial figure had presided over most of Durban's time at Derby. Clough, who had been in the throes of establishing himself as a Sunderland goalscoring legend when injury had prematurely ended his playing days, had waxed lyrical about north-east fervour and playing talent. Had Clough ever shirked a managerial challenge in favour of the 'soft option'?

The potential of Sunderland Football Club throbbed. It was almost palpable. Durban had witnessed the phenomenal devotion that had emanated from the visiting Sunderland support the previous season not only when they came to Stoke but when he had been on a watching brief at Coventry as Knighton's team had earned plaudits for their entertaining approach but finished with another defeat. It was the level of loyal support that fired Durban's enthusiasm, and he relished the challenge to harness this juggernaut. There was untapped energy here.

Mulling matters over in the tropical climate, Durban slowly, but unflinchingly, made the momentous decision. He would go where others had feared to tread; he would occupy the hotter-than-hot seats that that had been reserved for him on Wearside in the Roker Park manager's office and dugout. On Thursday, 11 June 1981, Alan Durban resigned as manager of Stoke City.

## Enter The 'Miracles' Man

As far as the Sunderland public were concerned, once the club's interest in making Durban their next manager had been revealed, matters moved relatively swiftly. There had been much media speculation that the deal would hinge on whether his former right-hand man at Shrewsbury, Richie Barker, was prepared to leave his assistant role at Wolves and renew their partnership on Wearside.

Having been deprived of their esteemed manager, however, the Stoke board moved for Barker and he accepted their offer to take up the reins. Working in a relatively successful spell under John Barnwell at Molineux, Barker's stock had risen, and this provided some consolation for the large portion of disappointed Stoke players and fans sorry to hear the news of Durban's departure.

Not for the first or last time, newspaper reports were wide of the mark; Barker's non-accompaniment was not the deal-breaker portrayed. It was the fervour of the Sunderland fans that had clinched Durban's decision, and he had even recommended Barker to the Stoke board as management material. On Friday, 12 June, the day after his resignation, Durban drove up from the Potteries and strode into Roker Park to be unveiled as the new Sunderland manager. On his arrival, as he walked towards the main entrance, photographers took the snap that would adorn the front page of the local evening newspaper. Holding his jacket and tie, and with loosened shirt-collar, Durban stood bathed in sunlight, exuding the aura of a man ready to get down to work. Allied with his proven management experience and tactical acumen, the overriding perception was that here stood a man who would, both physically and metaphorically, roll his sleeves up and graft for the cause.

As Durban was officially unveiled at the ensuing press conference, he chose his words carefully to convey a feeling of cautious optimism and to evade a situation where over-expectant supporters, starved of top-flight success, got carried away with unrealistic dreams of mixing it with the 'big boys' and challenging for major honours straight away, 'Don't expect miracles overnight. I hope the supporters will realise that we have the basis of a side to build on, but I am coming into a very tense situation – I would prefer to use the word tense rather than pressure – but I am confident that we can develop on what we have here.'

The chairman welcomed Durban, remarking, 'I have checked on his track record and am very impressed with his achievements. He has worked minor miracles on a tight budget and I believe he is qualified to take over a club of our status.'

Was this the first glimmer, on the very first afternoon of a new working relationship, that manager and board were not reciting the same mantra? Despite Durban's protestation that he could not transform a team of perennial strugglers overnight, Cowie had declared that here was a man who '*has* worked minor miracles'. Even an ardent Sunderland supporter might have afforded themselves a wry chuckle at the chairman's inflated reference to 'a club of our status' as he offered a stinting concession that Durban was adequately qualified to take the helm at such a 'big club', but most in the game felt that it was the club that had struck lucky.

Many supporters were not old enough to recall the last time that Sunderland had managed to persuade one of their top short-listed targets to assume the Roker hot seat. Not only that, here was an established *current* First Division manager who had proven his ability to keep a team in a relatively comfortable top-flight position. This was a situation almost unheard of at Sunderland who had all too often witnessed a string of convenient stopgap appointments or simply figures who failed to excite anticipation, and who usually affirmed these misgivings by producing a correspondingly disappointing level of performance before exiting.

Amazingly, for a man possessing such a wealth of experience, and in his managerial prime, Durban was only 39; he would hit 40 the following month. This job was not one for those who wished to preserve their youthful looks, but Durban touched on part of his motivation for moving to the north-east, 'I felt the enthusiasm and progress created within the club was not accepted by enough of the Stoke public. As a result I have felt a lack of enthusiasm myself.' Enthusiasm, devotion, mania; Durban would certainly feel all that now in abundance. The new arrival spoke of his immediate vision of attainable goals and, crucially, also identified those that should be considered non-starters. For the present at least, the primary aim would be one of consolidation, 'It would be stupid to talk about winning the championship but I can promise you Sunderland will do a lot better than they did last year.'

As an incoming prime minister might be taken to task over any deviation from victory-day pledges, Durban may have later regretted issuing what amounted to an assurance. Although the *Sunderland Echo* ran with the new man's 'Don't Expect Miracles' headline message, some supporters keenly latched on to the prospect of 'a lot better' immediate future. After all, a 'promise' had been issued that, for the majority of Sunderland followers, implied finishing well clear of the bottom three and not having to endure the emotional turmoil of a nail-biting final game with their First Division status teetering on the brink of the abyss. Yes, mid-table paradise; that would do very nicely Mr Durban, thanks.

Not one to court popularity, Durban went on to spell out the policy he envisioned, 'I will do what I think best, and if that means not playing entertaining football away from home then that is what we will do. I am not paid to entertain and my sole aim will be to get points.'

This was not unfeeling; it should be remembered that a large percentage of supporters would gladly swap a pulsating, unfortunate 3-2 defeat for a scrappy 1-0 win any day. Durban underlined his point, 'Sunderland were one of the best sides for entertainment last season but it got Ken Knighton the sack.' He might have added that an attack-minded policy had not compensated Sunderland fans for the frustrating repetitiveness of bright performances ending in dismal results.

It had been 60 days since the sacking of Knighton, who had been in charge of team affairs for 22 months and was still only 37.

One 'bright young thing' had made way for someone with similar attributes, but Durban was the finished article. He had the nous, and he possessed foresight. That vision for the future was evident as he reproached the club for a past major failing, 'Too many top-class players have left the north-east over the years and it is time this was stopped. You can go back years and reel off the names of players who have gone on to carve out international careers.'

Durban proclaimed caution, and had been plain-speaking enough to chide and mildly rebuke in crucial areas, but he also instilled confidence and positivity for the future. It seemed appropriate that this day of new beginnings should also see the publication of the forthcoming season's fixture-list. Sunderland would start against the two teams that had recently vied to be crowned champions, Durban taking his team to face Bobby Robson's Ipswich at Portman Road followed by a Roker Park baptism against Ron Saunders's Aston Villa. In these heady days, rather than provoking trepidation, the feeling generated by these opening fixtures was more of tingling anticipation. Sunderland had got their man, and the chosen one inspired confidence. These were days when optimism prevailed – and the sun shone.

## Send Back the Clowns

The new man's first-day comments had served notice of his fundamental priority 'to get points', and that providing entertainment would be a secondary concern. Such a stance did little to dispel a major myth that hung around Durban's neck; one that led some to think that a brand of drab, negative football would be the fare on offer for the coming season. The misconception sprung, primarily, from Durban's peevish riposte to some antagonistic journalists grilling him about his team's unambitious set-up in a defeat at Highbury the previous year. The version of that infamous remark subsequently bandied about usually has Durban 'growling', 'If you want entertainment, go and watch clowns.' The practice of trawling out and perpetuating the misquotation, while completely ignoring the context, has continued from many hacks and pundits lazily seeking to convey general sentiments about negative tactics.

Let the record be set straight. Are we sitting comfortably? Stoke arrived at Highbury in September 1980 having suffered a couple of heavy defeats in their preceding two away fixtures, and Durban's defensively-geared formation sought to stop the rot. It was very much a case of a manager applying a practical 'horses for courses' approach for that day's specific task. It was not an instance of some malevolently negative policy that he extended to home matches, or a tactic employed for every away trip. The ploy failed to avert a 2-0 defeat however and, at the post-match press gathering, an already fractious Durban eventually looked a plaintive journalist in the eye, saying, 'Who are we running soccer for? If you want entertainment, you could go out and get a bunch of clowns. If obtaining pleasure from matches is the only concern, then you could get rid of all the coaches and let the players go out and get on with it.' Anarchy!

Of course, it was the reference to clowns that was appropriated and twisted into a tasty sound-bite by the press and media. The butchered rendition of Durban's vexatious retort subsequently became an almost ubiquitous accompaniment to outpourings from football 'purists' bemoaning the state of the game. This was, and is, unfair. In subsequent years, many a manager has emerged fresh from suffering the agonies of an end-to-end, incident-packed match, and declared: "It was a good game for the neutrals". Being partisan shifts one's perspective dramatically. A team's true supporters will fret and panic throughout what non-committed spectators or armchair viewers rate an 'exciting' or 'thrilling' contest. Ultimately, some football 'experts' might sniffily adopt high-minded principles, and preach for the masses to be served an entertaining product, neglecting the immediate welfare of your beloved team. But, for the devoted, those who have a vested emotional involvement, it is not so simple.

Harking back to that 1980 episode, there is also the overlooked fact that Stoke's trip to Highbury was the first of two consecutive away fixtures. Seven days later, Durban marshalled his team to a 2-1 win over Malcolm Allison's Manchester City at Maine Road with goals from Loek Ursem and Lee Chapman. The facts plainly refute the many subsequent disparaging and misguided comments about 'clowns'.

Adding fuel to the myth for Durban's new congregation on Wearside was that two months after 'Clown-gate' Stoke were the opposition in one of the poorest matches seen at Sunderland that season as the crowd endured a goalless stalemate. However, supporters needed to accept that a lacklustre home team were as much to blame as Durban's visitors that day (to the extent that Knighton ordered his squad in for Sunday training). Nevertheless, it should have been apparent that, in the new manager's initial season, fans going to Roker Park would be foolhardy to expect a thrill-a-minute 'pleasure dome' extravaganza.

## Down to Work: The Machine Needs Parts

As Durban settled down to assessing the situation he had inherited, one of the initial tasks he earmarked for attention was to check on the physical condition of two of the club's prime playing assets, Shaun Elliott and Stan Cummins, who were spending the summer playing in the North American Soccer League. Experienced goalkeeper Barry Siddall had also been allowed to play with Vancouver Whitecaps. It had become a trend for clubs to generate extra income by 'leasing' their star men to USA franchises but, depending on their respective teams' progress in the play-offs, most players returned to Britain after the start of the domestic league programme.

This practice was one that Durban strongly disapproved of, and it was clear that a commercially motivated decision had been made at board level to the detriment of the playing side. An extra bugbear for Durban was that even if returning injury-free, there was the issue of men being physically jaded by playing through the year with little break.

In addition, Football League club chairmen had inexplicably voted to start the season two weeks later than usual, with a blank fixture weekend in November thrown in to help England prepare for their final World Cup qualifier. To extend a season's duration in what was to be a World Cup summer (1982) was baffling in itself, and made no allowance for the risk of a fixture backlog caused by a bad winter. Therefore, Durban was nonplussed by the schedule organised for the club's pre-season build-up, 'The players are due to report back on 23 July and expect to be match fit by 1 August, but there is no way I want them in peak condition by then with the league programme not starting until 29 August.' From the word 'go', the Sunderland executive hierarchy had succeeded in riling Durban with dubious decision-making that hindered his new team's preparations for the season ahead.

Sporting attention in the early summer of '81 had focussed on Ian Botham's battle to hold on to the England cricket captaincy for the Test series against Australia. Botham claimed not to be worried about being appointed one match at a time, 'Pressure doesn't bother me.' That was one story that would run. Although a keen cricketer, Durban was more concerned at the estimated late arrivals of Elliott and Cummins, 'It could be that we have to operate without two main cogs – and how much machinery can do that – then pitch them straight in the minute they arrive back.'

Another experienced player unavailable for immediate selection was Ian Bowyer. The midfielder had won league championship and two European Cup medals in the past three years with Nottingham Forest, and had been Knighton's penultimate signing in January. Rarely ruled out at Forest, Bowyer had sustained a serious knee injury in a March training session and now Durban regretfully reported that the medical team were 'unable to say how long he will be out'.

Ever a pragmatist, Durban turned his attention to matters he could do something about. Two pre-season fixtures were arranged against local rivals Newcastle United. Despite not possessing the insane intensity of later years, these Wear-Tyne 'derby' matches would serve as spicy appetisers before the start of the new campaign.

Another issue that Durban addressed was the appointment of an experienced captain. Defender Rob Hindmarch had been handed the position the previous season aged 19, and Durban had been scrutinising available TV footage. His admission that he would be seeking a change in on-field leader did not represent a criticism of the rookie skipper, Durban explaining that the switch was natural, 'Young Hindmarch is only learning the trade himself. From what I saw on the video recordings there was just no one to take the game by the scruff of the neck and slow it down.' Durban had been particularly disturbed at viewing the team's lack of resilience and caution as they conceded an injury-time goal in their final home game against relegation rivals Brighton.

Talking calmly and with common sense was all very well, but the one thing guaranteed to excite the imagination of fans and press alike was speculation over new signings. A couple of weeks into the job, a gaggle of reporters posed the inevitable questions about prospective breakthroughs in the transfer market. Durban responded by saying that he would not be 'poaching' from Stoke, as well as outlining his view on bringing foreign players to the country, 'I am a great believer in temperament and think the best players suited to our game are from Holland and Germany who have similar climates. I am not over-enthralled with the South Americans as it takes them too long to settle down and, basically, they are not suited to our game. They are great passers of a ball in hot climates but our game is based on running.'

Durban was unlikely to face any dissent on airing this opinion as Sunderland fans' memories were still raw over the record signing of Argentinean Claudio Marangoni for over £300,000 in 1979, and the player's failure to make an impact had hastened the demise of Knighton.

Durban favoured scouring the market much closer to home and, although not openly criticising the club's scouting system, he mused, 'It is amazing how few Scots are here and yet Sunderland are the nearest First Division club.' He then followed up remarks made on his arrival about the top local talent that had been permitted to slip through the club's fingers, lamenting, 'It is a disgrace that so many lads are going out of the north-east and it is time that it was stopped.

'For this to happen it is essential that the first team be successful so that boys want to play for the local team.' These were laudable ideals, but also flagged up a potential 'catch 22' situation – hoping that a young prospect's decision-making would not be predominantly swayed by the glittery attraction of how successful a club appeared.

In addition to strengthening the team, Durban was eager to secure at least one signing that would increase the club's general cachet, 'The fact that there are no internationals here reflects on the lack of success in the area and, as we are the only club in the First Division without one, we must do something about it.'

Presumably, Durban was referring to a lack of current internationals, or the seven England caps held by right-back Steve Whitworth were being harshly neglected.

## Do Things My Way (The Right Way)

Clearly irked that three of his senior players were playing in the USA, Durban emphatically declared, 'The position will not repeat itself. I am very much against players continuing to be involved in matches when they should be relaxing and recharging the batteries. It's too much of a strain.' Durban soon learned that Cummins was out of action with an ankle injury, and promptly wrote to the player suggesting he terminate his Seattle contract and return to the UK.

The manager also sought to remedy the inadequate scouting arrangements that he blamed for the club failing to secure the prime talent from the local area and Scotland. He made it plain that he expected the coaching staff to take in as many matches as possible in a scouting capacity. Although stating his desire to bring international experience to the squad, Durban ruled himself out of the running for Everton and former England centre-forward Bob Latchford who was a free agent, 'The last thing I want to be doing is patching up and make do with short-term buys. It is essential that I bring players here of character and proven qualities who, if things did not work out, would be saleable assets again. I don't like taking gambles on older players and I certainly won't be making any enquiries for Latchford.'

Exasperating as it undoubtedly must have been to be constantly harried over newspaper gossip about transfer permutations, Durban's almost throwaway dismissal of Latchford's suitability for his grand plan at Sunderland appeared somewhat hasty, and was perhaps borne from his irritation at media speculation. With the benefit of hindsight, Durban would come to realise that Latchford would have been an asset who, far from being a short-term buy, would still be a sought-after striker two years later.

Instead, the boss enquired about a current international centre-forward, Mick Robinson, who had been wanted by Knighton before the Eire striker signed for Brighton. Durban's predecessor had not been backed and, predictably, Robinson's value had increased. But, this was all academic as Brighton manager Mike Bailey issued a 'hands off' message. Far from welcoming any new signings, the only movement was outgoing as long-serving left-back Joe Bolton rejected a new contract and signed for Middlesbrough.

While waiting for the phone to ring in response to his transfer enquiries, Durban could appreciate the nation's temporary absorption with events at Headingley cricket ground as Bob Willis set up an historic victory, taking 8-43 in Australia's all-out total of 111. Botham had hit 149 as England won by 18 runs. Perhaps it was of greater significance that England, like Sunderland, had turned to a 39-year-old 'safe pair of hands' to steer the team. Mike Brearley, a fellow wily tactician with silvering hair, had the gifted capacity to motivate those around him to maximise their abilities and get the job done. Although the parallels are blurred, it would not be a far-fetched exercise to place photographs of Brearley and Durban from those halcyon 1980s days side by side and invite comparison.

## Big Sam and General Munro are Welcome

Six weeks into the job, and with most players and managers back from far-flung summer holidays, the media was abuzz that the new manager's first purchase was imminent; 'Durban Goes for International Star' being an *Echo* headline that whetted the appetites of supporters. Of course, such banner statements had to be treated with caution. It had not been unknown for exaggerated claims to be made about a fairly obscure 'name' that had picked up a couple of substitute appearances in relatively meaningless international friendlies. Never mind; it was all part of the rich tapestry, the game, of following your team's transfer rumour mill.

As right-back John Gidman had just signed for Manchester United from Everton, speculation was rife that United's Jimmy Nicholl was the targeted man. Nicholl certainly fulfilled Durban's stated wish to get one or two full internationals on board (being a Northern Ireland regular). The theory was stoked further by the fact that Nicholl usually operated at full-back, and might be viewed as a replacement for the outgoing Bolton for whom Middlesbrough had agreed to pay £210,000 without going to the next sitting of the transfer tribunal panel.

Whoever the mystery man was, Durban sent out a dynamic retort to his press questioners, 'I don't hang around.' He also emphasised that certain departures were not the foregone conclusions anticipated. When taking over the reins, Durban had immediately taken Whitworth, Bolton, John Hawley, and Barry Dunn off the transfer list so that he could make his own assessment, giving them opportunities to impress. The only reason Durban had not removed the name of Sam Allardyce from the pre-existing list was that the big defender was seeking a move for practical reasons. Allardyce had signed the previous summer but had been unable to sell his Lancashire family home. Third Division Carlisle United had made an approach but the Cumbrian club could not match the player's First Division wages. Now, Durban stressed that Allardyce was not only welcome to stay, but might be needed as cover, 'I am in no panic to get rid of Sam – especially with Shaun in America.'

At the end of July, it was announced that Stoke's Scottish international left-back Iain Munro was the 'star' expected to join his former boss. Durban had paid St Mirren £150,000 only the previous October, and this, arguably, meant that he was entitled to go 'poaching'. Besides, Richie Barker was obviously prepared to sell the 29-year-old who was duly unveiled as Durban's first signing. Commenting on the defender's age, Durban added, 'He will be able to pass on so much. He has a fine understanding of the game and is a versatile player, but left-back is his best position.'

Munro was not only signing for a man he knew much about but also a club. He had an aunt and uncle living in the Silksworth district of Sunderland and had visited since an early age. He fully appreciated the passion that football generated in the area, and was satisfied with the move, 'I could not ask for a better platform to try to win a regular place in the Scottish team [to add to his seven caps]. I am ambitious and would not be coming if I did not think that Alan Durban would be successful. Everywhere he has been he has done well on limited resources and I believe he is capable of big things. He is a realist. At Stoke he got the maximum out of his squad.'

Realism was an element often at a premium with sections of Sunderland fans but, at present, things were slowly but surely progressing as Durban strived to see more internationals come through the 'Home Team' doors. He had also brought in a man he knew could be relied on when the chips were down; a general both on and off the field. Munro was already familiar with Durban's working methods, and the standards that would be expected – he did not have to be taught.

## Strip to Tease but Not to Please

Another decision that the club had taken well before Durban's arrival was to break their partnership with kit supplier Umbro and embark on a new arrangement with Le Coq Sportif, a company that had come to prominence in the eyes of football fans the previous season through their association with Tottenham Hotspur's FA Cup-winning squad. Ostensibly, there was nothing particularly controversial about taking such a step, but the aspect that served to alienate many older supporters was the radical design unveiled for the new home strip. Rather than donning the traditional broad red-and-white striped shirts, the team would be running out in a predominantly white jersey featuring twin thin red stripes placed at intervals. Official club publications had described the stripes as 'candy red' which unintentionally conjured a sense of superficiality. As if that development was difficult enough for some to swallow, the usual black shorts had been abandoned in favour of the confectionary hue of red.

The London branch of Sunderland Supporters' Association were one group who made their feelings clear on the switch, a spokesman complaining, 'This news has filled us with anger and disbelief. Whoever is responsible for this has a lot to answer for.' Not surprisingly, the transfer of business to a new kit supplier was financially motivated, but the club could surely have dictated that the home-strip design should remain faithful to tradition. Not for the first time, someone on high was guilty of badly misjudging, or simply ignoring, the feelings of many supporters.

On Friday, 31 July, the new strip was modelled for the press. Defender Jeff Clarke sported the non-controversial light-blue shirt and navy shorts of the away kit, while local model Jane Davison lounged by his side in the offending home ensemble. It would be fair to say that most were distinctly unimpressed with the club's unveiled 'Autumn Collection', one prevalent expression muttered being 'pyjama tops'.

## The Players Return

Any kerfuffle over the revamped home shirt was a matter outside the new manager's control and, regardless of his own personal opinion, a decision he would have been powerless to influence. Of far greater relevance to Durban was that the squad had just returned to full-time training, and he was keeping a close watch for any bulkiness. One thing Durban assured his new charges was that anyone found to be over their prescribed weight would suffer a fine. About 30 players and staff made the short journey to Durham's Maiden Castle complex for the preliminary sessions featuring a short physical work out and five-a-side.

Durban was also viewing the player who was effectively a 'new signing.' Central defender Clarke had been voted player of the season in the 1979/80 promotion campaign but, frustratingly for all concerned, had suffered a cruciate ligament injury to his knee in the final away match at Cardiff. Ironically, the damage was sustained in a collision with team-mate Joe Hinnigan but the outcome was that Clarke had not featured the previous season. The *Echo* now heralded this potentially influential figure's readiness for action, reporting that Durban saw Clarke as his defensive 'kingpin' and admitting to being more concerned about that player's state of fitness than any other. Durban displayed a mixture of optimism about Clarke's condition as well as subtle appreciation of the psychological element involved after enduring lengthy lay-offs, 'Jeff looked as fit as anyone. Sometimes in these cases it becomes mind over matter when a player has had two serious injuries.'

While one welcome return was on the cards, another player appeared to be edging towards the exit doors. Although Durban had initially taken former Leeds striker Hawley off the transfer list with a view to assessing his capabilities in the warm-up fixtures, the player was now officially in dispute with the club after failing to agree new terms. Matters were certainly not done and dusted, however, and Hawley was included in the squad travelling north for the tour of Scotland.

## Strikers, and Scotland

Durban had noted the reported willingness of former Roker forward Dennis Tueart to return to his native north-east and, by now, the manager was aware that a new striker might become a priority depending on what he saw from his front men during their Scottish fixtures. However, with the possibility that Hawley might stay, and no imminent panic, Durban coolly remarked, 'Tueart is a good player, but I am not rushing in anywhere.' The Manchester City front-man was supposedly available for a fee of £75,000, and also fulfilled the much-vaunted wish to bring in players of international status. He certainly possessed quality and experience, and it would not be many months before Durban would belatedly acknowledge that Tueart's 'know-how' was just what his team badly needed.

With no further transfer movement, in or out, Durban's squad set forth for games against Hearts, Hibernian, Dundee, and Berwick. The surprise name touted as being set for an early first-team opportunity was Nick Pickering, who had mainly been operating as a full-back and was only just about to sign professional forms. Meanwhile, Durban could only look on with envy at the spending power wielded by Lawrie McMenemy at supposedly 'unfashionable' Southampton as they lavished £750,000 on stylish midfielder David Armstrong from Middlesbrough. It was true that spending money did not always guarantee success, but this was a prime example of a club acquiring quality in proportion to their outlay.

Sunderland experienced mixed fortunes in the city of Edinburgh. A 1-0 win was achieved against Hearts courtesy of a goal from Alan Brown (one of the existing strikers hoping to prove their worth) but the team's performance in a 3-0 reverse at Hibernian provided cause for concern. Two games into the tour, and upset by his team's evident lack of punch in attack, Durban was already painfully aware that he *was* in need of a goalscorer. The press speculated that he was 'ready to swoop' for Bolton's unsettled Neil Whatmore, a story fuelled by the fact that Sunderland could offer former Bolton defender Allardyce as a sweetener in any deal.

A 2-2 draw with Dundee followed, the team fielding four men across the middle: Gordon Chisholm; Kevin Arnott; Mick Buckley; and Pickering. Playing on his 18th birthday, Pickering received the unwanted 'present' of four stitches to a gashed leg. In the final game at Berwick, Sunderland won 2-0 with goals from Gary Rowell and John Cooke, but it was the introduction of 'retired' coach Docherty for the final 20 minutes that surprised the travelling supporters. Injury had brought down the curtain on Docherty's playing career and he had benefited from a Roker testimonial game in 1980. Against the odds, he and Durban were mulling over the practical and legal insurance obstacles of making a professional comeback. Durban knew that the midfield department lacked tenacity and leadership and was keen to have Docherty's bite back in evidence, a quality he could see was in short supply.

Almost as soon as the idea had been mooted, however, hopes that here was a cut-price solution on their own doorstep were quashed. Long-standing club physiotherapist Johnny Watters advised that the Doc's knee would not be up to full-time football despite the fact he trained every day with the squad and was still only 30. One door slammed shut; as manager of Sunderland Football Club it was an experience that Durban would become accustomed to. Sadly and frustratingly, it would all too often be the club's own upper hierarchy that performed the obstructing and wedging.

## Transfer Limits and Rebuffs

With the new season only three weeks away, Durban had recruited only one of the 'four or five' new players he had indicated to the board would be needed if the team was to win anything rather than merely survive. But, juggling a squad of 22, he knew trimming was also required. The local press appeared to be privy to certain spending parameters that had been laid down by the directors to the manager in an evening meeting held at Roker.

The precise amount Durban had at his disposal was unclear but it was apparent that he would be expected to do some 'bargain hunting' if there were to be more than one or two new additions. There would be enough made available for a striker, but after that the manager's resources would be somewhat 'stretched'. Durban remained tight-lipped about whether the club's reluctance to finance his hoped-for number of quality signings came as a shock.

Although previously linked with Second Division Whatmore, it was two top-flight strikers that Durban made official enquiries about. Firstly, he sounded out the possibility of Lee Chapman becoming the latest Stoke man to jump ship to Roker. By now, circumstances may have forced Durban to shelve any 'no poaching' good intentions. He also spoke to his former Stoke captain Howard Kendall, the new man in charge at Everton, about Peter Eastoe. As Durban waited, he enviously regarded the way ex-mentor Clough could splash out £425,000 to make Mark Proctor the latest star asset sacrificed by Middlesbrough. It was not long before news was received that Chapman had signed a one-year contract extension at Stoke. In a double blow, a polite-but-firm message came through from Kendall, 'Eastoe is not for sale.'

Pride was also a little ruffled by Chapman's subsequent comment on his decision to stay put, 'The only reason I wanted to move was to become more successful, and I don't think my chances would improve much by going to Sunderland.' Chapman's blunt assessment of the Roker team's immediate prospects was shared by the bookmakers who quoted 100/1 for Sunderland to win the championship.

Thus it was that the official pre-season photocall pictured a very-much provisional 17-man line-up. The fact that their number included players whose immediate futures were open to conjecture, such as Allardyce, Hawley, Whitworth and Dunn and another (Bowyer) who would not be available to play for some time, gave the photograph a deceptive aspect. At least any departures would be partially offset by the return of the three players from the USA. Pickering was not included in the first-team photo, but this was not so surprising given Durban's tendency to instil that young professionals should not take anything for granted, and to be recognised as a senior squad member was not a status to be conferred overnight.

## The Heat is On

Pickering was in the party that flew to Greece for a friendly match against Panathinaikos. Durban saw his team 'wilt' 2-0 in the torrid conditions but felt that the trip had been 'worthwhile'. Almost as soon as the squad returned they were preparing for the heat of two Wear-Tyne 'derbies'. Aware of the potential for crowd trouble, Durban stressed his hopes, 'I only want people to go to Newcastle who are interested in football. We have a new manager, a fresh strip, and a fresh season. The sun is shining and we have enough optimism. I want people to support the club and would like supporters to bring back more humour and knock out all the aggression.'

The first match was played at St James' Park on a Tuesday evening and there was 'no shortage of competitiveness' in a 1-1 draw. The *Echo* reporter observed 'the reluctance of the midfield players to get forward despite the pleas of Durban'. This offered an early indication of his attitude regarding the supporting role he felt should be performed by that department. Far from expecting his midfielders to adopt holding positions throughout the game, Durban would consistently advocate, sometimes plead, for players to throw off cautious instincts, and 'gamble more' by making runs into the box. Goals from midfield was an aspect always predominant in the thinking of their manager who had practised what he preached when he was a midfielder with a healthy goalscoring return.

Trailing before a crowd of only 9,882, a 40th-minute Pickering cross found Tom Ritchie who beat Kevin Carr with a low shot. Durban's post-match observations were wide-ranging, firstly criticising inadequate advertising, 'It is disastrous that 1,000 fans could not get in because they did not realise that they had to purchase tickets in advance.' He also remarked on his decision to watch one half of the match from the stand, 'I learnt more sitting upstairs in 45 minutes than I did in the previous games. It is surprising how you see certain situations from a different angle.'

The following night, Durban and Docherty were in Glasgow watching St Johnstone go down 4-1 to Celtic in the Scottish League Cup. Media speculation centred on the likelihood that Sunderland would join the posse of clubs chasing St Johnstone striker Ally McCoist, described as 'one of the hottest properties in Scotland'. Never easy at constant frenzied press speculation over transfers, Durban refused to confirm the primary focus for his Scottish sortie, 'All I was doing at the game was filling my bank of knowledge.' Middlesbrough had made a firm enquiry, with several other teams watching developments. Durban needed to prune his squad, but was swift to emphasise that one major purchase would be sanctioned by the board prior to offloading players from the wage bill.

Durban planned to put Allardyce in the 'shop window' for Saturday's return match against Newcastle as at least two managers had declared their intention of checking the form of the defender who had simply been unable to settle after being caught up in the recession in the housing market, leading to him making weekly drives to and from Lancashire. Durban would not be at the game, preferring to check the form of 18-year-old McCoist. After previously stating his reluctance to take 'gambles on older players', Durban was clearly not averse to backing his judgement on young potential. Meanwhile, one striker was on the move as Manchester United were ordered to pay Arsenal £900,000 for Frank Stapleton.

The 'second leg' against Newcastle attracted a mere 10,032 who saw Hawley score with a full-length diving header to put Sunderland ahead. Alan Shoulder beat keeper Chris Turner to equalise but, in the 56th minute, the other transfer-seeking man, Allardyce, flicked a near-post header past Carr. If 'Big Sam' was to go, then a winner against Newcastle was a positive note to end on.

Although Durban had wanted Allardyce to stay, the player asked to be allowed to move on and later admitted that a continued house-sharing arrangement with Hawley in Cleadon would have been detrimental as, to kill the boredom, both men had been temporarily drinking a little more than was good for them. On Monday morning, Durban officially confirmed Allardyce and Hawley's availability for transfer, as well as stating he was prepared to part with Whitworth, Brown, Cooke, and Dunn. Meanwhile, his scouting trip north of the border had provided the confirmation needed to lodge a club-record offer for the current brightest prospect in Scottish football, the much-coveted McCoist.

## A Swift Courtship: We'll Take More Care of You Ally

Sunderland faced serious competition for the signature of McCoist. Fellow First Division clubs Wolves and Middlesbrough had made substantial offers, while Glasgow Rangers (who, as an East Kilbride boy, the player held an affection for) had also declared an interest. There was a visiting list to get through, and the player's first journey was to the Midlands for talks with Wolves manager Barnwell. A contributory factor behind Durban's move for the youthful striker was that 26-year-old Hawley's injury record suggested he was highly unlikely to play enough games to contribute to the number of goals the boss sought his strikers to share in order to attain a comfortable league position. Brown and Cooke had also been listed as neither was showing signs of fulfilling the potential that had been fleetingly displayed in the past. With the following Saturday marking the season's curtain-raiser, the urgency for clubs countrywide to conclude transfer business was ratcheted up.

Events developed swiftly and the *Echo* proudly announced 'McCoist Opts for Sunderland'. St Johnstone had issued a statement confirming that the young 'goalscoring sensation' was travelling south with manager Alec Rennie who had provided protective guidance throughout. Durban was gratified with the successful recruitment of a player he envisaged would prove an asset for many years but, as on his own arrival, was mindful to downplay unrealistic expectations generated by the repeated hyperbole employed by the press alongside any mention of the talented striker's name ('hot-shot' and 'sensation' were particularly popular).

A delighted Durban declared, 'I am just pleased that he has selected Sunderland in an affluent market and not because of the money we have offered him but the future he sees at the club. He is a very mature lad but we have not bought him for now but as a long-term investment.' Pay attention! – *Not* for now! But, would the majority of fans have the patience? Durban spelt it out for anyone who remained in doubt, 'He is an 18-year-old novice in football terms and we must be very careful with him.'

That evening, Durban's mood turned to anger after watching his team falter to a 1-1 draw at Fourth Division Darlington whose team included young forward David Speedie. Pending the imminent arrival of McCoist, it was another Scottish striker, Ritchie, who netted Sunderland's 'face-saver'. After the game, Durban rapped his players, 'Too many of them have had it too easy for too long and one or two of them think they are prima donnas.'

That annoyance evaporated on Wednesday, 26 August as Ally McCoist ceremonially put pen to paper, on a sun-drenched Roker Park pitch, watched over by both his previous and new manager. Rennie spoke excitedly about the deal, displaying confidence that he had overseen a wise choice for all concerned, 'He's a natural finisher; some of the goals I've seen him score have had me out of my seat. The boy is exciting. Always looking for shots at goal and once he is settled into the routine of full-time training I am quite certain that Sunderland fans will consider him a "steal" [at £355,000].' Talent-spotter Alex McLintock endorsed these thoughts, having seen him playing for Fir Park Boys Club against Avonbank, 'It was December and the weather was atrocious but Ally's talent stood out like a beacon; one of the most naturally talented footballers I had ever seen.'

Rennie appeared to be genuinely pleased that McCoist had chosen Sunderland ahead of the chasing pack, 'He has had some marvellous matches for us, and although it would be terribly unfair to expect miracles from him straight away I certainly expect the Roker fans to take to him. Quite apart from being a smashing kid – he's intelligent and confident without ever being arrogant – he has the kind of natural talent Wearside fans will love.' Amid the intoxicating mixture of optimism and radiant sunshine, Rennie had proffered the same sage counsel promoted by Durban; that it would be 'unfair to expect miracles.'

Rational and perceptive advice had been forthcoming from two experienced managers, but it was inevitable that expectation levels would be accentuated by the 'record signing' label that would be a constant companion to any appearance of McCoist's name in local print.

Overall, the 'scoring sensation' himself displayed the intelligence to share his new manager's vision of 'slow-but-sure' progress, both for the team and his own development, 'Scoring goals is what my game is all about, though I am not what you would call a bustling centre forward. I like to play it around on the deck. I could have gone to Rangers who I'd supported as a kid, but Sunderland are very ambitious.'

McCoist would be 19 the following month, and many were unaware that he had been representing St Johnstone on a mere part-time basis. Only now could he enjoy the financial security of a full-time contract that would allow him to submit his resignation letter to the Overseas Development Section of the local civil service office where he had worked through the week. No wonder the young chap was doubly delighted to proudly declare, 'Now I am a Sunderland player, and I can't wait to play for them in the First Division.' McCoist had signed a five-year contract but, despite the 'slowly slowly' message preached by his new manager, the wait to see him play in the first-team would be considerably shorter than anticipated.

Overall, the signing represented the second part of an almost unprecedented double in the living memory of most supporters. It had been a novelty for the club to secure a top-choice managerial candidate, but for this to be followed by a highly rated player electing to join Sunderland ahead of the opposition provided a unique boost to the collective ego. It was a case of 'our cup runneth over' as, for now, the glowing sense of optimism (and the sun) remained in full ascent.

## Showtime Arrives with False Dawns and Discontent

On the same day that McCoist was unveiled at Roker Park, Newcastle United had their own incoming centre-forward to present as Imre Varadi signed from Everton for £125,000. But, for Sunderland, it was home-grown striker Alan Brown who would be the envied number nine on the opening Saturday as he was given the early nod to lead the attack at Ipswich.

Clarke had been made club captain, while Allardyce was given permission to speak with representatives from Millwall. On the eve of the season's opener, Durban outlined some of his hopes and expectations, 'My target is to be sitting here in 12 months' time with the club in a much better position and with a European challenge the next season a realistic proposition. We could not have had a more difficult start to the season. However, we will be taking over 2,000 supporters with us and if that is not motivation then I don't know what is.'

The manager then commented on the thinking behind selecting speed-merchant Brown, and hinted at the factor that would influence his final midfield selection, 'It is only logic that we need some pace up front; and if this heat continues it is important that we have players who won't give the ball away.'

The following afternoon in sultry Suffolk, Durban's first league team selection read: Turner, Hinnigan, Munro, Buckley, Clarke, Hindmarch, Chisholm, Ritchie, Brown, Rowell, Pickering, sub McCoist. The idea to use Brown's pace was sound in principle but it was undermined by the hot conditions as the striker tired. The upside was that the visiting hordes got their first opportunity to see the new record signing in action as McCoist entered the fray after only an hour.

Sunderland had, unexpectedly, not only scored first (a fine glancing header from Ritchie) but established a 3-1 second-half lead with two goals from Buckley. McCoist had contributed a subtle back-heel to play Buckley in for one of the strikes, but under relentless pressure from the rattled hosts the lead was lost as two Eric Gates goals had Ipswich level with ten minutes remaining. Bearing in mind that both Durban and Knighton had seen their teams crushed 4-0 and 4-1 at Portman Road earlier in the year, a 3-3 draw reflected a slightly surprising result against the league runners-up.

Durban expressed appreciation at the encouragement the fans had given the side throughout the match, and made sure to lead his players to the end where the bulk had congregated at the final whistle. He was encouraged by the runs workaholic midfielder Buckley had made into goalscoring positions; the sort of 'gambles' that Durban tried to instil into the mindset of his players.

On a less savoury note, there was some trouble at Newark on the return journey when travelling Sunderland and Southampton followers clashed. Durban switched focus to the problem of curbing trouble inside the ground, 'I don't like all-seater stadiums as they restrain people who want to let off steam, but if fans continue to cause trouble then the board of directors will have to look at all-seater stadiums.' This remark may have caused some consternation within the Roker boardroom, but Durban had a propensity for plain speaking, no matter if some 'establishment' feathers were ruffled.

One player who had certainly been ruffled at not being included in the starting line-up was talented 22-year-old midfielder Arnott who responded to his manager's decision by slapping in a written transfer request. Durban did not appear to be overly perturbed by the development, offering a pragmatic overview, 'I don't believe in standing in the way of players if they want to go. I am not really surprised or annoyed but after all *it is only the first game of the season*. I explained to him and Hawley in front of the rest of the players why I was leaving them out. There are two options open to him. He can either stay, and buckle down to win his place back, or move on.'

Durban recalled his own experience of being left out of the team for an opening match when at Derby. He had not responded petulantly, and his reward had been to regain his place in the team and finish the season clutching a championship medal.

The implication was clearly that he thought Arnott's reaction had been hasty.

The players would have to adjust to Durban's motivational style, as Gary Rowell recalls, 'He was not the sort of manager to put an arm round the shoulder and praise you to the skies, massaging a player's ego; he liked to challenge you, or give players a rocket at times.'

Durban was more concerned with expending his energies on preparing the players who were willing to fight for their place rather than attempting to placate moody ones, and a mouth-watering midweek home fixture against reigning champions Aston Villa was now in his sights. Cooke (who had scored only one goal in 14 top-flight appearances) was to be given another chance, the boss explaining the rationale, 'Brown is short of match practice. Cookie must improve his goal ratio. Buckley proved on Saturday that he will get his fair share of goals by going in where it hurts, and Cookie must stop playing at being a professional and improve his attitude.' Durban did not believe in pulling punches.

The boss also had thoughts on the new three-points-for-a-win system that was in its debut season, 'I want to see goals coming in from all over the place as a draw is almost worthless.' The latter assertion was bordering on the melodramatic; surely he would welcome his team scoring a last-minute equaliser and gaining a point rather than lose. Also, if you salvaged a draw, there was the bonus of knowing that the opposition had been denied two points. Durban appeared to have temporarily thrown logic out of the window on that score. What was certain, was that he required his team to produce an up-tempo showing against the powerful opposition that awaited, 'The only way we can use the crowd is to keep the pace going from the start and, against a side like Villa, we must match their pace and running.'

## The Sound of the Crowd

Despite missing defender Ken McNaught and striker Gary Shaw, Ron Saunders was able to leave an expensive close-season signing, midfielder Andy Blair, on the bench. Villa lined up: Rimmer, Swain, Gibson, Evans, Ormsby, Mortimer, Bremner, Donovan, Withe, Cowans, Morley. Two interested spectators at Roker Park that evening were Shaun Elliott and Barry Siddall, who had completed their USA stints. They were being given a short break to recover from jet-lag and what Durban considered to be general overplaying. However, Elliott was feeling aggrieved after being forced to leave his erstwhile Seattle team-mates enjoying a luxury end-of-season sojourn in Hawaii, a mood further inflamed by his new manager's initial greeting including an explicit indication that the returnee was regarded as his 'midfield dynamo' – hardly Elliott's preferred role.

With the vaunted 'Roker Roar' very much in evidence, Villa did their best to subdue the atmosphere and in the 23rd minute Terry Donovan went wide of Turner to score from an acute angle. Sunderland responded and Jimmy Rimmer produced two outstanding saves to deny a Hinnigan header and Ritchie drive. But, Ritchie was not to be denied when a 36th-minute Pickering free kick was headed back into the middle by Clarke for the forward to turn quickly and sweep the ball just inside the post. Peter Withe should have restored the lead before the break, but the England striker headed wide when unchallenged at the far post.

Three minutes into the second half, Sunderland went ahead after Kenny Swain fouled Rowell on the edge of the penalty box. From Buckley's curling kick, Ritchie's header was palmed out only as far as Rowell who nodded in. Villa gradually took over as they penned Sunderland deep into their own half, with Tony Morley giving right-back Hinnigan a torrid time. But, with the energy of Buckley finding an overdrive gear, Sunderland held out. The home crowd did get to see a cameo appearance from their star signing, but by the time McCoist replaced Cooke for the last ten minutes it was backs-to-the-wall stuff with little opportunity for the enthusiastic youngster to show his ability.

In the immediate afterglow, Durban set a cautionary tone, 'We have not got to get carried away with a couple of results as there is a long way to go. We have got to get it right against West Ham who will come here flying' (the Hammers had beaten Tottenham 4-0 at White Hart Lane with four goals from centre-forward David Cross). Durban believed he had detected welcome signs, but there was also a warning, 'We were better defensively, and I can see a pattern emerging similar to my previous clubs. But, it will be harder as we will not catch anybody by surprise now.'

Villa boss Saunders was astounded by the support from the near 30,000 attendance. 'It wouldn't matter here if they turned out their reserve side as the crowd would get behind them. I have never known an area for its passion and loyalty to its team.' This independent assessment confirmed something Durban already knew, and validated his decision to leave the relative indifference that had manifested itself at Stoke despite successfully consolidating the team in the top flight.

Another striker who had hit four midweek goals was Hawley, in front of watching scouts as the reserves mauled Doncaster 8-0, and Durban indicated he would be disappointed if there was no ensuing transfer activity. Almost immediately, Norwich City's Ken Brown held talks with a view to signing Hawley as a replacement for Justin Fashanu who had signed for Nottingham Forest for £1m. That huge deal paved the way for another as Trevor Francis was allowed to leave Forest for Manchester City, the £1.2m deal making Francis the first player in history to figure in two separate million-pound transfers.

The movements of other strikers may have been in the news, but the priority was the one who had just joined the club. What were McCoist's first impressions? The remarks voiced in the *Roker Review* programme indicated the stamp of a player who shared his manager's reluctance to be easily satisfied. On the draw at Ipswich, he commented, 'Of course I enjoyed that back-heel, but we were all sick at drawing after leading. No matter that we faced the UEFA Cup holders on their own ground and got a point. We had three for the taking.' On his impressions of the pace in the top flight, McCoist noted, 'It was a bit quick to say the least after Scotland. I have a lot of hard work to put in.' The spotlight was also turned on his hopes for the future, 'I came to Sunderland because of their great traditions, their terrific potential and because I was impressed by Alan Durban's obvious ambition. Let's just say that I know I made the right choice. I'm thrilled to have worn a Sunderland shirt in the First Division.'

Durban reinforced his long-term vision, 'Ally's one for the future. Any new player needs time to settle in and he needs support and patience from supporters and new team-mates. In Ally's case this is particularly true with him being a part-timer in Scotland. We'll not see the best of him until he has had the benefit of full-time training over some months and gets the feel of First Division football. But I do consider it a feather in our caps that he has chosen Sunderland when other clubs were pressing him so strongly.'

McCoist echoed his manager's sentiments and showed that he shared the drive to succeed, 'I've a lot to learn. But the great thing is that I have a lot of time on my side. I'm determined not to let the fee bother me. What dominates my thoughts is scoring goals. I know I could have had the chance to play European football with Rangers, but I'm hopeful that the European scene will come to Sunderland before too long. It certainly will if Mr Durban has his way. He's tremendously ambitious to build lasting success at Roker Park and I'm with him all the way.' Unfortunately, the big question was would the chairman and fans be with Durban all the way to see his long-term vision for Sunderland greatness achieved.

These were still early days, however, and optimism remained the predominant emotion, 'My first taste of English football really made me appreciate how much I'm going to enjoy playing in front of the Sunderland supporters. There were thousands of them at Portman Road and their vocal support was out of this world.' McCoist also eulogised another ultra-talented Scottish forward, 'Kenny Dalglish – a superb team player and a terrific individual talent.' The young protégé's admiration for the 'team player' side of things was a quality that would endear him to the dressing room throughout his future career. This was one man who was an asset at a club, whether in the team or on the sidelines biding his time. Finally, McCoist pondered on 'such things as dreams are made of', 'I want the day to come when Sunderland are as successful as Liverpool have been for so long. That would be something.'

Well, quite; but north-east fans would have to absorb the message of slow and steady improvement. Bill Shankly's Liverpool had not achieved instant success; Clough had not transformed Nottingham Forest in a couple of seasons, and Ron Saunders had been allowed several years to mould Villa into champions. Patience had been a virtue.

## Learning Cruel Lessons: Back to Reality

Another crowd in the region of 30,000 was expected for the visit of newly promoted West Ham. Immediately after the midweek win, Durban had been downplaying expectations and preaching caution. A day later, however, he made statements out of kilter with his previous demeanour. Firstly, he was asked about any special provision to stymie the visitors' form striker, 'I think David Cross has had his share of goals for the week; Clarkie will put him in his pocket just like he did with Mariner and Withe.'

True, those two England strikers had failed to register goals in the opening matches, but other players had breached the Sunderland rearguard. Moreover, Durban's bold remark about Cross being put in the defender's pocket would doubtless motivate the striker to disprove the boast. Or, was Durban simply trying to puff up his own player's chest, reinforcing belief that he was capable of shackling the danger man?

The hyper-bullish attitude did not stop there, 'If we play as well as we did against Villa then I think we will win by more than one goal.' More than one goal; as if a 1-0 win would be considered a minor disappointment! But Durban was hoping that visiting teams would not shut up shop, 'The last thing I want is for them to start playing around at the back. Villa tried and that type of image would harm football. I would like to see a rule introduced that would not allow the ball to go back to the goalkeeper once he parted with it.'

There seemed little danger that a team coming fresh from a big away win would play it negative, but Durban's prescient comments anticipated the future rule changes that restricted back-passes. Overall, his pre-match views marked a departure from a manager who was generally tough on slapping down on any sign of complacency. It was one thing to express confidence in your own team's ability to do a job, but his comments constituted a dismissive prediction that any threat the opposition posed would be handled comfortably. This appeared to be either a case of reckless talk, or a manager playing calculated psychological games. Either way, things went sadly awry.

Sunderland supporters were well versed in the art of anticlimax, and the ensuing 2-0 defeat fed that trend. The *Echo* reporter asserted that 'the class of West Ham proved too much. The pace and commitment which had been the hallmark of Sunderland's previous two games were not sufficient.' Alan Devonshire set up West Ham's first for Paul Goddard and there was a second-half clincher from Cross who was conspicuously nowhere near a certain defender's pocket throughout. 'We needed a tin opener and mine's in America,' quipped Durban, referring to the creativity he felt that the absent Cummins could have provided, but Rowell, Cooke, and McCoist had all spurned gilt-edged chances. There was worse news to come off the pitch after a group of supporters went on the rampage, and 30 arrests were made. The first clouds had appeared across the previously sun-filled sky of Roker optimism.

At the next reserve team fixture at Roker, Arsenal manager Terry Neill, who had been Hawley's boss at Hull City, was present to check on his former centre-forward. Newcastle manager Arthur Cox, in the first of what, decades later, would seem an incredible number of enquiries to take Wearside players across to Tyneside, had got in first and agreed a 'cut-price' fee of £45,000. Of course, Cox had a strong affinity with Sunderland; he had been the coach to the Second Division Roker team's momentous 1973 FA Cup triumph when they defied heavily stacked odds to defeat Don Revie's formidable Leeds United outfit. Cox held lengthy talks with Hawley but was not prepared to be kept waiting while the forward waited for options to develop. A no-nonsense stance was evident as Cox vented his displeasure, 'I have pulled out of the deal. I made Hawley an offer yesterday, but he wanted to play last night and give people an opportunity of seeing him. He wanted a chance of being better off financially. If he didn't want to join Newcastle United at the first time of asking then I don't want to know. I have other irons in the fire.'

Durban gave Siddall the chance to stake his claims for a swift return to league action as Sunderland beat Middlesbrough

2-1 in Jim Platt's testimonial at Ayresome Park, but it was keeper Platt's fellow Northern Ireland international George Best who had attracted the limelight. The 35-year-old flew into the country from the USA (where he played for San Jose Earthquakes) and guested for Boro to the delight of the 7,425 crowd. Best showed enough to suggest that he still had much to offer. It was the wayward genius who set up the chance for David Hodgson to drill a low drive past Siddall in the 49th minute, but the game's outcome was turned on its head by goals from Pickering and Hinnigan.

Cox came calling again, but Durban ruled out Newcastle's desire to take Arnott on loan, 'I told them at the moment I would not consider it.' One deal was completed when Hawley got his move to Arsenal, Sunderland's next opponents. In this period, there was a strange lack of clauses in deals preventing a player from turning out almost immediately against their former employers. Durban was aware of the potential danger of the situation, 'We will have to be careful as he knows our tactics and dead-ball situations.' With the transfer market moving too sluggishly for Durban's requirements, it may well have been a gamble he felt worth taking rather than delay the paperwork until after the weekend and risk the deal falling through.

As England prepared to meet Norway in a World Cup qualifier in Oslo, Durban had warned the national side to take the Norwegians as a serious threat. Of course, England sank to an abject 2-1 defeat in a game perhaps best remembered for the Norwegian commentary that bellowed a diverse list of famous English names, including 'Lord Nelson, Winston Churchill, Henry Cooper and Lady Diana', before goading the Prime Minister, 'Maggie Thatcher, can you hear me? Your boys took a hell of a beating.' Durban offered more measured criticism on team selection, 'You have to pick winners and not just who you think are the best 11 players. If Ron Greenwood wanted a winger, why didn't he play one instead of trying to make Trevor Francis into one? Tactically Norway were green but we couldn't exploit it. The side was overbalanced with flair players and not enough grafters.'

On the topic of grafting, Durban felt obliged to swing the axe for the match at Highbury. Disappointed by the player's attitude in training, he dropped Cooke from the 13-strong party. Durban demanded high professional standards to be maintained, 'I expect players to train to their absolute maximum and don't like to see talent going to waste. It is time Cookie decided if he wants to work at his game or play at it.' There was also confirmation that McCoist would win his first start, 'We have used four number nines and, apart from the odd goal, not one of them has produced the goods. We have eased him in.' The manager revealed that Elliott would also start but could yet change his mind about who to drop, 'If I thought at 2.15 tomorrow that the attitude of a certain individual was not right I would have no qualms leaving him out.'

This would be a common threat brandished by Durban to guard against players taking their place in the starting line-up for granted, or thinking they might get away with slacking off in training.

Gordon Chisholm was the unlucky man to make way, as Durban embarked on an ultimately doomed quest to turn Elliott into a midfield performer. But, the manager was not forced to make a difficult decision over the goalkeeper position as it had been found that Turner had sustained a wrist fracture in a clash with Peter Withe ten days before and had only just discovered the extent of the injury. Fortunately, Durban had a capable replacement available in Siddall. In his first full game, McCoist looked sharp and displayed the confidence to run it alone, but did spurn a good second-half chance after bursting into the penalty area with only Pat Jennings ahead, the keeper parrying his shot. A 1-1 draw was salvaged ten minutes from time when a Buckley free kick was flicked on by Ritchie for Rowell to shoot in via the upright.

Durban revealed that Rowell's inclusion had not been a formality and that only his goal against Villa had kept him in the team. In goal, Siddall had displayed fault-free handling, 'I was very pleased with Barry who seemed to give us maturity in the last ten minutes.' On Chisholm's omission, Durban praised the Scot's willingness to support his team-mates, 'It was a difficult decision, but I was delighted with his attitude. There was no sulking from him; in fact it was great to see him encouraging the lads from the dugout.' There was a message to Arnott there somewhere. There were also signs that Durban's selection options were about to be increased as Cummins was due to report for training the following week.

Back at Roker, Durban dispensed some unpleasant medicine in the form of a few home truths, 'Sunderland can't go on tradition forever. They must be winning something to be classed as a big club.' Durban was delivering a reality check; one that many blinkered locals knew to be correct but had difficulty swallowing. Graeme Souness would adopt a similar tack when taking over at Newcastle United over three decades later, pointing out that there had to be something fundamentally amiss when no silverware had been won, and that people were fooling themselves when talking about the club as a giant. In 1981, Durban was spelling this out for the Wearside faithful and boardroom alike.

The manager could see the green shoots of potential however; there were grounds for optimism – if he was backed to the hilt, 'The club is one of the biggest in the country in support, and the signing of McCoist is the first step on the ladder in attracting top players here. The lad has potential to become another Dalglish but we must be aiming at signing really top players. Players like Fashanu can pick their clubs and that is why Sunderland have been forced to go for players who cost considerably less. My aim is to bring players here who want to win something and, with our location, I will be looking to Scotland. There are few successful clubs that have not got any Scots in it.'

With the benefit of hindsight, Fashanu was not the most convincing example of the recent expensive movers to name, but Durban's essential point remained valid. Meanwhile, there was light at the end of the tunnel for 30-year-old Bowyer whose midfield steel Durban had been unable to call upon. The player had battled through a summer of lone training and it was anticipated he would be on the brink of competitive action in weeks. It was hoped that the return of this seasoned pro would achieve much the same impact as a new signing.

Allardyce eventually completed a £95,000 move to Third Division Millwall who, unlike Carlisle and Bolton, had somehow been able to match his top-tier wages. Predictably, Sunderland had suffered yet another loss on a player, having spent £150,000 on the defender the previous summer. Coupled with the £45,000 realised from Hawley's move (he had cost £200,000), Durban hardly had a fortune at his disposal but was in no hurry, 'I will just keep it ticking over for now and hope that I can sell one or two more before bringing in new faces.' The manager needed much more spending power to have any chance of enticing the 'really top players' he coveted but, less than three months later, he would ruefully reflect on his reluctance to make concerted moves for the more modestly priced men he had been monitoring as his 'supportive' chairman slashed the unimpressive transfer kitty even further.

In the music world, the newspapers reported that 'Antmania' was resurgent and that, after only a few days on sale, 'Prince Charming' would put Adam Ant at number one in the pop charts. But, Sunderland supporters were hoping their own prince elect would provide them with a fairytale scenario as they looked forward to McCoist's home debut against one of the teams he had turned down, Wolves. Durban offered an appraisal, 'The lad has a lot of confidence and imagination and has settled in really well but what he needs now is a couple of goals under his belt. He has changed his outlook on football from a hobby into a full-time profession but I feel, with his make-up, he will make the transition very comfortably.'

There was certainly a less secretive approach over team selection back in this period as many managers freely disclosed their planned starting line-up, sometimes as early as Thursday. The press informed readers that the home team would be 'unchanged for the first time' but, of course, it must be appreciated that clubs operated with comparatively small squads with which to spring surprises compared to later decades. Durban's message to his players was to capitalise on home advantage as much as possible, 'It is no good grafting away like we did last Saturday if you throw the benefits away in home matches.' After four games, Ritchie, Rowell, and Buckley had two goals each, 'It is about time one or two others got off the mark and I expect goals to come from all over the place.' Goals from all over the place; great! A mere two months later, it might have been understandable if the battle cry had changed into 'goals from anywhere, anyone, please'!

## Imagination Needed (On and Off the Pitch)

A barren 0-0 deadlock was not the stuff of fairytales, and Durban conceded that his team had been too predictable in their efforts to breach a Wolves team that, after three straight defeats, had been intent on preserving what they had started with. Durban pinpointed the amount of 'wasted' corner kicks, but it could have been worse had Siddall not twice denied Wayne Clarke with fingertip saves. Elliott had not looked comfortable in midfield, 'It is unfortunate that our best players duplicate positions. I know that Elliott's best position is in defence, but I don't want to take out either Hindmarch or Clarke.'

Durban also highlighted a stark reality that he felt supporters should not forget, 'Apart from a couple of changes, I am working with the same players who just escaped relegation last season so people just can't expect things to change overnight.' This was a justifiable point pleaded by future managers too.

The *Echo* generally backed the new manager, reiterating the well-worn sentiment that he 'could not work miracles overnight', but also delivered more sobering observations, 'The fact that Sunderland could not beat bottom-of-the-table Wolves at home only confirms how far Durban is from making his side capable of making a realistic challenge for honours. Perhaps the Roker boss arrived on Wearside with a reputation for producing defensive-minded sides and although Sunderland are beginning to struggle for goals, they cannot be accused of being negative. If you can't win then the object of the exercise is to make sure that you don't lose and defensively Sunderland are looking much more sound.'

Durban contemplated where his approach might be flawed, 'Perhaps it is my fault, in that I am selecting a team that will play better away than at home. The results away last season were depressing but what we must protect against is losing what we had at home.' The report promoted the long view in a common sense analysis, 'It will take time for Durban to bring the class players he feels are necessary for Sunderland to make a realistic challenge. I only hope the Roker fans have the patience for the new manager to fulfil his ambitions.' It was worrying however that that this sort of reminder was felt necessary after only the fifth league match, and having suffered only one defeat.

## Clough Reunion, but Away-day Blues

With the return of the three players from the USA and the arrival of their record signing, a fresh squad photograph was taken. At the same time, Middlesbrough were pulling out of a proposed deal for Arnott as their manager Bobby Murdoch angrily commented on the fee Durban had quoted, '£350,000 for a player who can't even get into their side is a joke.' Meanwhile, Durban added the name of 17-year-old midfielder Barry Venison to the squad for the midweek match at Nottingham Forest, 'I don't think Venison will get a game on this trip, but I am certain that he will before the end of the season.'

At the City Ground, Durban would be pitting his wits against his former boss Brian Clough, 'Only two managers have won the league championship with different clubs; Cloughie and Herbert Chapman. While he was successful at Derby he was always reminding us of the north-east connections in their side with the likes of Colin Todd, John McGovern, John O'Hare, and John Robson, and this must be our aim.' Durban's latter remark underlined his intentions to focus greater efforts on scouring the local scene for talent. It was apparent that Clough held his former player in similar high esteem, 'If I had had a vote, I would have nominated Alan as manager of the year last season for what he did at Stoke. People don't realise what kind of job managers do at unfashionable clubs but nobody needs to tell me of Alan's capabilities. I had the greatest admiration for him as a player and he's just carried on the same way since going into management.'

Alas, for all the mutual goodwill, Sunderland flattered to deceive as they went down to a 2-0 defeat. Surprisingly, Arnott had been reintroduced to the midfield, and Cummins made his bow. After matching their opponents for an hour, Sunderland were undone by two of Clough's expensive recruits. On 68 minutes, Proctor raced clear down the right after receiving from Fashanu and crossed for the other £1m striker Ian Wallace to flash a header wide of Siddall. Five minutes from the end, it was Wallace's turn to find Proctor who scored with a low drive. On Arnott's recall, Durban warned that the talented midfielder must be prepared to 'fit into the pattern and do it my way.' The manager was encouraged by the performance but realised its futility, 'That was the best we have played all season and it gave me as much pleasure as when we beat Aston Villa, but to come here and put on a show like that and finish up with nothing is so disappointing.'

Wary that defeat at Swansea at the weekend could see his new team hit the bottom of the league, Durban indicated that the more adventurous approach might have to be jettisoned, 'I am fully aware that we have scored only one goal in the last four matches, but if we continue to lose then I must take action. I would rather bore people to death and get a point away from home but really we must start and score more goals from set pieces.'

Durban wanted to make room for the return of Elliott who he regarded as one of the very few in his squad exuding genuine class, 'I did not realise the problems the lads coming back from America would cause. I keep writing the side down and will continue to do so until I see what is right. Our position is immaterial to me at the moment. I have said all along that it would be the end of November before we get a realistic view of the position.' That was over two months away, but Durban knew a change of tactics might prove necessary much earlier.

Newly promoted Swansea had emerged as a surprise package, and had beaten Tottenham in midweek. Aggravatingly, the striker Durban had said he was not interested in 'taking a gamble' on, Latchford, had been contributing goals and 'assists' aplenty as Swansea revelled in their top-flight adventure. An injury to Munro meant Elliott came in at number three, but he was luckless when a Latchford effort looped off him and over the stranded Siddall for Alan Curtis to head in. Sunderland strove for an equaliser and Ritchie looked as if he was held in the box before Dai Davies saved from Arnott. But, a breakthrough came at the other end when Leighton James foraged into the area and went down under

Clarke's challenge. The Welsh international's well-placed spot kick sealed Sunderland's fate. In a post-match interview, an aggrieved Clarke remarked, 'I tried to play the ball back to Baz, failed to connect cleanly, and the result was James went down. But I never touched him.'

On his return to his native South Wales, an irritated Durban considered that the scales had now well and truly fallen from his eyes, 'I never thought that I would be gullible. What I have done in these last two games was entirely against the principles which have carried me through my managerial career. I was forced into a situation of having to field attacking sides; but even though we have had as much of the ball as our opponents I had the feeling we would not win. If we continue to try to entertain it will get me the sack, get the club relegated, and sicken our supporters who made another long journey to see the team lose.'

Durban knew many would demand the supposed 'quick fix' foray into the transfer market, but felt that such a response would merely paper over fundamental shortcomings, 'There is no way I am going to try to buy my way out of a situation. I want to pick a settled side. The time for experiments is over. I will be working for a blend and regular pattern.' The boss conceded he had erred, 'I felt obliged to fit lads in and have a look at them. I feel that McCoist should now be playing, but we must change the shape of the side and stop conceding. It is ridiculous for the away team to be caught on the counter-attack as we were. I must select a team that can adapt for home and away games as I don't like making changes.'

Despite seeming to be torn between goal-hungry and ultra-defensive approaches, Durban's attitude did inspire a degree of confidence that everything would work out all right in the end. There was a sense of 'You worry if you want to; the manager is not for worrying.' As a final defiant riposte, Durban offered some advice, 'See what odds you can get for us finishing out of the bottom six – and get your money on it.'

## Winds of Change

On 29 September, news emerged that revered manager Bill Shankly had died during the night in an intensive care unit, three days after suffering a heart attack.

From this sad news, the football world flipped to the bizarre with the announcement that FIFA has called for a ban on hugging and kissing by professional players to celebrate a goal. A FIFA spokesman asked, 'Can it be that in modern football goals have become so rare that scenes must occur every time one is scored?' He then stated that the organisation's technical committee felt that goalscorers should be congratulated by the captain, or a player making a vital pass, and sanctions should be imposed on those who overdid the jubilation. Regrettably, there had been little danger of seeing scenes of joy unconfined at Roker Park recently.

Striving to make inroads to improving the footballing infrastructure at the club, Durban made plans to win the reserve team admission to the Central League. He was painfully aware that the current North Midlands League did not 'lift' or stretch players anywhere near sufficiently to prepare them for first-team action. This was the type of quiet organisational groundwork that Durban realised was essential, but would not bear fruition at first-team level for a couple of years. Here was another area where he would be relying on patience being extended by a fickle boardroom and large proportion of fans.

The weather had changed, and there was an autumnal nip in the air coming from the North Sea as Sunderland prepared to meet Dave Sexton's Coventry. The news was that McCoist would start, Durban observing, 'He is the only one that has had genuine efforts at goal and even if he doesn't score he is gaining valuable experience. It can take up to a year for him to really settle in; so any goals in the meantime would hasten his progress.' Durban knew McCoist needed service rather than striving to create his own opportunities, 'I am hoping that Cummins will be able to give us that bit of magic that has been missing in our last two home games.'

Elsewhere, big money was being splashed out in Manchester. United's Ron Atkinson raided his old club West Brom to sign Bryan Robson for £1.5m, while City paid an exorbitant-looking £350,000 for 30-year-old Asa Hartford from Everton. The feeling emanating down to Durban was that he would be consigned to trying to turn things round with his existing squad, 'We must try something different. West Ham's John Lyall summed it up when he said we were too predictable but now that we have Cummins playing in his first home game I am expecting a lot of open football. We have lacked imagination and flair from the flanks but Stan can give us something special. We need someone in the side who is unpredictable and can give us width.'

At this stage, Durban consistently praised and generally talked-up the potential of 'tin opener' Cummins. Things would turn sour between the pair, but what mattered now was that the club's forwards should find some form, 'It is essential that they get double figures if we are to finish the season in a mid-table position. The situation we are in doesn't really surprise me at present but if we are in a similar position in six weeks' time then obviously there will be cause for concern.' Although it may have sounded like an excuse, Durban continued to vent his annoyance over the USA fiasco, 'We have had a more than difficult start to the season and disruptive few weeks because of the American scene.' However, he appeared to relish the arrival of the chill in the air as if it was a harbinger of some 'proper' football from his charges, 'I sense a change over the last couple of days. The sunshine at the start of the season made it all a bit unrealistic, but the rain is more like it.'

Durban was upbeat about the fans seeing a more uplifting spectacle, 'It will be a different game against Coventry who are well known for their attractive play as I am sure that will be the way Dave Sexton will want to play it. They have had to build their team on a successful youth policy. Last season, I made an enquiry for Garry Thompson whom I have seen destroy one or two of the best centre-halves in the country but not many have shown against our two central defenders this season and I don't think tomorrow will be any different.' Tempting providence again?

In the event, Thompson and his fellow forwards were kept in check, but the end product was another sterile afternoon for a restless crowd. Pickering had been given 'a breather' on the bench, but Cummins had proved as ineffectual as his cohorts as he was stifled by right-back Danny Thomas. Before the break, Gerry Daly streaked clear and was only denied by Siddall's desperate dive at his feet. There was some drama midway through second half when Munro body-checked Steve Hunt and was shown the red card. Under the newly introduced disciplinary procedure the dismissed player would receive a two-match ban enforceable 14 days after the offence. Durban complained, 'You can call it a professional foul but I did not see it as violent. I am not condoning Munro but what bothered me was the reaction of the Coventry players. I have never seen anyone sent off for obstruction.' Meanwhile, the *Echo* reporter felt that the incident overshadowed Sunderland's problem in front of goal which he felt was 'rapidly becoming an embarrassment'.

There was a redeeming feature but, as Durban acknowledged, not one that the press or fans would be in a receptive mood to hear, 'We kept a clean sheet, but that is not enough. Those are games that I expect to win if we are to finish in a respectable position, but I sensed that the players are not accepting responsibility; too many are playing supporting roles.' Durban exuded the aura of a man with shoulders broad enough to bear the burden and deflect the heat from his players, but he needed the crowd to exhibit understanding and encouragement rather than impatiently dishing out 'stick', 'I don't want the players to take the pressures – that's what I'm paid for – but they can't do it without the backing of the supporters.' An undaunted boss issued a reminder that he was only here now because things had been far from rosy before, and asserted, 'I have no qualms that we will get it right.'

The local report still sympathised that Durban had canvassed from the start for an 'injection of quality players' to his squad, but also pointed out the catch that would interfere with that objective, 'Sunderland must prove that they are going places to attract them.' Arguably, the general attractiveness, or lack of it, had already been a factor when Durban had made moves to entice players to the north-east; Lee Chapman was one who had articulated his lack of enthusiasm for the move. Now that Sunderland were lying in the basement, the task would become even more difficult. Of course, that was if the chairman opened the purse strings, a prospect looking increasingly unlikely. At the weekend, reserve winger Barry Dunn signed for Tommy Docherty's Third Division Preston for £12,500 – barely an amount to set pulses racing and send Durban reaching for the chequebook.

## Honeymoon Period Well and Truly Over

Some hope of movements in the transfer market were raised after the Wolves chairman instructed Barnwell to prune his squad to finance the new stand at Molineux. It was looking as if the frustrated boss would be forced to sell star striker Andy Gray (rated at £1.2m). If so, he was rumoured to be interested in buying Cummins. But this was speculation, and a stumbling block was that Barnwell might not receive *any* of the incoming cash to spend. The fact that some clubs' managers were enduring more straitening working restrictions than at Sunderland did not provide much consolation. Not for the last time, Durban disparaged media hype, 'This is all pie in the sky. I would sell a player if I thought I could strengthen the team with a replacement; every asset in a house has its price.' At Stoke, Durban had sold Garth Crooks to Spurs for £600,000 but had used the funds to improve the overall strength of his squad by bringing in Munro, Peter Hampton, and Paul Maguire.

Times were not desperate (yet) but Durban intended to shake up the dressing room. Press and fans had been voicing a degree of disillusionment as the goodwill extended to an incoming manager had cooled. In turn, Durban believed his relationship with the players had to change; it was time to abandon the gentle touch and demand that players demonstrated total commitment, 'Clubs need contention between the manager and dressing room. It suddenly hit me that we have had enough time assessing, now is the time to make some decisions. Maybe it's time to take the pin out of a grenade and toss it into the dressing room. We have kept the boat in fairly calm waters up until now. I want to rock it and see players' reactions. I have had a chat with one or two, and got some answers I wanted and some I didn't. It's not the dressing room that's comfortable, it's the wage packets.'

Mixed metaphors aside, Durban was clearly concerned that certain individuals were not giving maximum effort. Something had to give, and it would not be the manager who would have to change his approach, 'I am finished with threats.'

On the pitch, there was the distraction of a second-round League Cup tie against Emlyn Hughes's Rotherham. A disappointing crowd of 10,450 saw Whitworth and Elliott in defence as Sunderland achieved a first-leg advantage with a 2-0 win through first-half goals from Rowell (penalty) and Ritchie. Although Rotherham were Second Division opposition, Durban saw enough to boldly announce, 'Elliott will be our kingpin. Playing at the back is his favourite position.' Durban's efforts to convert Elliott into a midfielder seemed at an end as he spoke of the player's importance, 'I saw things which I can improve. I think he still has to mature as a player and realise his potential, and start taking the responsibility that his ability merits. But he came to see me and said that he wanted to play at the back and be successful there, so that gives me something to build on. It was not an easy decision to leave out Rob Hindmarch but he took it like a man.'

There was an injury blow to deal with as a badly bruised ankle ruled Buckley out of the visit to newly promoted Notts County. Not possessing anyone in the same all-action mould, Durban turned to 17-year-old Venison, but concentrated on the benefits sometimes gleaned from a forced change, 'Injuries have not helped what I had in mind, but I will have no hesitation in playing Venison if he is in the right frame of mind. He has looked good in reserve-team games but until you throw them in you don't know. This is what happened to Nick Pickering and he has proved to be our most consistent player. I expect him to play in the rest of our games this season and within two years he should be pushing for a place in the England under-21 side.' That graduation would come to pass sooner than predicted.

A pleasing debut by Venison in the number four shirt was a rare crumb of comfort at Meadow Lane as the team, despite dominating possession for large chunks, slumped to a 2-0 reverse. Tiresome failings up front undermined the effort, Ritchie being guilty of botching a close-range chance over the bar, while Trevor Christie twice exhibited the basic finishing ability that Sunderland forwards looked incapable of replicating. The press message delivered to supporters at home was, 'unless a remedy can be found then it's going to be a long hard slog to avoid the Second Division.' The sun had long since disappeared behind the clouds of pessimism.

Durban echoed the despondent mood, 'We were two leagues ahead apart from putting in the goals. I have never been so flat in my life about one result. There's not a lot more I can do with the team. I'm finding it tougher going than at Stoke.' Briefly engulfed in the general gloom, Durban hoped the sluggish transfer market might buck up, 'I have got to start to find some answers very quickly. I would buy if I could improve the side but it's no use spending money on players unless they want to come here. I have spoken to someone today but I don't expect anything to happen. If the Andy Gray deal goes through, however, it could open a few doors.'

## The Dice Were Loaded from the Start

As Sunderland were slumping at Notts County, and Durban hoped for transfer doors to slip ajar, Allan Clarke's Leeds United were reported to have offered £750,000 plus a player for Andy Gray. Leeds had already spent heavily on recruiting Peter Barnes, Frank Gray, and Kenny Burns, and this latest bid meant that these fellow strugglers had backed their manager with the best part of £2m – a scale of outlay that all on Wearside could only imagine.

Meanwhile Durban planned to instil some confidence before Saturday's encounter with Tottenham. 'I am hoping to arrange a match against a side we know we should score some goals against. I have been through all this before and the lads have got to play themselves out of it. The hardest thing is to keep the spirits going. Once the goals stop going in, the players at the back are going to be deflated.' Durban was encouraging others to hold their nerve and keep the faith, 'A couple of good results can change the picture completely. I have tried every combination up front but will not panic into buying players. If we had received three good hidings and could not see the light it would be very worrying.' In the manager's eyes, the situation as it stood was only mildly worrying.

Durban soon returned to the shift in recruitment culture that he had pushed for on his arrival, a policy that would enable Sunderland to enjoy a treasure of local riches as opposed to scouring the market for overpriced or stopgap solutions. Midfielder Mick Hazard was set to play for Spurs at Roker – against his hometown club. He had been widely pursued when playing for Sunderland Boys, a fact Durban found galling, 'I appreciate we cannot take all the lads from the area but when 12 clubs are after one, then he must be something. Had he come here I am certain that he would have had a couple of seasons under his belt instead of only a handful of first-team games.' Hazard was now 21 and, given Sunderland's record, would likely have been a first-team regular with over 100 appearances had his home club persuaded him to reject London's calling.

In the practice match designed to boost morale, McCoist scored a hat-trick in a win over Darlington, but Durban indicated the Scot would have to bide his time before returning to the First Division pressure-pot, 'I am trying to get something fairly solid going, and I am not keen on chopping and changing. Ally took his goals very well and it will have done him a lot of good. But it is a big step from part-time football; I don't think he has attuned mentally to everything yet.'

In other news, bottom of the Second Division Orient appointed previous Roker boss Ken Knighton as their new manager after Jimmy Bloomfield had resigned following the sale of John Chiedozie to Notts County. At least Sunderland were not in the parlous financial position of Wolves and Orient who were being forced to sell prize assets simply to ensure survival. Another north-east club, Middlesbrough, had sold the 'crown jewels' and would still find themselves in penury. Tom Cowie did have justification in highlighting such predicaments when being lambasted for perceived tight-fistedness.

## A Sorry Consistency

Problems were mounting as seven of the first-team squad were unavailable through injury and suspension, and now Durban had another dissatisfied player in his office. Gordon Chisholm had been left out of the team before a hamstring injury curtailed his push for a recall, but Durban explained that the player's immediate concern lay in another area, 'Chis feels that he should have had an improved contract at the end of last season as there was a differential between him and some of the lads of his own age [21]. I knew that he had not been happy for a while but if he wants to go then I will not stand in his way. I have enough problems without sitting down coaxing players to stay here – it is not my job.'

Well, technically it was the manager's job to do exactly that if the situation warranted. However, Durban always maintained that it was simply counterproductive to have discontented individuals hanging around, and obviously felt his energies were more usefully engaged in mobilising fully committed players to arrest the alarming slide.

Despite the predicament, Durban enthused, 'We are going for the double. Having seen off the league champions we're now after the cup holders.' He also awaited the opportunity of comparing McCoist with Crooks. 'I see a lot of similarities between Ally and Garth; McCoist drifting into space in the box better, while Crooks does not need a big backswing to shoot.' The manager also made this game the time to initiate a tradition of allowing one lucky boy or girl to be the matchday mascot and have the thrill of running out on to the pitch with the team. This was typical of Durban's approach; connecting with the community and nurturing the vital young fan base. Although often besieged with onerous managerial responsibilities, Durban liked to apply a personal touch to thoughtful little details that would mean so much to the recipient.

A crowd of over 25,000 saw Tottenham inflict a 2-0 defeat on their hosts who duly hit the bottom of the league. What hurt even more was that they were outplayed for long periods, the *Echo* reporter finding it difficult to detect positives, 'Limitations were cruelly exposed. Spurs were so far ahead in skill and vision that it just wasn't true.' Another 18-year-old had been thrust into the fray, Colin West replacing the hapless Whitworth who gestured angrily at the Fulwell End boo-boys before disappearing down the tunnel in an episode that seemed to indicate he had worn a Sunderland shirt for the final time.

Thus it was that the home side had four teenagers trying to get to grips with the star-studded opposition. Along with Pickering, Venison, and McCoist, West battled manfully in what was a lost cause. Salt was rubbed into the wounds by the fact that it was local lad Hazard who sidestepped Siddall and rolled in the second goal. Hazard had also supplied Glen Hoddle in the build-up to the opener as an unmarked Steve Archibald nudged the ball home from close range.

Scrambling for sparks of consolation from the game, Durban maintained that McCoist was 'going to be gem', but the record signing needed a better supply. By this point of the season, it was significant that the veteran striker Durban had passed over in his considerations, Latchford, had notched seven goals for Swansea. But, the boss was perturbed that his own senior players appeared incapable of providing the necessary strength of character for the side's young hopes to lean on, 'It's not fair to put too big a burden on their shoulders.'

Apart from the cruel barracking directed at Whitworth, the crowd had soon become fractious and critical. Durban warned, 'It is essential that the fans don't turn on the players, if they want to criticise take it out on me as I can take it.' The *Echo* column conveyed Durban's ultimate confidence that 'when he has a full squad available he has the resources to climb away from the relegation zone.' It also pinpointed what might become the insurmountable obstacle to achieving any of the manager's medium-to-long-term aims, 'What he asks for is time and patience from the fans – whether he gets it remains to be seen.'

Despite the goal famine, Durban wished to strengthen a defence that was looking increasingly brittle and naïve. He revealed that he would be 'going to the continent to watch a cup game', but one potential answer lay much closer to home. It had not escaped his notice that former Sunderland and England lynchpin Dave Watson had been dropped by Southampton at the weekend, and the short-term acquisitions Durban had been intent on resisting were looking a more likely proposition with every passing game.

In midweek, Durban watched the reserves beat Middlesbrough 3-0 with Bowyer playing left-back, and Whitworth playing at the request of Bolton manager George Mulhall, who was set to sign the defender in a £25,000 deal. After the Tottenham match, Durban realised a swift departure would be beneficial for all concerned, 'He needs a fresh start, and we are keen to help him on his way for his own sake.' West scored twice in the win, and Durban was pleased with the forward's progress, 'The lad has come on a lot. He had a spell at the back for a couple of months which will have given him greater insight; now he knows what causes problems for defenders.'

Switching from youth to experience, Durban indicated that Bowyer was set to be eased back, 'Ian may just be lacking in sufficient fitness to play in midfield, but he could probably slot in at left-back where it can be less physical.' But the likelihood of a clash between Sunderland and their next opponents, Leeds United in the Elland Road cauldron, being anything other than physical was always going to be a forlorn hope. Mick Docherty dubbed the fixture 'the crunch', and the press labelled it 'Fallen Giants v Sleeping Giants'.

Durban's mission in Belgium turned out to be another cul-de-sac. He had watched 27-year-old Zoran Jelikic play for Hajduk Split in their 3-2 UEFA cup win at Beveren, but was not impressed, 'He is not the type of player that I am looking for, and certainly no improvement on the present squad. He did not communicate particularly well with the people around him; a bit of a follower rather than a leader. But, I had a day in Holland and established a lot of useful contacts.' Therefore, the only transfer activity saw former captain Whitworth complete his move to Bolton.

Away from the pitch, the annual report of directors was issued, which revealed that the previous year's deficit of £489,568 had been transformed into a loss of just £1,381. Meanwhile, several players paid a public relations visit to nearby Wearmouth Colliery and spent three hours underground. Despite being bottom of the league, this was the kind of reality check that put any perceived football hardships into context.

## Animals

On the evening prior to the 'crunch' Elland Road fixture, Durban prepared to employ Venison and Pickering as 'emergency' full-backs (with Munro suspended and Hinnigan injured). Understandably, the manager stressed his confidence in young Venison's ability to cope, 'I have no qualms about playing him at right-back as he has the right attitude.' Durban remained generally upbeat, 'Apart from 20 minutes against Ipswich and Spurs I don't think any team has really got the better of us. We must be careful in these situations that we don't expect to go a goal down and get into a rut if we miss chances. Leeds are a solid team and, like us, won't go down.'

This turned out to be another suspect prediction, although it was probably intended to underscore confidence in his own team's ability to pull themselves out of their predicament. Leeds had been bottom before beating West Brom 3-1 the previous weekend.

In the end, Leeds won 1-0 through an 80th-minute Eddie Gray goal, but the game was better remembered for Kenny Burns's 70th-minute flying 'tackle' that left Venison lying in agony, and fortunate to escape serious injury. The scenes that followed could be loosely described as pandemonium. Docherty and Durban led the protests, and believed that an automatic sending off could be the only reasonable outcome. To their disbelief, the inexperienced referee only booked Burns – for 'ungentlemanly conduct'! Later, the official took similar action when Trevor Cherry brought down Cummins as he was set for a clear run at goal.

Not fazed at all by the frenzy his 'assault' had sparked, Burns offered his own recollection, 'I sailed in for a 50-50 ball and must have caught his knee.' This was Burns's second successive booking for his new team, and his nonchalant description that he had 'sailed in' certainly implied a degree of recklessness, if not intent. At the post-match press conference, Leeds manager Clarke tried to switch the emphasis as he accused Durban of being a disgrace and trying to get Burns sent off, 'Sunderland made a meal of the incident. Football is a physical game.'

Apart from surviving (just) the physical battering, it was Sunderland's two rookie full-backs who emerged from the battle with most credit. Venison had snuffed out the threat of expensive England winger Peter Barnes, while Pickering had demonstrated his vision for the quick break and proved that he could operate effectively in the number three jersey. Up front, however, McCoist had squandered a great chance in each half and his side's league goal drought had now passed the 11-hour mark. Oh for a slice of luck similar to that enjoyed for Leeds's winner! Not only did Gray's shot deflect off Burns (who arguably should no longer have been on pitch), but Elliott led forcible appeals that the ball had not crossed the line after descending from the underside of the bar.

Later, Durban maintained that, following Burns's horror challenge, the prime motivation that had prompted him to leap from his seat in the directors' box and join Docherty on the pitch was to check on his youngster's welfare, 'I stayed out of the press room, and put a ban on the players saying anything about the incident as they could have filled newspapers with descriptions. I told them just to get on the coach as quickly as possible. I only wish I'd known that Allan Clarke had called me a disgrace as I never gestured that Burns should go. I went on the field to see the state of Venison's injury. He has cuts above the knee which are just above the height of a cricket pad.'

Overall, Durban believed that he and his players had exhibited self-control and not reacted in a hot-headed fashion to a tackle he regarded 'to a large degree, the worst I have ever seen'. Recalling the 'X-rated' challenge, Venison remembers, 'It was a bad tackle; cut me in two on the halfway line; sliced my knee open, and I felt like I had been hit by a truck.'

If the back page of the local paper was not bad enough, the front page led with the aftermath of the home match against West Ham, 'Eight fans were fined a total of £1,200 when they appeared before magistrates today. The eight all behaved like a pack of animals, said the chairman of the magistrates.' The prosecutor told how three West Ham supporters had come out of Roker Park to look for a telephone. Shortly afterwards a gang of 15 to 20 Sunderland supporters came after them and forced them to run into the coastguard's station to escape. The eight, who pleaded guilty to breach of the peace, were all fined £150 and bound over to keep the peace for two years.

## Storm in a Teacup

The following evening's front page also featured a football-related headline in what must have been a day particularly short of news. 'Durban Drops Ally McCoist' trumpeted the leader. The story recorded that McCoist had been left out of that evening's League Cup second leg at Rotherham for 'disciplinary reasons' and, instead, would turn out for the reserves at Mansfield. At this point, Durban would only give a vague explanation, 'I don't think he has prepared properly for a tough game. I don't want to say any more.' The record signing was to have led the attack alongside either Rowell or Ritchie, but his exclusion would allow the club's joint-top scorers (with two apiece!) to team up. Durban was anxious that there would be no slip-ups, 'Anything but a good result would harm the spirit.'

In an entertaining game, Durban saw his team go 3-1 up through Ritchie (2) and Cummins, but two quick-fire goals from the home team applied pressure. Munro was back after completing his two-game ban, but was booked as early as the ninth minute for a foul on skilful winger Tony Towner, and five minutes later it was deemed necessary to switch him to midfield, and allow the more mobile Pickering to take over at left-back. With ten minutes remaining, Hindmarch came on for Arnott to stiffen up a defence which had conceded three headed goals in a 12-minute spell. After the game, Durban remarked, 'We lost a bit of composure when they started winning the balls in the air and, on reflection, perhaps I should have sent Hindmarch on a bit earlier. All I hope for is a good home draw in the next round.'

Meanwhile, McCoist had grabbed all four goals in a convincing reserve-team win. Durban now deemed it appropriate to relay exactly what had taken place, and prevent unnecessary speculation. The young striker had been disciplined after failing to report when the party was due to leave for Matlock in preparation for the cup tie. His car had broken down at Gretna, and while he was telephoning Durban another car ran into the back of his vehicle. Durban explained, 'I was annoyed that he just took off and then headed back down on Monday morning. I am pleased at the way he responded as I have never doubted his character.'

For his part, McCoist had taken his medicine in a mature manner, and was now focussed on the important business on the pitch, 'The four goals will do my confidence the world of good. I felt much more relaxed and did not snatch at the chances which I have been doing in the first team. I realise I was to blame for what happened, and the boss was right to punish me.'

Both manager and player were clearly united in their view that McCoist had made a relatively minor error of judgement, would learn from experience, but had to receive some form of tangible admonishment from his manager (and he had already seen his car written off). Both parties had amicably moved on to focus on the next match. The sensationalised nature of the headline was a reminder, not that Durban needed it, of the local obsession with Sunderland Football Club.

## Not to Worry, It's Only Liverpool and Manchester United

As his squad prepared for the visit of European champions Liverpool, Durban received the news he had hoped for; a home League Cup draw against Second Division Crystal Palace. He also made an enquiry for Rotherham right-back Gerry Forrest, who had impressed in the previous round, but felt that the valuation was exorbitant.

Although McCoist was concerned about his first-team goal drought, he knew that none of his team-mates had produced the goods either. His manager's confidence remained steadfast, 'I have no qualms about Ally whatsoever. I think he felt the Leeds result more than anyone else. The time to start worrying is when the chances stop coming. He knows that he should have scored. He has shown in training what he can do. I am just waiting for him to take off.' Durban also emphasised that there would be no sense of being overawed against Liverpool, 'We have just got to believe we can do it, and not go into the game with apprehension and hand the initiative.'

In reality, a crowd of 27,854 saw Sunderland completely outplayed but, despite their dominance, the nature of Liverpool's opening goal in the second half riled the Roker crowd. Presented with a free kick just outside the area, Souness's first unsuccessful attempt was whistled back by referee Trelford Mills, an official who gained a reputation for being involved in controversial incidents. The retake saw Souness's sweetly struck shot powering like a bullet into the top corner. Another defeat was rubber-stamped when Terry McDermott volleyed home a left-wing cross from Dalglish. Throughout the encounter, the midfield zone had been dictated by Ray Kennedy, McDermott, and Souness, the trio stamping their international quality on proceedings. Against such a strong unit, Buckley and Chisholm had a forlorn task in winning any room for Pickering to embark on any foraging runs. Up front, the attack had looked woefully inadequate.

Durban conceded the vast discrepancy in quality, 'It was like schoolboys against men. They were better than us everywhere, and gave an indication of how far we are from being a top side.' The manager had previously stated his resolve not to crowbar individuals into the team if they did not complement the game plan, but this intention had evidently fallen by the wayside, 'I must stop trying to accommodate the best players and find a blend; against sides like Liverpool it is suicidal to compete with only three in midfield. There will be a big difference against Manchester United next week.' The supporters were not holding their collective breath.

Durban had other business to attend to before new league leaders United rolled into town. An FA commission had invited the Sunderland boss to submit a written account of the incidents at Leeds. Durban also met Arthur Cox at Roker and discussed players he was prepared to let go on loan. Brown, Arnott and Cooke were the primary names discussed, and they would all play in that week's reserve-team game. As well as meeting his Newcastle counterpart, Durban held 'a showdown' with his squad where he voiced his theory that too many senior players were not accepting the responsibility necessary if the club were to climb the table, 'I want to know who wants to battle and who wants to take the easy way out. I always judge people under pressure and not when everything is rosy.'

In a busy week, Durban also had another transfer request to contend with. Gary Rowell had been dropped for Saturday's game, but the manager was becoming bemused by the reactions of a number of players when they were left out, 'I have never come across a situation like it here where they want to know why they are dropped. I had a straight decision to make between Pickering and Rowell, and in my opinion Pick has been the better player.'

Regardless of Rowell's request, Durban had renewed his interest in former Roker favourite Tueart, and a £60,000 deal appeared to have been lined up. But, not for the first time, Durban was frustrated by the erratic conduct of John Bond. The City manager was prone to feed news to the media before the fellow manager with whom he was meant to be negotiating, and was reported to have had second thoughts on parting with the former

England international, offering him a new contract. Durban was annoyed that Bond informed the press before telephoning him.

Although Tueart would be 32 the following month, Durban viewed the player capable of injecting some goalscoring power into his attack, 'For what he was going to cost us over the next 18 months or so, it was worth the gamble. Dennis can give us character and he has unquestionable ability. When I saw him play on Wednesday against Stoke he was as fit as anyone else after two hours.' Learning from his reluctance to move for Latchford, Durban was now saying a veteran was 'worth the gamble'. However, when one was talking about proven former internationals of this calibre, there appeared to be relatively little risk involved. Age was now a secondary consideration to quality, 'It does not matter how much trouble we are in, there will be no second-rate buys. We are crying out for a Tueart who would improve our goalscoring record and he has the north-east connections which would give him the appetite to do a good job for us.'

Cox was at Roker for that week's reserve game, but Burnley were also believed to be keen on Alan Brown. Contemplating the possibility of an exchange deal, Durban and Docherty took in Burnley's 1-0 win over Chester City with their main interest believed to be full-back Brian Laws. Meanwhile, the club waited to hear whether former boss Knighton would agree to pay the £60,000 asking price to take Cooke to Orient. However, the only movement came with the announcement that Brown would start a two-month loan deal at Newcastle. The forward had underachieved, netting 15 league goals in 84 appearances, but Durban stated, 'I want him back for the FA Cup, and I think he will do very well for them. He has two months' aggravation to get out of his system.' Durban was hoping the recent showdown meeting would pay dividends, and pointed out that good performances and fighting qualities would benefit those seeking moves, 'The attitude in the dressing room Monday to Friday reflects on Saturday's performance. I want people to look at the club's situation and not personally. The success of the club will guarantee success for the individual player.'

The task facing whichever line-up Durban fielded would be formidable. Manchester United had racked up three successive wins, but a young striker would win his first start, 'I am not expecting Colin West to lead us out of the wilderness but we might be able to feed off his strengths.' West certainly had a physical presence that none of his fellow front-men possessed, but midfield was proving a headache for the manager, 'Suddenly we have six players competing, and most of them are left-sided.' He also hoped that a 'back to basics' approach would yield an upturn in fortune, 'I don't feel that we have had the rub of the green lately. I'll take anything now to give us a win. We have simplified things in training, and I have told the players to cut out the frills. We have been taking too long to get the ball forward but I am sure that if we can get a couple of goals or a win it will give us our confidence back, and restore pride.'

Against United's table-toppers, another crowd topping 27,000 saw the first-team return of Bowyer who donned the number four shirt, and Wallsend-born West made his full debut at centre-forward. Trailing to a scrappy Kevin Moran goal, there was a shock to the system for the home crowd after 38 minutes when a dynamic run by Pickering finished with Cummins shooting home at the Roker End to end 768 minutes of league action without a goal. Level at half-time and generally matching their opponents thus far, the Fulwell End rang out to the chant of 'We have scored – we have scored – we have scored.'

The mood was a combination of semi-delirium and self-mockery, and perhaps recognised that it might do to milk the moment while it lasted. What followed was that they witnessed the complete dismantling of their team by United's collection of multimillion-pound internationals. Bryan Robson rifled home a Coppell corner and Stapleton added two headers, before Gary Birtles added a fifth to inflict the heaviest home defeat since a Bobby Moore-led West Ham had achieved the same margin of victory in 1967.

The *Echo* report acknowledged that injuries and the early unavailability of the NASL trio had disrupted the side 'but it is to be hoped that the experimental stage is over.' This hope of 9 November was perhaps reminding Durban that he had indicated that 'the time for experiments is over' following the Swansea defeat at the end of September. There was the hope that Bowyer's experience could start to galvanise those around him, but the manager had already complained it had been some of the more experienced men who had been guilty of 'hiding'. Durban found his team propping up the First Division table, seven points adrift of a safety position, and the upcoming 'derby' at Middlesbrough would signal the completion of a third of the league programme – alarm bells were clanging loud and clear.

## Ten-Year Plan with Tweaks

Durban was unwavering in his belief of what constituted the right approach to eventually deliver enduring success, 'I've never been associated with an unsuccessful situation. I know I'll continue to do what I think is right, in that if I am going to bring someone here it will not be someone who is going to cost us an awful lot of money and who we'd be looking to discard at the end of 12 months. It was right to buy the youngster with the best potential in Scotland. It was a lot of money, but he's one for the future. He'll be going for another ten years.'

McCoist was not the only long-term prospect, 'We've pulled Pickering and Venison from out of the reserves and they look as if they're going to be with us for ten years, provided they're handled properly. We've gone to the bottom of the league, but you still must do what is right. We have to get out of the bottom three and stay out. It's a simple case of survival. I did not want to contemplate anything short term. Now we've got to have a re-think.'

This was not an isolated instance where Durban was forced to reassess, but some principles would never be compromised, 'We must not be obligated to long contracts to paying out top money for some years. The economic situation at the club still has to be considered even in this desperate state. We don't want to be in a position where we've paid out a tremendous lot of money, still fail to recover, and are stymied for the future.'

Durban was well aware of another glaring feature of the club's past dealings, 'We cannot afford to make a loss on transfers. It prevents ground development. We need to improve Roker Park and our training facilities. We must do this while we consolidate and be successful as a top-class First Division club. A manager's position is only reflected to the general public by the first-team's performance, but the development of young players is now going to be the base on which most successful clubs will have to rely.' Durban was certainly a man who had to juggle many important priorities, but one message and guiding principle remained constant, 'I am looking for quality and character. *The club is about tomorrow.*'

## Keeping the Faith

One change was implemented without delay as Durban relieved Clarke of on-field captaincy responsibilities (he remained club skipper), 'The players respect Jeff but I am looking for a captain who will give us more drive on the field.' Durban duly announced that Munro was the man for the job, and spoke of the player's leadership credentials, 'Iain has played at a higher level than anyone we have got. He has only been here a couple of months but he cares more than several players who have been here for years. Everything he does is intense. Part of Pickering's development has been because of Munro's influence around him.'

The new captain was swift to endorse his manager's view of the potential present at the club, 'The youngsters are really tremendous. There's depth of talent everywhere you look.' Munro also backed Durban's policy of looking to only import 'quality and character' to nurture such prospects, 'They learn from experienced players and from the right type they can learn a lot. The wrong type can destroy them.' He also spotlighted one of the features of the English First Division that fellow Scot McCoist was trying to get to grips with, 'They move the ball quicker. In Scotland they want a few touches.'

McCoist confirmed his new captain's observation, 'You've got to think what you're going to do quicker. You don't get much time on the ball. But the physical side's the same. It's just as physical in Scotland. It's the speed here. You've got to do in one movement what took two before. Defences are tighter.' One thing that might have eased the striker's transition would have been to team him with an experienced man with a greater physical presence than the ever-willing Ritchie or Rowell, 'I played with a big lad at St Johnstone. He could hustle and bustle, put himself about, and things would happen off him.' Once again, the decision not to make a move for Latchford looked increasingly regrettable.

McCoist found it difficult to believe the position his new team were in, and thought they had put in some good performances without reaping the rewards, 'I think after a game that it can't have happened. It shouldn't have happened. The manager comes in – and he knows we've played well and tried our hearts out.' The young striker did not attempt to shirk his share of culpability for the predicament, 'I've been snatching at them.' However, McCoist's irrepressible optimism shone bright, 'I think it'll come good. There's no depression. I've been coming back in afternoons. If I work at it, it should come better.' It would indeed, and many a Sunderland supporter would wish that Durban's 'ten-year plan' for the prodigiously gifted young forward had been fulfilled at Roker.

Shaun Elliott was another to admit that he could do better, but confirmed that the manager had promoted belief and spirit in the squad, 'I can see us pulling through. The lads know they have the ability. The dressing room is very, very alive.' Midfield dynamo Mick Buckley was in full accord, his remarks echoing his work-hungry, enthusiastic playing style, 'It's a terrible position at the bottom. Every game becomes a hard one. But we'll move up. The spirit is tremendous. Once we get a result under our belts. Once they start going in. We've been creating chances, and not putting them away. We're working hard. We'll come through. Alan Durban will come through.' Go tell it in the streets Mr Buckley; there were difficult times looming and the natives had become restless.

## Trying Things and Trying Times

Despite the situation, the manager knew a rash dive into the transfer market was not the solution, 'We have a team problem, and not an individual one. For an hour [against United] we showed what we are capable of, but for the last half hour we showed why we are in this position. It is about playing with heart. When we went behind again, we were poor and short of leadership.' Durban knew that United had spent heavily, but a crucial difference was that they were able to attract the class players who viewed Sunderland as an unappealing destination.

Realising he could not afford or entice a 'top' player to commit himself to the club in their present state, Durban made a more realistic (but still ambitious) attempt to bring Liverpool's Craig Johnston to Roker on loan. Johnston had been unable to command a first-team place since his £650,000 move from Teesside, but the Anfield club rejected Sunderland's approach. Durban claimed that the loan arrangement would have been with a view to persuading the player to eventually sign on a permanent basis, but the fee involved would surely have made his chairman blanch.

One player who arrived on trial was Želimir Vidović, a 27-year-old defender from FC Sarajevo with three caps for Yugoslavia. Durban flagged up the economic practicalities of importing from that part of the European market, 'It will cost us about £100,000. It could save us a lot of money for an international and another good thing is the Yugoslavs don't demand cash on the nail.' It was revealing that Durban had to concern himself with details of the stage-payment nature of any proposed transaction – a team manager had to be a man of many parts. Vidović could play anywhere along the back four, and Durban remarked, 'I need to bring in a full-back. Venison has done very well but he is now being given too much responsibility, and I would prefer to use him in midfield.'

Venison was not the only bright talent the boss was contemplating deploying in midfield. McCoist had begun his career there before his 22-goal season as a forward catapulted him into the radars of bigger clubs, 'McCoist will never blend in with Cummins as a pair, so if he is going to break into the side he has a better chance of doing it in midfield where we are looking for goalscorers.' This sounded logical reasoning, but also of a man whose potential solutions were being exhausted.

It had been easy to forget that Durban had not signed a contract, and it was now revealed that he had been offered a fresh five-year deal, 'I am only interested in Wednesday's cup tie and getting us off the bottom of the table, but if the board feel that signing a five-year contract would bring stability to the club then I would.' Chairman Cowie pledged faith, 'The more I work alongside Alan Durban the more convinced I am that he was exactly the right appointment.' At this point of their working relationship, Durban could derive genuine comfort from such a pledge of backing from the top.

One manager denied a vote of confidence was Crystal Palace's Dario Gradi, who was sacked the day before Palace arrived in Sunderland for the cup encounter. Chairman Ron Noades had brought Gradi with him from Wimbledon in January to take over from Malcolm Allison. In a statement that contained a chilling relevance to future events at Sunderland, the Palace board articulated their regret at Gradi's departure, 'The directors appreciate that he has laid the foundations of a successful long-term youth policy which should produce positive results in the years to come.' A fine way to show appreciation! Coach Steve Kember was named as caretaker-manager, and Durban was aware of the danger of the 'wounded beast' – the eagerness of players to impress a new boss, 'We have a good home draw; it would be criminal to waste it. By selecting the same side it shows that we have done enough switching and experimenting and are on the right lines.'

An apathetic attendance of only 11,139 were at Roker Park to witness that Sunderland most certainly were *not* 'on the right lines' at present. The *Echo* lamented, 'Sunderland are again the laughing stock of the football world following another embarrassing and humiliating defeat.' A 58th-minute Jim Cannon goal won it for Palace as they advanced into the fourth-round draw. The bemused reporter told readers that their team had resorted to 'hitting aimless balls into the middle to an 18-year-old youngster'.

The cutting comments marked a dramatic departure from the more moderate tone that had accompanied disappointing results earlier in the campaign. For this correspondent, breaking point appeared to have arrived with an almost farcical miss, and the disdain was evident, 'Firstly, Cummins preferred to take a dive and look hopefully for a penalty which referee Worrall quite rightly ignored. Bowyer's follow-up was cleared off the line, and fell to West who somehow managed to hit a post from a couple of yards when a tap-in would have sufficed.'

The young blonde striker had been guilty of a howling miss, but had been only one of many poor performers. His youth did not save him from scathing criticism, 'How Colin West is preferred to a player the manager has paid £350,000 for is beyond me as Ally McCoist must surely have tucked away about Sunderland's only chance in a performance that borderlined on pathetic.' The manager was not about to escape the firing line, 'If that is Durban's idea of the best side available then the relegation fight ahead is not worth thinking about.' It looked as if some white flags were being hoisted by the local media. Had they fallen out of love with the new man? Had they lost faith that the long-term vision was achievable?

Durban was not one to hide, 'I can take a beating but not the humiliation for our supporters [who] are the best in the country, and once supporters start losing faith, that's when you know you have a major problem. I know how badly the players will feel but that defeat really hurt.' The boss then reasserted his anger over a repeating trait, 'There's a difference between playing badly and not accepting responsibility, and I will be looking for those who want to roll their sleeves up, and sorting out those who don't. I realised after two minutes that I had made an error in selection; but I wanted to keep faith with the same team.'

However difficult, Durban knew this sorry chapter had to be closed as soon as possible, 'We have still got something precious to fight for and we must get a run going to redress the balance.' On a more personal note, the FA had been satisfied with Durban's reply concerning the incidents at Leeds, 'There is no case to answer, and no disciplinary action will be taken. I must make sure, however, that I don't go on to the field of play again.' This was a small crumb of comfort on a night to forget.

The day after a disastrous early cup exit was not the best timing for a new manager to attend his first club annual general meeting, but it did crank up the drama. Chairman Cowie played the politician and his declaration that there would be 'no U-turn' set him up for a comparison with Margaret Thatcher who had responded to critics the previous year with the line, 'You turn if you want to. The lady's not for turning.'

Returning to less histrionic language, Cowie emphasised the imperative task of putting the club on a sound financial basis, and that they must look to the youth policy to save the club from relegation. While the hopes pinned on Venison, McCoist, Pickering, and West providing the basis of long-lasting consolidation were genuinely felt by the manager, he and the supporters must have been disheartened to hear this public intimation that no major buys would be sanctioned.

The influx of young potential that Durban had overseen was intended to reap dividends aplenty, but in the medium term. The manager had not expected the full onus of clawing the team out of immediate trouble to fall on the shoulders of his raw youngsters.

Shareholder and local property businessman Barry Batey voiced his dissent at the chairman's policy, whist former director Bill Martin indicated his concern over money matters, being perturbed at the wages (in the £25,000–£30,000 bracket) paid to three players (assuming they were Knighton's final three signings Allardyce, Bowyer, and Ritchie). He was also unhappy about the change of strip but Cowie assured him that financially the change was well worthwhile. The chairman went on to say that the club had paid exorbitant fees for players in ill-timed moves that had lost the club money. He was confident that the club now had the manager to pull them through, but appealed for supporters to be *patient*. There was that word again.

## Stopping the Rot

The club released more cash it could ill afford when they reached a settlement with the sacked managerial team of Knighton and Frank Clark, who accepted an increased compensation offer. In return, the pair dropped their claim for unfair dismissal which had been due to be discussed by an independent tribunal.

On the pitch, Durban wielded the axe for the upcoming Tees-Wear derby as Arnott, Rowell, and West were omitted, 'The players will be relieved that they can go and play away from home when things are going this way. From my experience, they must relax but still give 100 per cent, and try to take the tension out of it. Our survival depends on how many players are prepared to commit themselves to the cause, so I am looking for a big change in attitude.'

Middlesbrough and Sunderland remained deadlocked in a match that demonstrated the reason both teams were at the foot of the table. Siddall turned a close-range Billy Woof header over the bar, while Ritchie mis-hit a close-range attempt straight at Platt and failed to improve from the rebound as he lost his footing. After the break, the standard of finishing maintained its dismal standard; Bowyer scraped a post when he had time and space, and Hodgson shot well wide after fashioning an opening. Meanwhile, the forward who had gone out on loan did find the net as Alan Brown scored in Newcastle's 4-1 win over Charlton Athletic.

Following their recent torrid time, Durban was grateful for a bore draw, and that local honour had been preserved, 'I don't normally use superlatives on players but Hindmarch was absolutely outstanding, and for the first time I saw the reaction I am looking for from somebody out of the side. He had it written all over his face that he won't be left out again.' Elliott had been deployed in midfield only a month after Durban had declared the intention to make him his defensive 'kingpin.' The boss's attitude was uncompromisingly simple, 'I will do what I think best for the club and not the individual', and he emphasised that the player was 'just as pleased as anyone that we have stopped the rot'. The enthusiastic backing supplied by the away support, despite the recent failings, continued to impress Durban, 'When the bus pulled in at the ground they gave us a magnificent reception and the lads responded.'

A practice match was arranged to assess the capabilities of Vidović, who made a favourable impression, 'The lad can play there is no doubt about that; I think he will be joining us provided they like the method of payment which would not tie up any cash we may want to spend on a striker. Our problems at full-back are minimal compared to the front-men.'

This indicated that some money was available, but was the boss giving supporters (and himself) false hope only days after the chairman had publicly implied funds were sparse? Whatever the real financial situation, a suitable deal for Vidović failed to materialise, and Durban soon distanced himself from any early incoming transactions, 'Patching up is not the right thing to do. Buying is not the answer to all our problems and I will not buy second-rate strikers just to be seen to be doing something.'

Durban then took his team to face an Everton side managed by the man he had mentored at Stoke, Howard Kendall, and there was a boost when Buckley was declared fit to play against his former club. Trailing to a 60th-minute Eastoe goal, Durban left the directors' box to sit in the dugout. Minutes later, he sent on Ritchie for a struggling Pickering, and Kendall introduced Kevin Richardson for his first league action. Both substitutes would be heavily involved in the 75th-minute moment that reshaped the final outcome. With Cummins preparing to shoot following a fumble by keeper Jim Arnold, he was brought down by Richardson. Despite having only been on the field a few minutes, Ritchie took responsibility and tucked away the penalty. The Scot was modest when recalling the incident, 'With Gary Rowell out of the side, and Stan feeling groggy, I asked if he wanted me to take it. I knew where I was going to put it but the goalkeeper moved so that helped me.'

Six minutes from time, Arnold failed to hold a McCoist drive, and Elliott gratefully swept the rebound into the roof of the net. Durban's reaction to that goal was that it would boost Elliott's confidence and 'help him to believe that he can be a good player in midfield.' Ritchie's general attitude evinced a sense that the Sunderland dressing room had managed to retain its solidarity, 'That was great for the lads and they deserved it. I knew that if we got one goal then we could go on and win it, and that made up for the disappointment of being made substitute.' At one stage, it looked as if Sunderland were going to finish with ten men after Cummins needed treatment from Docherty, Durban reporting, 'When Mick came off he had a handful of bits and pieces of Stan's teeth.'

Scotland manager Jock Stein had been present and had seen Munro put in a good performance, but it was the Sunderland boss who had greater call to be satisfied, 'Those last two results have given me a lift, and I hope that they have had the same effect on the players and supporters as we have now given ourselves a lifeline. Two home games give us the chance to get in the ruck. We are not going to fly our way out of trouble, but we have got to fight and make the most of these games.'

## A Step Forward, and Two Back

Durban was contemplating his transfer war chest receiving a welcome injection after Brown notched another two goals as Newcastle defeated league leaders Luton at St James' Park.

'We have not agreed a fee' he stressed, but it was evident that Brown's form had strengthened Sunderland's bargaining position. Meanwhile, a loan deal for Arnott was arranged with Blackburn boss Bobby Saxton, 'It is better for Arnott to be playing Second Division football than North Midlands League which is the deadest I have seen.'

Nevertheless, it was telling that, despite the current precarious position, Durban judged Arnott's services to be dispensable. Days later, it appeared doubtful whether Newcastle would be able to buy Brown no matter how much he impressed after the Tyneside club announced debts and liabilities amounting to £987,342, the primary causes cited being losses on transfers and lower gates.

All three of the north-east's 'big three' had their financial problems, but the mood in Durban's Roker camp was buoyant for the upcoming home matches against Forest and West Brom, 'We have got to give the crowd something to shout about. I can sense the dressing room. Hindmarch has made a big difference to the side since his return and Elliott more bite to the midfield.' The attitude being displayed was encouraging, but a glance at the bottom five league positions offered a sobering sight: Birmingham 15 points; West Brom 15; Leeds 15; Middlesbrough 11; Sunderland 11.

Constantly quizzed about the prospect of new signings, Durban had little encouragement to offer the long-suffering supporters, 'All we are doing at this stage is looking at the merits of another Yugoslav for I know when I took on the Dutch lad [Ursem] at Stoke it took him a long time to settle.' But, Durban's mind was focussed on that evening's return fixture against Clough's Forest as he mulled over his team selection, 'I want to see what mood the players are in. It is important that we maintain our improvement. We have managed only two league victories and each time we have had to come from behind to do it. So it would be nice if we could get an early goal.'

The match would afford the chance for Bowyer to impress against his former club, 'Ian gives us know-how and his experience of playing in the back four, like that of Elliott, enables them to sense danger more quickly.' During this period such players' senses must have been heightened to overdrive; there seemed to be danger every time the opposition had possession. Sunderland remained unchanged, with Bowyer donning the unfamiliar number nine shirt. Perhaps the apathy inflicted by the United and Palace debacles had struck deep; despite the weekend win at Everton the attendance of 17,419 represented the lowest league gate at Roker since the final game of the 1977/78 season when 16,718 had seen a 3-0 win over Charlton.

The match started in dramatic fashion. After only 20 seconds, Forest skipper Einar Aas fell awkwardly as he turned a simple ball back to goalkeeper Peter Shilton and had to be stretchered off. Five minutes later, McCoist cleverly back-heeled the ball to Cummins who went wide of Shilton only to find the side netting. In a familiarly depressing pattern, however, John Robertson sent Colin Walsh clear to shoot past Siddall while the crowd bayed for an offside flag. Six minutes into the second half, Peter Ward (again looking suspiciously offside) sent in a cross-shot which was stabbed home by the lurking Fashanu for his third goal in as many games.

The mini revival that followed was both encouraging and cruel. On 62 minutes, Bryn Gunn brought down McCoist and from Pickering's free kick Hindmarch powered home a header to record his first senior goal. Ritchie came on for Buckley and was involved in the 78th-minute moment that all Sunderland had been yearning for as his mishit shot inadvertently set McCoist up with the opportunity to strike the ball under Shilton to send the crowd wild. The ground suddenly resounded to the chant of 'Ally – Ally – Ally' which enjoyed the same timbre and rhythm as that used by boxing crowds to serenade former heavyweight champion Muhammad Ali.

Inspired with hope of an upturn in fortunes, all was cruelly dashed with five minutes remaining, and an erratic refereeing decision was not something Durban and his team of battlers deserved. John Hough penalised Munro's challenge on Ward, and Proctor's free kick was headed past Siddall by David Needham. Captain Munro later commented on the injustice, but also of the resolve to set things aright, 'It was no foul as I won the ball cleanly. The lads were tremendously disappointed but we are not deflated. We will be rolling our sleeves up and battling all the way as our spirit is still intact and we can't wait for Saturday to come.'

The two goalscorers were also taking away positives from the defeat, McCoist harbouring the hope that a psychological barrier had been removed, 'It is great to get off the mark at last, but disappointing to lose to a goal like that. I must admit not scoring had been at the back of my mind a wee bit but now I have broken the ice I hope to score a few more.' Hindmarch commented, 'The Doc told me to get up there and make some early runs, but the defeat has taken away the pleasure.'

Although this was the club's fifth successive home loss, Durban had been given grounds to back up his consistent optimism, 'There is no way we will go down if we continue to battle the way we did. The team showed tremendous spirit but we can't expect to concede and come from behind to beat sides like Forest. I thought that was a perfectly fair tackle by Munro and a bad miss by Cummins. But that's the way things go when you are at the bottom.' The match had been quite entertaining and Durban hoped supporters recognised that a positive approach had not been discarded, 'It's nice to get among the goals for without them you can't get anywhere. I hope that those fans who had given up the ghost saw some light and that as long as we are giving them value for money they will bear with us.'

That message was not heeded three days later when the already diminishing support dwindled further for the visit of a West Brom team that included Martin Jol in midfield. Durban got his wish for the team to get their noses in front, and it was defender Hindmarch, not McCoist, who notched a second senior goal. Alas, the novelty of grabbing a lead did not change the ultimate outcome as two second-half lapses, and missed chances, gave the impression of a doomed outfit.

Seeking the cushion of another goal, McCoist went clear but his control let him down before the ball broke off keeper Mark Grew and Buckley fired the rebound over the bar. Then a misguided decision by Clarke proved costly when he ran out in an attempt to play offside as Cyrille Regis broke clear. Though Siddall parried, Ally Brown forced home the rebound. Bowyer then side-footed the ball wide after Cummins had squared the ball across the face of goal, and that bad miss would be rued 15 minutes from time when the away team were gifted the game in a manner that many in the crowd found hard to stomach.

Right-back Venison was hesitant as he contemplated finding his keeper, then looked to see if he could play the ball up the line before eventually reverting to his initial plan. The delay was fatal; Regis had anticipated, and the striker gratefully intercepted the back-pass and beat Siddall.

The *Echo* reporter was sympathetic with the manager's difficulties, 'Surely he can't be expected to carry the can for ridiculous goals being conceded and chances spurned. When experienced players are letting the side down it is no use expecting the youngsters to see you through. As good as the present crop of kids are, the confidence is gradually being drained.'

Durban lamented, 'We are our own worst enemies. We gave them it. From having everything under control, we went to a side with no confidence. We had done the hardest bit by scoring against the wind and I said that if we kept our heads and didn't do anything silly we would win it easily.'

Durban was annoyed and frustrated at the basic errors, but was not about to 'crucify' the young player who made the most prominent blunder, 'One of the biggest crimes in football is to pass back to the goalkeeper, and I rollicked Hindmarch on Wednesday, yet we do the same again. That's the easy way out, but Barry Venison won't do it again. He may kick the ball into the crowd the next ten times in a similar position but at least he's learnt at 17, and not 27 like me. It's not as though it's the same players that are letting us down.'

## No Substitute for Experience

The manager recognised that a capable and experienced head was needed to steady the ship, and provide on-field stature and resilience. Given their league predicament, however, a straightforward signing was looking increasingly unlikely. A sweetener would need to be thrown into the mix if anyone possessing real quality was to be tempted to join the relegation dogfight.

In the dying embers of November, Durban offered the position of assistant manager as the bait to attract Ipswich and England defender Mick Mills, and the 32-year-old mulled over a £150,000 deal. Both clubs were annoyed at news leaking out, accusing each other for the breach, and Durban hoped that it would not jeopardise his chances of landing a current international, 'Mills's age may not be ideal but it is immaterial as I have checked his fitness. He is a top-class player who to capture in their prime we would have to pay £1m. I have known Mick for a long time and if he comes he will *upmarket* the club considerably and let everyone know that we mean business. It is all about timing and I believe Mick is ideal management material.'

Durban revealed that if Mills joined he would play at full-back, and Munro switch to midfield. There were complications; Mills had three sons at school, and would hold talks with Bobby Robson at Portman Road to clarify the likelihood of retaining his first-team place. Mills stated, 'Alan Durban wanted to fly down and see me but I will not be leaving Ipswich in a hurry. There is no way I am going to be rushed into making a decision.'

Durban recognised that the player was also hopeful of being part of the England team for the forthcoming World Cup in Spain, but reckoned any move to Roker 'should not make any difference as he will not have to give up playing.' But, Mills planned to ask Ron Greenwood whether joining a team at the bottom of the league would be detrimental to his immediate international position. Durban had done everything he could, 'The ball is very much in Mick's court. Our meeting went very well and I have outlined what I want on the playing field and what his responsibilities would be. He must decide.'

The Roker boss added that Elliott's name had cropped up during negotiations, 'Bobby Robson inquired about Shaun and I told him how much I wanted, but he has not been back and said nothing about the price I quoted.' Durban may have been better advised switching Elliott to his favoured central-defensive role, as the manager acknowledged that the man he had envisaged as the rock to build his defensive unit around, Clarke, had been distinctly 'wobbling'. The manager was certainly dismayed by recent error-strewn displays, 'We are starting to give goals away from nowhere and I have never seen anything like those two on Saturday. When we get outnumbered at the back we think playing offside is the answer but the video confirmed that Regis was onside, and we paid the penalty.'

As Durban continued to work at achieving a much-needed transfer breakthrough, rivals Middlesbrough were claiming a major coup; 35-year-old George Best had apparently agreed to sign and was due to meet manager Murdoch to sort out the details. Best's signature was being somewhat prematurely spoken of as 'a formality' with only a wait for international clearance. Durban had his own agenda and was in bullish mood about there being more than one new arrival, 'Should we sign Mick, our priority would then become a midfield player and a striker. I don't want to overload the club with older players but I feel that we must sign tried and trusted players who can do it, and not gamble at this stage.' This was an interesting deviation in Durban's mindset; now experienced men were *not* the 'gambles' he had implied before the season kicked off. The view from the foot of the table had transformed perspectives.

Still hopeful of a 'yes' from his principal target, Durban outlined that Mills's initial responsibilities would be aiding an upturn in results, and he could learn the managerial ropes when the dust had settled, 'Mick has all the qualities and experience to stay in football, and though there is much more to this side of the game than first appears, he will not have much time for it as he will be training and playing.' One rumour that Durban distanced himself from was the possibility of an exchange with Sheffield Wednesday involving Terry Curran and Cummins whose former manager at Middlesbrough, Jack Charlton, was an admirer.

Enjoying the reserves of energy permitted by boyish fitness, Pickering and Venison played in a Youth Cup win at Hull. At York meanwhile, Hinnigan was not fit enough to turn out for the reserves, and Durban answered the emergency to play at full-back. The *Echo* report is revealing, 'The atrocious standard of the North Midlands League was once more underlined. No more than 12 paying spectators were present at kick-off.' Durban played the full 90 minutes, 'At the age of 40, he looked more than capable of handling the threat from York strikers half his age' (one of these was future Eire international John Byrne).

## Frustrating Days

While Queen and David Bowie topped the pop charts with 'Under Pressure', the Sunderland boss was attempting to shield his shell-shocked troops from the strain of life at the bottom as they made the long haul to Brighton. For a second successive match, Durban saw his team take the lead before crumbling. In the 21st minute, McCoist sent Ritchie clear to round Graham Moseley and slot the ball in. This was a step forward, as Durban had been used to seeing his team spurn such gilt-edged openings. But, defensive failings resurfaced as Gordon Smith was left unmarked to equalise. A 'backs-to-the-wall' affair followed, but yet again there was a sense of injustice about Brighton's 80th-minute winner when substitute Andy Ritchie appeared to push Clarke before shooting. The squad then travelled on to the Isle of Wight for a Monday-night friendly against Newport. A 4-1 victory saw McCoist notch a couple of goals, while the interesting full-back pairing was Durban and Bowyer.

Back in the north-east, the George Best 'formality' had predictably developed hitches. San Jose Earthquakes accused Middlesbrough of 'arrogant discourtesy' over the lack of direct contact, and were insisting that a fee would be payable. The culmination was that on the day that Best had promised to sign a contract (worth £1,500 per game) he instead flew back to his California home for an 'easier life.' Murdoch fumed, 'People said Best was a reformed character, but I think he has let everyone down. We had to ring his agent Bill McMurdo [to find out]. I think he was too embarrassed to ring us.'

As for Sunderland's prime target, a major sticking point for Mills was that Ipswich were handily placed in the league, only goal difference placing them second. Mills acknowledged that he had received a 'fabulous offer' from Sunderland, but 'my greatest ambition is to win a league championship medal. This season may be my best and last chance.' Although coming as no major surprise, it was a heavy blow to Durban when Mills's rejection arrived, but he remained in determined mood, 'The search will go on. Right now I am interested in any quality right-sided strikers.'

The next player to emerge as having been approached, however, was a central defender. Willie Young had just signed for Forest for £175,000, but revealed, 'Before setting off for Nottingham, I was informed that Sunderland had come in for me. I thought it was only fair as Forest had been in for a long time that I spoke to them first, but had things not worked out I would certainly have talked to Sunderland because there was no point in me carrying on in Arsenal reserves.'

Despite the knock-backs, Durban reissued his intention of acquiring reinforcements, 'The team and the supporters need a spark from the transfer market and we must get someone in the near future.' In the interim, Durban moved to take 22-year-old Gateshead striker John McGinley on a fortnight's trial, with the local public generally viewing this 'unknown' as another woefully inadequate stopgap. They awaited the 'spark'.

No sooner had he reassured supporters of his determination to make a breakthrough signing, Durban had to deal with another disappointing request from a want-away player. The man whose return both manager and fans had been hoping would add the 'know-how' Durban craved, Ian Bowyer, had (as the *Echo* phrased it) 'opted out of Sunderland's fight for First Division survival.' Durban stated that the player's primary reason was that he had 'not settled here', and 'when he asked to be put on the list I had no hesitation in making him available.'

The timing was suspect, however, and it was fair to say that Sunderland supporters had been disappointed with the player's lacklustre form throughout his short spell at the club. Bowyer's struggle underscored the malaise of a team lacking confidence. It could come as no surprise to see McCoist, a teenager from the Scottish Second Division, struggle to adapt to life in the top tier when such a seasoned pro as Bowyer (boasting league championships and European Cups) was also appearing bereft of confidence.

The arrival of frost and snow put paid to the home match against Southampton and, as the weather deteriorated, Durban beavered away via telephone from his Yarm home hoping to secure a signing ahead of the FA Cup deadline. The press went as far to suggest a 'double swoop' might be imminent, linking the Roker boss with Jimmy Nicholl and Frank Worthington. Hopes of signing the 24-year-old Manchester United international in a £250,000 deal hit snags from the outset. Although Ron Atkinson was under pressure to recoup some of his recent massive outlay, Nicholl was not enthused about a permanent deal, 'I am wary of joining a club threatened with relegation, but going on loan would put me back in the picture for World Cup selection.' Durban had also enquired about Watson and Dave Swindlehurst, 'I have made initial contact for a player who was available at £400,000 earlier in the season, but I am not sure how badly he wants to come – and that's important to me.' This was Swindlehurst. Although Derby were reluctantly forced to sell, the former Crystal Palace man had declared a preference to return to the south. Birmingham's Worthington was the one Durban had not moved for – not on this occasion.

## Nothing Straightforward

Dave Watson appeared to be the most immediate candidate for a permanent move as Southampton were prepared to let him go for a fee of around £50,000, but much would depend on the 1973

FA Cup hero's personal terms. Watson was currently languishing in the reserves, and apart from a bid by Arthur Cox to tempt him away, inquiries had been scarce. The press did not wait long to associate the Sunderland manager's name with other targets. Winger Peter Bodak had been fined by Coventry for making public a written transfer request, but Durban quashed elements of the newspaper rumours, 'I have not bid £100,000 for Bodak as reported. They wanted one of our better players in part exchange and I told them I was not interested. He is only one of many players that we have made inquiries about.'

Durban watched Watson in action at Brisbane Road as Southampton reserves beat Orient and remained hopeful over the prospect of a new face being in the team for the weekend, 'The situation can change with a phone call. Jimmy Nicholl was the one, and I am hopeful that the deals which were on earlier in the week will go through as I have never said that they were dead.' Durban then offered some insights concerning the modern complexities of transfer business, 'Until a couple of years ago the hardest part of signing a player used to be agreeing a fee between the clubs, but now it is with the player. I don't think the players have been unreasonable in their demands but our position geographically and in the table has not helped us to sign quality players. The club's lack of success in recent years is another factor, but I want to find out how badly players want to come to the club as it is amazing the different excuses they have come up with.'

Despite the wintry weather that had hit the country, Sunderland's fixture at Manchester City looked as if it would go ahead. Then, a breakthrough of sorts cheered the Sunderland camp as Nicholl agreed to join on the loan basis he preferred. Durban had extended flexibility, but still hoped to make the move permanent. Nothing about this deal would go smoothly. There was a frenetic start when, following a phone call, Durban and Docherty dashed to Manchester to complete the formalities; a telex was sent, but the player could only make his debut provided the registration forms reached league headquarters at Lytham St Anne's before the 3pm kick-off, 'The motorways were so bad there was no chance of us going on to Lytham; we are now in the hands of the Post Office. I am still looking for players of quality to strengthen the side, and hope that this is only the start.'

In a bid to arrest the slide, Durban was planning to implement a sweeper system, and had earmarked the loanee as the man to assume the role, 'I hope that the introduction of Nicholl will help us stop conceding goals through the middle and at the same time we must look for an attacking flair.' The sweeper position was not alien to Nicholl and was an aspect of the move he relished, 'The first thing that Alan Durban said was that he wanted me to play sweeper and I was delighted about that as I played in that position for my country; but I would like a long spell there.' Unlike the unsettled Bowyer, Durban was delighted that a quality player had 'opted in' for the fight ahead.

'Twas the week before Christmas but, as far as fresh signings were concerned, there were going to be no new presents to open. Watson had been expected to fly up to Manchester before the match in order to sign in time to be eligible to play in the third round of the FA Cup against another of his former teams, Rotherham (again paired with Sunderland). But the move had hit a snag, the media speculating that, with Watson nearing the end of his playing career, he was seeking lucrative financial terms that Sunderland were not prepared to meet. Durban did not give this theory any credence, and remained hopeful, 'The deal is not dead but there is no chance of him signing today.' To complete a morning of frustration, Nicholl's registration forms failed to arrive, and then Munro was ruled out. This meant a late call-up to the squad for the unsettled Rowell.

## A Glimmer of Festive Cheer

With his options narrowed, the line-up that Durban sent out to face high-flying City was: Siddall, Hinnigan, Pickering, Hindmarch, Clarke, Elliott, Buckley, Ritchie, McCoist, Rowell, Cummins, sub Venison. The decision not to play Nicholl was only taken at 1.15pm, and the player was unaware of the paperwork hitch until after the pre-match meal when Durban was forced to break the news. Clarke took over as captain, while Hinnigan was thrust in for his first match in ten weeks. Maine Road's undersoil heating meant that the game was one of the few that had beaten the weather, and had therefore attracted far greater attention than might have been expected. There was live national radio commentary of the second half, and the ITV cameras were there to record highlights for the following day's *The Big Match*. They struck lucky.

A couple of minutes before half-time, Ritchie swung a fine pass across for Cummins to cut inside and unleash a tremendous shot past Joe Corrigan from 20 yards. Tueart was in the City side, but had to be helped from the pitch just before the interval after going down with no other player near him. The striker failed to reappear, but the abandonment of the plan to adopt a sweeper system looked as if it was going to cost Sunderland dear; in-form Trevor Francis equalised two minutes into the second half, and ten minutes later was sent clear through Sunderland's vulnerable belly to beat Siddall. Another bleak midwinter experience beckoned, and this feeling increased in the 70th minute when McCoist made a hash of a glorious opportunity to equalise. An ill-advised Caton back-pass went straight to the record signing, but with time and space he screwed his attempt wide. There was no place to hide, and to McCoist's credit he continued to make runs looking to be played the ball. It appeared as if it was to be a case of the same old story for Durban's team, but an unlikely fairytale end was about to materialise.

In the 82nd minute, with Hinnigan running on empty, Durban sent on Venison with instructions to 'push forward'. Venison ran on to the pitch, and immediately received a pass. His first touch released Cummins on the right wing, and his cross was swept home with almost simplistic ease by the recalled Rowell. Venison tore back wheeling his arm in delight. If he was elated about the equaliser, the best was yet to come. Five minutes later, Cummins jinked past a couple of challenges before McCoist hooked the ball to the supporting Buckley who sent in a cross. A City head partially cleared but, as the ball bounced up on the edge of the penalty area, Venison lashed an unstoppable half-volley into the top corner and was engulfed by jubilant team-mates. This time, there was no late twist of fate to deny Sunderland, and the 3-2 win would have stood out even if the league programme had not been in a depleted state that day.

After the match, Durban's first thought was for Nicholl, 'It was probably a bigger disappointment to the lad himself. Had he came in as sweeper then I would probably not have used one of the defensive midfielders.' The manager was not pretending that he had played a masterstroke, and went on to say that the substitution was borne from necessity, 'I sent Venison on as it looked as though Joe Hinnigan thought we were winning 3-1; it was not until he came off that he told me he had cramp. I told Barry to push forward down the right as I knew Cummins would give [Bobby] McDonald problems.' Durban was also swift to pick out some of the unsung heroes of the day who had embodied the 'rolled-up sleeves' attitude he had urged, 'Shaun Elliott was the one who kept us going; he tried to do something about it.'

Durban candidly admitted he had not foreseen the game's dramatic turnaround, 'There was a blizzard forecast, and at 4.15 I was wishing that it would come.' It later transpired that Tueart's injury was a ruptured Achilles tendon – he was out for the remainder of the season. The player later realised he had been carrying the niggle for weeks but it had been misdiagnosed and treated with anti-inflammatory tablets. If Tueart had signed for Sunderland a couple of months earlier, his Achilles time-bomb may well have exploded a few weeks into his return to Roker.

## No Movement in the Freeze

Once again, the press had been wide of the mark, the hitch in the Watson transaction had been Southampton trying to wring out more money by inserting a clause whereby a further £20,000 would be payable after 20 appearances. Durban and Cowie discussed how far the 35-year-old international could be pursued without bursting the Roker payscale wide open. The outcome was that Sunderland would submit a final offer, but were not prepared to be held to ransom, 'I don't want to use all the cash we have available when something else may happen over the next weeks.'

The following day, Durban officially pulled out of the deal, 'I feel that in having Nicholl on loan, the cash for any Watson deal could be better used elsewhere. The money involved for 18 months was a lot, but I want to stress that Dave has played fair with us on wages. Dave is sick, he just wanted the chance to play first-team football again but the overall package was just too much.'

With the next scheduled match to be at home, Durban indicated he still planned to use Nicholl as sweeper, 'The way I operate the sweeper's role will not give us a defensive attitude, but the type of goal Francis scored on Saturday was similar to too many that we have conceded.' By this time, Durban seemed to be getting accustomed to dealing with unsettled members of his squad, and news of Chris Turner seeking a move was treated as an almost inevitable by-product of trying to keep two senior keepers satisfied.

Switching attention to the other end of the pitch, Durban offered thoughts on the struggles faced by McCoist, 'Goalscorers have the greatest responsibilities, but you have to be missing regularly to be scoring regularly. Ally has lost his gambling instinct and has been told that he should be more like his old self. In Scotland he would shoot from outside the box and, though we see him doing it in training, he is not doing it in the First Division.' Durban also praised McCoist's irrepressible spirit that would serve the striker well throughout what would be a long and distinguished career.

The 'big freeze' continued to take its toll on fixtures, and Sunderland's Bank Holiday games were postponed; the Roker Park pitch was under an inch of snow with a frozen surface beneath. Already denied his debut the previous weekend, Nicholl's one-month loan arrangement was beginning to look like an exercise in futility. Amid the general frustration, it was barely any surprise when an agreed £150,000 deal to sell Brown to Newcastle broke down. Cowie dismissed suggestions about any medical issues, 'There's nothing wrong with Brown. [Chairman] Stan Seymour rang me and said, "I have been to the bank and I cannot raise any more money. Could I have Brown on an extended two-month loan?" My reply was, "No."' Durban confirmed, 'The deal was called off before he had a medical; because Newcastle could not raise the money.' Although the incoming fee would have bolstered his spending power, the manager's primary concern was for his player, 'He is seeing our own specialist. I would not be surprised if he was fit and playing in a fortnight; all I want now for Alan Brown is peace of mind.'

With the fixture list on hold countrywide, it was clear that the prospects for Nicholl and the club to have a good look at one another within the month's loan were rapidly diminishing. Durban concentrated on the opportunity that might create for Venison, 'He is threatening both Hinnigan and Buckley for places. Barry has coped so well since he came into the side. He has crammed more into a couple of months than some players manage in a career. He has played Peter Barnes out of the game, been involved in that incident with Kenny Burns, laid on a goal for West Brom [!], and then turned the game at Maine Road. The lad is very mature for his age.'

As 1981 came to an end, Sunderland were set to incur another major loss on a transfer deal. Bowyer was having talks with former club Forest with a view to the £285,000 January signing returning to the City Ground for a cut-price £45,000. In his six appearances that season he had failed to impress, before citing problems in settling in the area as his reason for seeking a move. Durban had subsequently omitted the want-away player and realised that concessions would have to be made to offload one of the club's highest wage-earners, 'We have agreed terms with Forest so it is now up to Bowyer to settle his personal terms.'

When details of the New Year's Honours List emerged, a few wry smiles were afforded by the inclusion of Tom Cowie's name. Some fans suggested that the only OBE they wished to see conferred on the Sunderland chairman was an 'Out Before Easter'.

## New Year, Same Problems

In the FA Cup at Rotherham, Towner gave the home team the lead and, apart from a glaring early miss from Cummins, Sunderland struggled as an attacking force. They were not helped by the 'monsoon conditions', but Tom Ritchie, celebrating his 30th birthday, was singled out for praise by Durban. With 20 minutes remaining, and Venison stripped to come on, Pickering got to the byline and his cross to the far post was knocked back by Ritchie for Rowell to drive in the equaliser.

Durban was grateful but demanded more from Rowell in the future, 'It shouldn't be necessary to leave him out for nine matches to get this response. His goalscoring record shows he should be one of the best midfield players in the business. Gary is the sort of player who thrives on goals.' It is noteworthy that, at this stage, Durban still regarded Rowell as a midfielder, albeit one with an eye for goal. The manager also suggested that the player had perhaps benefited from a luxury not enjoyed by all – having some success early in his career.

On the transfer front, it was interesting that Leeds's Argentinian midfielder Alex Sabella had been transferred to Estudiantes for £100,000. This was the man Knighton would have committed over £600,000 to purchase two years previously had he been able to persuade Mrs Sabella that the north-east town was a cosmopolitan destination (a car tour through the district had not convinced the couple)! However, the player had failed to make any impact at First Division level following his move from Sheffield United. If he had flopped at Roker, it would have been an even more expensive 'error' than the Marangoni deal.

Those days, when Sunderland were capable of entering the running for such expensive recruits, had gone. Now their manager was reduced to inviting hopefuls for trials as he scoured the market for 'bargains'. The latest to turn up at Roker was 27-year-old St Mirren midfielder Lex Richardson. Durban had also been linked with Liverpool's Ray Kennedy, but at present was concentrating on the vital cup replay, 'I have not got over the debacle of Crystal Palace. I feel that we are getting done on occasions through lack of know-how and experience. I want no diversions, and anybody who does not prepare properly knows what to expect.' A welcome boost was received when, after being knocked out of the competition by Watford, Manchester United gave permission for Nicholl to play.

The freezing weather was relentless and the Roker replay was repeatedly postponed. In the enforced hiatus, some transfer action materialised, but not exactly the sort to set pulses racing. The headline 'Durban Goes for Cheapie' was uninspiring, and it transpired that the player was the Gateshead triallist McGinley, 'We hope to take him until the end of the season (for £3,000), and there will be more cash in it for Gateshead if we keep him. The lad has a lot of potential, and though he is not ready for the First Division we hope to see what effect full-time training will have on him.' The word 'potential' would have been more acceptable in less urgent circumstances, and the statement that the player was 'not ready' would have to be rethought after only a few weeks as the manager's options for sparking a revival dwindled.

One player in, but Bowyer was dragging his heels as he neared the Roker exit doors. The fee had been agreed, but incredulous supporters were being informed in the press that the player was 'hanging out for settlement of part of his contract which he feels he is entitled to'. Even if legally correct, the impression created was that, after making only a handful of generally disappointing appearances, Bowyer's stance was a morally unreasonable one. One deal that did go through was Watson joining Stoke for a quoted £50,000. It was debatable whether Southampton had dropped their insistence on the £20,000 add-on clause that had proven a 'bridge too far' for Durban.

The next two league fixtures were also postponed and, amid a national fixture pile-up, fingers were being pointed at the mass of club chairmen who had voted to start the season two weeks 'late'. Meanwhile, two players departed, Bowyer travelling to Nottingham with the forms to complete his return to Forest just a few days short of the anniversary of his journey in the opposite direction, while Richardson returned to Scotland with Durban taking a philosophical view, 'It has not worked out. The cup replay and weather has not made it an ideal situation.' Although there was no prospect of a game, Durban decided to exercise caution when McCoist and Venison reported heavy colds, 'With the threat of an epidemic I thought it best to keep them all away from the ground.'

'Ultimatum to On-loan Nicholl' was the next headline to dominate the back page. A £250,000 deal has been agreed by the clubs, and despite not seeing any competitive action, Durban thought the player had enjoyed sufficient opportunity to gauge his potential new environs, 'Unless he is committed to joining this club then I will not be asking to extend his loan. I have read quotes that it would suit Jimmy to spend the rest of the season with us on loan, but that would not suit us.' Nicholl was a player who satisfied Durban's required quality criteria; he was no triallist. Eventually, welcome news emerged that the loan agreement had been extended, Durban being convinced, 'the lad is genuinely interested in signing for us on a permanent basis.' Personal terms were not a stumbling block but the player wanted to keep his options open as he was set to become a free agent after the World Cup finals.

Durban then contacted Bob Paisley to check whether the asking price for 30-year-old Kennedy was still £175,000 after noting that the player had been linked with Stoke, 'I would not have liked to find out afterwards that the fee had been dropped to £100,000.' The manager now revealed that the only reason Kennedy (with 17 England caps) was not already a Sunderland player was that a deal had broken down six weeks previously when he felt unable to match the player's personal terms. If Liverpool were to drop the asking price, however, there might have been room for compromise, 'Kennedy is from the north-east [Seaton Delaval] and that is our best hope of attracting experienced players to the club, but we would still have to discuss the merits of signing him if the price is right.'

With the rematch against Rotherham looming, Durban's squad tried to cram in some necessary work to reacclimatise, 'Our groundsman is not very happy at the thought of us using the pitch for training but we have not trained on grass for three or four weeks.' Meanwhile, Durban was honouring a contract pledge he had made to 17-year-old Venison. From being an apprentice on £25 per week plus expenses, Venison accepted a two-and-a-half year contract, 'I said that when he had made 15 first-team appearances I would offer him a full-time professional contract and but for the weather he would have done so by now.'

Monday night football; the cup replay was on. With a home draw against Liverpool up for grabs, Durban stressed the importance of not slipping up, 'I toyed with the idea of using Nicholl as a sweeper but I dare not experiment for such an important match.' The manager had taken the 15-man squad to a local hotel overnight to prepare, 'We are playing for a big prize and we must not flatten our supporters again. I am happy with the mood of the players and the spirit is better than at any time this season.' The combination of Nicholl's debut, and the fact that Sunderland had not been in action at Roker since November, was expected to attract a decent attendance, 'A cup run would probably get us back 10–15,000 fans who have given up, and I would like nothing better than to see the ground full.'

In the end, 14,863 saw Sunderland progress. Rotherham player-manager Emlyn Hughes had stepped in at right-back and was soon booked after barging over Cummins. Early in the second half, Pickering delivered a right-footed cross for Buckley to bullet a winning header into the top corner. This was a match where the result was deemed far more important than the performance, but Durban acknowledged that it had been an anxiety-ridden display, 'We were so tense, so much on edge that we couldn't even murder a Fourth Division side here at the moment.' He did feel able to heap praise on Nick Pickering, 'He could find himself going to Spain. It is surprising how many of our goals this season have come from his involvement.'

One player taking practical steps to try and exorcise some of the tension from his game was McCoist, and the approving

Durban reasserted his belief in the young striker, 'Ally decided that he would like to come in for a bit extra training. He is far too tense and you can't play any game if you are not relaxed. Striker is probably the hardest position in which to play, and there is nothing worse if you are not hitting the target regularly. I said it would take a year to judge him and perhaps the lad is trying too hard to justify the big fee. He is trying to beat men before he has got hold of the ball, but he has tremendous spirit and you will never break that.'

Durban was now being harried by the press over the possibility of a signing, 'I am only interested in beating Liverpool at the moment and have nothing to say on reports that Kennedy is coming for talks.' The boss remarked on the huge hurdle his team faced, 'They are still the most formidable team in Europe. We know we must knock them out of their stride as they will come strong in the last 20 minutes as Liverpool just don't run out of steam like most other sides.' The squad's preparation included another overnight hotel stay, 'The Liverpool game could be the stepping stone for if we can beat them we are good enough to go all the way.'

'Going all the way' very soon seemed a million miles away after Dalglish had breached the Roker defence twice in the opening quarter of an hour. Clarke was replaced by Brown at half-time but Durban refused to make the defender a scapegoat. Liverpool missed further chances before Rush added a third. Apart from an acrobatic save by Bruce Grobbelaar from McCoist, the visitors' goal was rarely under threat, 'We were leagues apart. We didn't settle, or set about them.' Kennedy was also returning to Merseyside as Durban dismissed the fee and wages demanded as 'excessive'.

Liverpool may have been uncharitable, but Durban did not display that trait as he rang former Roker caretaker manager Billy Elliott to see what help he could offer Elliott's Darlington who had held a public meeting in a last-ditch bid to raise cash after their chairman had warned that the club could fold within six weeks. Durban sympathised with his counterpart's plight, confirming that economy measures had been put in place since his appointment at Sunderland, 'We are saving more than £1,000 per week on players' wages but we will have to double that next season.'

Kennedy soon found a club prepared to meet his demands as Swansea tied up a £160,000 deal. Durban emphasised that the player's 'excessive' personal terms had been the primary obstacle to the proposed transfer, and made his buying policy quite clear, 'We don't want north-east lads coming to us at the age of 30-plus having spent their best days elsewhere. What we must do is attract them at the age of 20.'

Durban was not convinced that Kennedy was capable of providing a service to the team as high as his wage demands, an opinion eagerly endorsed by his frugally minded chairman. In the short term, Kennedy made an early impact at Swansea, but there would be a sharp downturn and recriminations between himself and manager John Toshack over his on-field contribution, as well as with the club when they regarded such high wage-earners as a contributory factor amid a later financial crisis. It would gradually become evident that Durban's gut instinct had been sound.

At the end of January, Nicholl spent two days in Manchester trying to iron out details for the agreed permanent transfer but was unable to make progress, and Durban was becoming reconciled to another deal biting the dust. The prospect of seeing two international players arriving at Roker Park had evaporated, and the double blow meant that the pressure would be cranked up on an already beleaguered squad. There had been an end to the intense cold snap, and the next match was away to managerless Wolves. Nicholl's extended loan meant he was available for selection but, ironically, Durban now had grounds to hesitate,

'What I have to decide is whether we will be better off playing those who are committed to the club. I never had any qualms about signing Nicholl, as I felt that we would get our money back, but there were always doubts about Kennedy.'

Bristol City became the latest club to announce a financial crisis. Durban believed many players would be facing dole queues, and had been spelling out some realities to his squad, 'I have had a meeting with all the playing staff and told them what is required of them until the end of the season. What they put in during the week will determine team selection. Any player who is not worth £50,000 in the transfer market is in danger of being out of a job. It has taken the recession a long time to catch up with football. When I first came here we were fielding a reserve side of highly paid professionals.'

Durban still believed that the salvation of the club lay in the hands of local youngsters. One player to progress through the youth policy, Chisholm, was on the threshold of a return, 'If I decide to continue with Elliott at the back then Chis, who has looked good in training this week, would do the anchorman's job in midfield.' On the eve of the trip to Molineux, Durban decided to omit Nicholl from consideration, 'I feel the lad has been upset this week, and not in the best frame of mind to play.' The manager also outlined his intention to give some of his younger players occasional breaks in the hectic series of rearranged fixtures that awaited, 'I will be spreading the load and expect the senior players not only to look after themselves but others too.' But, reliance on the senior men had not panned out so far.

## Soldiering On

Discontent was in the air at Molineux, and a group calling themselves 'The Frustrated Wolves Supporters' boycotted the first 15 minutes of the match. As well as tinkering with the formation,

Durban handed Cooke a surprise recall, 'When I knew we were going to be without Ritchie, Nicholl, and Munro I didn't have any option but to play four in midfield. Cooke has looked good in training, and it will also help to take the pressure off Ally.' Wolves were a club in financial turmoil and struggling in the league. A measly 11,091 saw Durban's bottom-of-the-table side come away with the fillip of a 1-0 win. The goal came in the 56th minute after Siddall saved superbly from Colin Brazier and Mel Eves. Venison's clearance was picked up by Chisholm who released Cooke through the middle and the teenage striker maintained enough composure to slip the ball past the advancing keeper.

Acting independently, Nicholl had travelled to Molineux to watch the game; the sort of supportive action that impressed Durban. The Roker boss was also aware that it might be a question of 'all hands to the pump' as the team strove to claw themselves out of their predicament, 'The injuries are going to be a problem with so many matches over the next few weeks, but I think changes to the side can be a stimulant rather than a hindrance. John Cooke was a perfect example of that on Saturday.' The player towed the line, acknowledging previous shortcomings, 'My attitude has never been what it should have been.'

There was to be a swift return to the Midlands to face Villa on Tuesday, and the preceding evening saw McGinley as the 'star of the show' in the reserves' 3-2 win at Hull, scoring the first and setting up the others. Having been thwarted in his attempts to strengthen the squad with experienced internationals, Durban derived a little satisfaction in declaring, 'McGinley was a revelation. He has the ability to go past players. He enjoys playing out wide which is something we have lacked, and if he continues to produce this form he will be considered for the first-team in a few weeks.' This was the player supposedly not yet ready for the First Division now being touted as a starter. As the club's situation deteriorated, weeks would become days. Rowell, unhappy at being omitted again, had more talks with Durban who mused that the 24-year-old might well benefit from a 'fresh start', 'I think we will circulate clubs to test the market.'

Things did not go well at Villa Park. Already without Buckley and Cummins, Chisholm pulled a hamstring early on, Ritchie twisted a knee, and worst of all, Pickering was stretchered off after keeper Rimmer caught him as he beat the midfielder to a through ball. When play was halted, Docherty raced on to the pitch but immediately called for a stretcher. Sunderland did not manage a shot on target as they were outplayed throughout, and Withe's second-half knock-down was swept into the net by David Geddis for the winner.

Defeat was bad news, but Durban was devastated about the injury sustained by the player who, despite his inexperience, the team turned to for energy, 'Pickering got a bad cut above the knee and it is very deep. The injuries to the other midfield players can be overcome but Pickering's is a disaster.' Pickering gave his view of the incident that would interrupt his season, 'I thought the full-back was going to get there first, but when he slipped I went in for the ball. Jimmy Rimmer came out with his studs high and caught me just above the knee. I felt sick when I saw all the blood but I am more sick now having to miss matches.' Yet Durban maintained confidence in 'the youngsters' to fill the breach, adding, 'They will do a job for me.'

Next, the boss had to deal with news that details of the financial arrangement surrounding Nicholl's loan had been divulged – paying United £4,000 per game plus wages. A stumbling block was that the player's parents were in a club house and he felt there was 'no way' he could move before they were settled. However, the player had been oblivious of the financial burden that Sunderland were shouldering and now understood Durban's hardline stance, 'I realise now what a gamble it was for Sunderland. If I had played say ten matches and then decided not to stay they would virtually have given away £40,000.'

Reassuringly, if he did eventually sign then the accrued match fees would be knocked off the final sum. As well as that press leak, Durban was annoyed over Bobby Murdoch's outburst about an 'overpriced' Rowell, after Middlesbrough were quoted £200,000, 'I am disappointed when clubs have confidential discussions reported on the back pages of newspapers, and I don't think other managers should be putting valuations on my players.'

Meanwhile, Darlington's Billy Elliott had phoned Lawrie McMenemy requesting permission for Keegan to guest for Sunderland in the friendly match arranged at Feethams to raise funds. Instead, McMenemy offered to bring his whole team for another friendly later in the season. Elliott also expressed his confidence that the region's teams would eventually come good, 'I am sure that the north-east fighting spirit will win through. Alan Durban is a no-nonsense sort of person who does not have any fancy ideas and just gets on with the game. He's had to struggle for everything he's won so far, and he can only be good for Sunderland' – wise counsel from the former Roker stalwart.

Arsenal were the next visitors to Roker Park and the crowd endured a drab goalless draw. West was employed in central defence and a restored Nicholl shone in the number eight shirt. But, as both sides packed their midfield, a stalemate always looked likely. It was widely assumed that Nicholl would sign permanently if the club were continuing to incur match fees. Such payments were not new; Sunderland themselves had collected cheques from Newcastle for Brown and were receiving money for Arnott (now in a third month's loan at Blackburn). However, they were not raking amounts in the £4,000 bracket.

Durban asked Docherty to play for the reserves against Lincoln City, stating, 'I am hoping that he will be able to teach the kids what should be done and see what difference it makes to them when they have a talker in the team.' The following day, Docherty was nursing a sore knee, underlining that there had never been a realistic chance of him making a return to the full-time professional ranks. There had also been another triallist on show – former Coventry forward Don Nardiello. The Welsh international (two caps in 1977) was a free agent after his American club, Washington Diplomats, went bust. Durban commented, 'We will have another look at him in training and take it from there.'

In other news, Newport County dismissed former Sunderland full-back Len Ashurst as manager and appointed Colin Addison. Their chairman said that despite spending £300,000 on 'strengthening' the team, results had disappointed. Newport had lost eight of their last 14 and languished eighth from bottom in Division Three. It was reported by the press that the terms of settlement included Newport honouring the remaining 17 months of Ashurst's contract and proceeding with a planned March testimonial against Manchester City. Ashurst had benefited from a testimonial at the end of his playing days at Sunderland, and was now being granted another after four years in charge at Newport.

## Bleak Outlook

Another home match came quickly, Durban pitting his wits against Stoke for the first time since his departure, and he revealed there would be a surprise debut as the gangling McGinley's promotion in the pecking was expedited, 'I don't really want to throw him in at this stage but when you're in a tight corner then you have to gamble. Durban was looking to the former bricklayer to provide width from the flanks to end a five-month spell without a home league win, 'McGinley can give us a variation to our play.' Brown had scored two goals for the reserves, but was only named as substitute, 'He blows hot and cold. You never know what is coming next.'

It appeared to be an ideal opportunity of climbing the table with Sunderland only two points behind fourth-bottom Birmingham. While Durban felt compelled to blood his non-league 'cheapie', his former club had the luxury of including a £350,000 midweek signing, Sammy McIlroy from Manchester United, not to mention the player that Sunderland had missed out on, Watson.

After the Arsenal bore draw, the attendance dipped to below 15,000. The discouraging news did not end there as Sunderland flattered to deceive before slumping to a 2-0 reverse. In the first half, McGinley caused problems, and Peter Fox magnificently saved two Buckley drives. Early in the second half, a good ball from Hinnigan put McGinley away but he overran the ball, allowing Fox to smother. Their ill luck and lack of composure would be rued. On 65 minutes, Chapman beat Hinnigan in the air and raced clear down the right, before delivering a fine cross for Brendan O'Callaghan (Durban's first signing as Stoke boss) to shoot past Siddall. Seven minutes later, McIlroy glided past Elliott and Nicholl before slotting the ball into the corner of the net.

As Sunderland became the team with the worst home record in all four divisions, Durban and Docherty had a 'clear-the-air meeting' with the players, 'The game is not just about going out and playing but also taking responsibility. To fetch a player out of the Northern Premier League who turns out to be your best player in his first Division One game is frightening. It is an indictment to the others. All we can do now is get three of our better players fit and go out and improve results; but our forwards are not scoring goals – and don't look like getting them.'

Supporters hearing Durban's comments could have been excused for wondering who these 'better players' were who were going to get fit. Sunderland had looked similarly inept with Cummins, Pickering, and Munro in the line-up; why would that change now? Discouragingly, for the first time, there was a certain resignation about Durban's tone, 'We had to do something remarkable to get out of trouble – and now we have to do something extraordinary.'

One player who would not be joining the fight was Nardiello. Durban recognised that something more was required, but invited the player to stay and train for a few days. Worryingly, the manager now seemed to be preparing the fans for the relegation scenario, seeking to convey the harsh realities, the 'signs of the times', 'The days of this club, and others like us, losing out in the transfer market are gone. Our future lies with the kids. We must develop our own players from an early age. They are our future, and we must look upon them as a solid base on which to build. Our spending days are over. Look at Nottingham Forest; they just put three £1m players on the list. That sort of money isn't around now.'

The message was clear, but it was foul-tasting medicine to swallow. Durban remained resolute and resilient; he would not shirk the mammoth task, provided he was permitted to try, 'Our fans must be patient. Things will be put right here, but it is a long-term job, and one that I am determined to see through.' There were encouraging signs regarding the first batch of youngsters that Durban had promoted as crucial to the club's future. Sunderland had drawn 0-0 at red-hot favourites Tottenham Hotspur in the FA Youth Cup, 'What a marvellous result that was. We didn't play Venison and Pickering; in fact we had two schoolboys in the side.'

Bobby Robson then chose this moment to try and deprive Sunderland of one of their 'better players', bidding to take Elliott on loan to cover a short-term injury crisis at Portman Road. Durban, understandably, dismissed the almost comical suggestion, 'It's a barmy request considering our own position.' Sunderland's next opponents, fellow relegation candidates Birmingham City, sacked manager Jim Smith the day before the game at St Andrew's. Nicholl would make his fifth appearance (ramping up the ongoing cost to £20,000) and, as United wished to reduce a massive bank overdraft, no further blocks were anticipated to a permanent deal being tied up. Not deterred by Sunderland's awful position, Nicholl declared, 'I'm happy, and the club has a great bunch of players.'

The team's slide towards the relegation precipice was gathering momentum, however, a goal from Tony van Mierlo putting the hosts ahead. Sunderland pressed in the second half and Nicholl was unlucky to see a fierce free kick cannon off the angle of post and crossbar. Frank Worthington scored at the death to apply some gloss to the scoreline, and Durban lamented, 'We had enough of the ball, but we were too powder-puff.' Grasping at hope, he noted, 'We are a bit fortunate that one or two other clubs are still in trouble but we must get some fire from somewhere to improve our position.'

In a quirk thrown up by the rash of postponements, Sunderland were scheduled to have four consecutive home matches. The press latched on to this as a 'now-or-never' chance for redemption. There was also some 'Nicholl must stay' clamour, but Durban found himself in an embarrassing situation as the board suddenly shackled their manager with a 'sell first, buy later' policy. Although bitterly disappointed, Durban adopted a pragmatic tone, 'Our position is no worse than any other club but the main reason why we were unable to complete the Nicholl deal was that Newcastle didn't buy Brown.' It was simple economics, and the squad had to apply themselves, 'We have had a ghastly eight days. We must battle with what we've got and put a bit more fire in our bellies.'

On his aborted move, Nicholl seemed as shocked as most, 'Until Tuesday night I was certain it would be completed.' Durban commented, 'Breaking the news gave me one of my most difficult moments as a manager. Jimmy's attitude, in training and even at reserve-team level has been first class.' The boss was heartened that a quality international had been willing to sign, 'It confirms the standard of players who want to come here, which means we are working on the right lines.' That message was endorsed when the youth team beat Spurs in the cup replay with a Venison penalty, a game featuring a series of saves by goalkeeping prospect Mark Prudhoe.

The first of the four sides to visit Roker would be Swansea who had just moved into fourth place after defeating Liverpool 2-0. Durban acknowledged it would be tough, 'You can't expect 17-year-olds to get us out of our position. I want to pick a settled attacking side for these four home games, and if we graft away and steer clear of injuries we have a chance.' On the eve of the match, Durban reasserted his attacking agenda, 'Our fans have been tortured all season. All they have seen in our home matches is the team trying hard and falling easily. One has only to look at our goals record. We have not yet got one league penalty this season [at home] which shows that people are not prepared to take on opponents in the box.'

Another poor crowd watched the recalled Brown's pace threaten to cause problems, but this early promise dissipated. After 22 minutes, Leighton James was allowed to take aim and thump a 25-yard drive just inside Siddall's left-hand post with the goalkeeper, seemingly having lost his bearings, making no attempt to save. Three disaffected fans vented their feelings by holding a demonstration in front of the directors' box, and scarves were thrown into the dugout. The *Echo* remarked that it was the missing thousands of supporters 'who issued a sterner warning to the board', and that the Nicholl 'saga' had exacerbated the sense of disillusionment. Durban's pack-shuffling permutations were almost exhausted.

## Desperate Times – Desperate Measures

The decision of the board of directors to block any incoming transfer deals until players were sold led to Durban officially putting all but four of his squad up for sale. The honoured exclusions were Elliott, Pickering, Venison, and McCoist. The manager regarded the move as one of the few options left open to him, recalling how he had sold Garth Crooks at Stoke in order to strengthen the squad with three purchases. The difference at Roker, however, was that there had already been substantial pruning: Bolton, Hawley, Allardyce, Dunn, Whitworth, and Bowyer had been sold; plus Brown and Arnott sent out on loan. Apparently, this was insufficient, and the manager had been fitted with a transfer straitjacket.

In another desperate attempt to end their latest goal famine (five matches) Durban named ten of the beaten side for that week's reserve match against the part-timers of Mansfield. The boss insisted that this wholesale measure was not a form of punishment, but one designed to restore confidence, 'We have got to find a bit of a settled pattern and get accustomed to scoring again.'

Durban still had the never-ending task of cajoling and placating unhappy members of the squad, or else agreeing to circulate their availability to other clubs. The latest parley was with Cummins, who felt unwanted and reckoning he may as well be put up for sale straight away, 'Stan told me a month ago that he would probably want to go, and if the money is right I will be willing to let him.' Against Swansea, Cummins had been replaced by West, 'He was not too happy about being brought off, but I only did it to give us a bit more height up front.' Cummins then reported he was feeling the effects of 'a slight groin strain' and dropped out of the reserve match which produced a far-from-convincing 3-0 win.

This did little to reassure Durban that his players would be capable of hitting the goals trail in the First Division, 'One or two things are starting to emerge when a team play together regularly but when you dominate a game as much as that then you should be reaching double figures. But the attitude was okay, and they worked well, and it was certainly better than a training session.'

In a recurring trend, new lows were being set, the last attendance being the poorest since 1978. Durban did not condemn the absentee brigade, but called for solidarity in adversity, 'I am not going to start knocking fans that stay away. I am only grateful for those that are still coming as their patience must be at the end of their tether, but it is only common sense that we must all stick together.' The lower league placings confirmed why: West Brom had 28 points from their 21 games; Birmingham 24 from 24; Coventry 24 from 26; Leeds 24 from 22; Wolves 20 from 26; Sunderland 18 from 25; Middlesbrough 14 from 24.

As Fourth Division Hull City called in an official receiver (similar to Bristol City), the front page of the local *Echo* trumpeted 'ROKER PARK CASH CRISIS'. Chairman Cowie was in Churchillian mood, 'I have no intention of resigning. That would be a cowardly way out.' He proceeded to make an appeal for support, 'We are facing a cash crisis, and it will not be resolved by the fans staying away. If Sunderland supporters want First Division football they must support us through thick and thin. We have got to make the best of our present playing strength because there is no question of buying in at the present moment. The managers are our professional advisers. The trouble today is that Alan Durban is getting the stick for clearing up the problems he inherited. All I can offer is blood, sweat, and tears, with a policy of sell first and buy later. This is a personal appeal to the fans. I can promise you success in the long run but we must have your support in the short term. The answer does not lie in lambasting the club.'

The principal 'rebel' shareholder, Barry Batey, was 'disturbed at the club's present position' and had served formal notice for an extraordinary general meeting, 'Tom Cowie has been a disaster.

There are men waiting to take over who would not have hesitated in coming up with the cash to buy Kennedy and Nicholl. The board does not seem to understand the facts of business that to improve the team would benefit all the other aspects of the club.' Not responding specifically, Cowie merely commented, 'I am pleased to hear that he is willing to invest money in Roker Park. I would be pleased to discuss this.'

While the chairman was being bombarded with criticism, on the playing side, Durban refused to make a scapegoat of Siddall for his recent howler and handed the keeper an early vote of confidence by naming him in the team for the visit of Notts County, 'I know Barry dropped a clanger last week but we all make mistakes and I just want to see if he is big enough to handle it. To have any chance of survival these are the games we have got to be winning.'

The boss also dismissed another unsatisfactory proposal to take one of his players on a loan basis which would only serve to deplete selection options without improving his spending power. Bob Stokoe, the manager who had led Sunderland to their 1973 cup glory, wanted to take Rowell to Carlisle to replace the Vancouver-bound Peter Beardsley, but Durban justifiably felt that there was 'no merit in such a move.'

After the last home defeat, and no new signings to parade, it was no surprise when the attendance dropped again for the visit of unfashionable County. Pickering was fit to return, but Elliott had sustained a black eye in a training collision with Cooke, handing McCoist the number six shirt. Winger Chiedozie proved a handful and after Munro obstructed one of his runs outside the penalty area, Rachid Harkouk sent the resultant free kick into the net and reeled away delighted. However, the referee had indicated the kick was indirect; a rare moment of fortune for Durban's team. Almost immediately after this reprieve, Cooke replaced an erratic McGinley and with his first touch sent a deep cross to the far post for Cummins to head back across the face of goal where Brown flung himself forward to head into the net. The second goal drought of the season had been broken. Goal-den Brown.

Entering the final ten minutes, and seeking to hold on for much-needed points, hopes were shattered. A towering clearing header from Brian Kilcline caught the defence square and put Iain McCulloch clear; Siddall scurried from his line but then hesitated. The goalkeeper was about to back-pedal when the striker coolly chipped the ball into the empty net from a few yards. Although a hammer blow, it could have been worse. Ten seconds before the final whistle sounded, County full-back Ray O'Brien sent a free kick against the bar with Siddall beaten.

As if the situation was not already a dire one, the end-of-season run-in was looking daunting as Sunderland were set to finish the season with four away fixtures out of six. Supporters' hopes were then raised by the back-page headline 'Durban Lines Up Mystery Striker', the manager planning to field a guest player in the fundraising match at Darlington. Expectation levels soon dropped, however, when it was disclosed that the mystery man was another non-league player. Durban would also use the Darlington trip to experiment with a recall for Rowell, 'I want to see how Gary does up front.' But, he was tight-lipped about the guest striker who would partner him, 'I don't see why I should help other people. By revealing his name, it could alert other clubs who will then have the opportunity of watching him. I will see how it goes, and if we are impressed only a small fee will be involved.' It went without saying that the fee would have to be small!

Darlington boss Elliott was grateful for the support that had been forthcoming from his former home town, 'The Sunderland people have been magnificent. I was at Grindon Social Club and was presented with a cheque for £250. I hope the match will do a bit of good for both clubs, and Alan Durban has done us a hell of a favour by bringing his first-team here.' In a light-hearted warm-up contest an All Star XI and Radio Tees played out a 2-2 draw, with Malcolm MacDonald and Durban netting for the All Stars.

The triallist on show turned out to be Graham Bennett from Bangor. The 26-year-old engineer was the top scorer in the Northern Premier League, his 45 goals that season being instrumental in helping Bangor to top the league and reach the semi-finals of the Welsh Cup. He scored twice as Sunderland won 3-1, and Durban was impressed by the player's composure, 'We would be trying to negotiate a deal on similar lines to that of McGinley. I have never been so sure of anyone scoring in the last minute like that.'

The McGinley arrangement was £18,000 if 15 first-team appearances were made. At this point, Durban's only hope of strengthening the squad was from the 'bargain basement', and he would take in Bangor's weekend match against South Liverpool. Elsewhere, less than 24 hours after benefiting from his testimonial at Newport, Len Ashurst was being installed as manager of Cardiff City.

Returning from his non-league watching mission, it emerged that Durban's quest to find quick solutions had encountered obstacles, and he decided not to pursue the interest in Bennett, 'I am not prepared to pay the sort of money Bangor are asking.' Cowie had already warned of severe cuts in the staff for next season, with some likely to be given free transfers, and the onus was on the manager to cut the wage bill (standing at £200,000). Bangor's chairman complained that he thought it was a done deal before he received a phone call. Durban contested this version of events, '[After two hours of talks] I never shook hands on any deal, and could not pay £34,000 on what I saw on Saturday.'

As well as anger and frustration, there must have been a degree of embarrassment that a manager of a top-flight club had been reduced to haggling for cut-price non-league hopefuls. It was a sorry state of affairs for Sunderland whose spending power in the 1950s had seen them dubbed 'the Bank of England club'.

## A Touch of Magic in the Night

Two goals from Paddy O'Donnell helped the youth team to win at Villa Park and progress to the FA Youth Cup semi-final. The team was being coached by the club's former goalkeeping stalwart Jim Montgomery. Docherty noted the contribution of the young keeper he hoped might emulate his mentor, stating, 'Mark Prudhoe kept us in it.'

For the first-team, the next visitors were Southampton who had just ascended to the top of the table. Brown had received a knock to his knee, so Rowell would be handed the chance to impress as an out-and-out forward. Durban confirmed that Turner would return in goal following Siddall's vital errors of judgement in two successive games, and outlined his immediate hopes, 'If we are to make a recovery then it has to be from here. Blatantly, our goal form at home is why we are struggling but, generally, there is more atmosphere for night matches and I just hope we don't waste chances. Southampton are one of the best one-touch sides in the country and we will certainly have to be more alert. So many people have written us off that to get back into the fight will be a bonus.' The boss also expected players to react to the announcement of a mass clear-out, 'That was no idle threat, and should make them give 100 per cent effort, not only to the club but for their own future.'

Durban was concerned about the pace of the free-scoring Saints attack and he drafted in Chisholm to bolster midfield, allowing Elliott to resume defensive duties. The manager acknowledged that the failures of other teams had given Sunderland hope that might have been long extinguished in past seasons, and he rallied his troops to do something to capitalise on the unexpected lifeline, 'We have a new combination up front in Rowell and McCoist as we are still trying to find the right blend, and Turner was in goal the last time we won a league game at home [in August].'

The size of the immediate task was highlighted by the huge discrepancy between the two teams' scoring power. The previous week, Keegan had notched his 24th goal of the season – the Sunderland team had managed a combined total of 18.

A crowd of 15,747 braved a biting breeze to watch; half-time was reached on level terms, but the home faithful had seen this all before. Why should tonight be any different? Five minutes into the second half, the script changed as their team took the lead. McCoist supplied Buckley and from his cross Pickering rose to send a header high and wide of keeper Ivan Katalinić. But, particularly at Roker, Sunderland had blown encouraging situations throughout the season. Why should tonight be any different? In the 70th minute a right-wing cross from Mick Channon found an unmarked Keegan, and the Roker crowd winced, waiting for the inevitable. But the England captain jabbed his close-range shot over the bar for a major let-off.

Southampton had upped the pace in search of an equaliser and, with a couple of minutes of normal time remaining, Sunderland were clinging on. It was one-way traffic, and even at this late stage a Southampton leveller was not only dreaded, but half expected. Cue a touch of magic as McCoist demonstrated his 'record signing' class with an exquisite goal. Receiving a Buckley knock-down over 20 yards out, the young Scot sidestepped a challenge, looked up, and curved a left-foot shot to perfection, leaving Katalinić a spectator. On the bench, pent-up tension and frustration were released as Durban and Docherty jumped out of the dugout to join in the celebrations of the ecstatic crowd. The referee managed to find four minutes of injury time as the crowd bayed for the final whistle that signalled the end of over six months of Roker Park league heartache.

The performance represented a team effort with commitment in abundance. Turner had been faultless on his return, and Elliott looked far more comfortable in his favoured defensive position, but it was a player not included on the night that underscored the camaraderie still present in the beleaguered squad. Tom Ritchie had just returned after failing to agree terms to join Second Division Barnsley on loan (an arrangement acceptable to the club on this occasion because Ritchie was one of the top wage-earners), but he was one of the first into the dressing room to congratulate 'the lads' on their magnificent win.

A delighted Durban gave a measured overview, 'Perhaps the turning point was the miss by Keegan, but I am absolutely delighted for Pickering who got his first goal and McCoist. When I signed Ally, I was told that he would not score a lot of ordinary goals, and that one was really something special. Ally is a better player now although he has not been scoring. I thought he worked very well with Gary Rowell who took up some excellent positions to create space for others. I felt I wanted a job doing on Alan Ball, and Chisholm took care of him very well.' Southampton boss McMenemy was gracious in defeat, 'On the night Sunderland deserved to win. You can't take it away from them.'

Keeping things in perspective, Durban realised that, after attaining such a high, they had to refocus quickly for Saturday's visit of some fierce relegation rivals, 'Leeds will tell us whether we have a chance of staying up.' That same night, Leeds had lost 1-0 at home to Manchester City, Burns had been sent off, and they were without a goal in seven matches. What could possibly go wrong?

## Intoxication Turns Cold

Only days after being dropped, Siddall informed Huddersfield manager Mick Buxton that he was not prepared to join the Third Division side on loan, 'I have spoken to Alan Durban who has been very fair and, as my contract is up at the end of the season, I want to make the right decision.' With Prudhoe making great strides, Durban indicated that one of his senior goalkeepers would be allowed to leave as he sought ways of reducing the wage bill. Further down the north-east coast, there was a shock for Middlesbrough fans who believed there was cash available for the manager to spend after amassing over £1.5m from the sales of Johnston, Armstrong, and Proctor. But, chairman Charles Kitching revealed that the club was over £500,000 in debt, and were losing thousands every week because of small gates.

Encouraged by midweek events, Saturday's crowd tipped the 20,000 mark to watch an unchanged team. Crucially, there was a change in the Leeds side as Allan Clarke had dipped into the transfer market again in an effort to arrest their famine. The new man, from Birmingham, was 33-year-old Frank Worthington and his arrival proved an untimely one for Sunderland. He not only led the line superbly, but rattled in the second-half shot that settled the result in a match that represented a massive anticlimax for Roker fans.

Turner admitted he should not have been beaten at his right-hand post by Worthington's crisply struck free kick after organising the wall to protect the left side, but Durban recognised the problem lay deeper, 'We never picked up the tempo. The crowd come here with fire and passion but we have sent them home flattened and, unfortunately, that is nothing new.' The pressure had got to his team, and Durban knew it, 'I would rather have beaten Leeds than Southampton. We had nothing to lose then, but the onus was back on our team – and they couldn't handle it. We have now reached a make-or-break situation.'

Remarkably, Worthington was one of seven players with international experience that Leeds had fielded against Sunderland, but that was no consolation following this kick in the teeth. The much-heralded 'four-in-a-row' home matches had yielded only four points from a possible 12, and although the transfer deadline was looming Durban had already intimated there would have to be a big clear-out in the summer, 'Ideally, I would like an all-local side. That has to be our aim for the future. Obviously, there will have to be one or two exceptions as every side needs a wise old head. I find it remarkable there hasn't been a testimonial here since Bobby Kerr's in 1976. At one time players made cash out of bonuses, and not through moving to other clubs. That's what's wrong, and until you get more players morally obligated to the club then we will never get anywhere.'

Elsewhere, the subject of prolonged transfer finance arrangements was highlighted as Bristol City struggled to pay Newcastle the outstanding fee for Mick Harford while they awaited incoming payments due from Crystal Palace for Kevin Mabbutt, Manchester City for Gerry Gow, and Sunderland for Ritchie. A Bristol spokesman exonerated Sunderland who had 'honoured their payment arrangements' and were expected to pay the balance of £15,000 within a couple of months.

After failing to cash in on their run of home fixtures, Sunderland were now faced with consecutive daunting trips to Liverpool and Manchester United. On a reconnaissance mission, Durban and Docherty watched United lose 1-0 to Coventry before the boss put the spotlight on Elliott, who he thought should be staking international claims, 'If you want to play for England, Anfield and Old Trafford are the places where you get a lot of publicity.' Durban was hoping that his side might be able to reproduce better form when they were not expected to succeed, 'We have got to go out and give it all we've got. Our only hope is to attack them as we couldn't defend even against Leeds. If we are going to get out of trouble we will have to produce something dramatic.' There was nothing dramatic at Anfield, where a 14th-minute Rush strike was enough in a one-sided affair.

## Shuffling and Recycling

Early the following week, Ritchie joined Carlisle on loan for the remainder of the season. Although the tall forward had been a good team man to have around, the lucrative nature of his contract meant that the club were eager to remove him from the wage bill. Docherty speculated, 'If we transfer one or two more for a nominal fee we may have the basis for bringing somebody in.' The loan system at the time allowed two players per club in a season.

As Ritchie exited, Durban terminated Arnott's four-month loan at Blackburn, also indicating he planned to throw the midfielder into the fray, 'As there seems little chance of Rovers coming up with any cash, I have decided to bring him back. If he shows anything, he will come into contention.'

That was not the only change Durban hoped to field, 'I have asked to borrow some good players, those who can improve the side, and we won't do that from the lower divisions. I would prefer to use an exchange basis, but other clubs are only interested in our best players.' The day before the deadline, he reported, 'I've spoken to a lot of managers. Everyone seems to be waiting for something to trigger things off. There's been a lot of talking and no action.'

Although he may have been feeling sorry for himself at being unable to make the forays into the transfer market he wished, Durban could maybe afford a wry chuckle at news that the 'Buy a Player' fund organised for Newcastle had only succeeded in raising just over £1,000. The fund's failure was blamed on 'the public's suspicion of previous directors and managers' – a familiar tale.

Arnott was named in the reserve team at home to Chesterfield, with Chisholm used in central defence. Durban would be watching closely, 'We will see how badly Kevin wants to play for Sunderland tonight. If he does well he will get his chance.' Arnott scored in a 3-0 win, and McGinley set up two goals for West. The *Echo* reporter was effusive about Arnott's merits for a swift recall, 'Arnott is fit, in form, and ready to add his talents to Sunderland's struggle. The elegant midfield man showed all the flicks, chips, and curved passes that made him a favourite with the fans.' On this occasion, Durban was in agreement with the pressman, saying, 'Arnott will play on Saturday.'

As time ran out before the deadline, Durban went back to Stoke to make a loan signing. Loek Ursem was the 24-year-old former Dutch under-21 international who he had taken from AZ67 three years previously for £60,000, but had played only once in the first-team this campaign. Another effort was thwarted when John Bond rejected a move for son Kevin. Although the City boss was also in the position of having to unload players or deal on an exchange basis, the managers failed to reach an agreement. Durban explained, 'There was no way I was going to part with Shaun. He is a good mate of Kevin Bond who I thought would do a good job as sweeper, but John Bond did not fancy any of our players [apart from Elliott].'

Another deal involving a First Division striker had been set up, but it depended on Sunderland selling first to raise £100,000 as the club concerned were only interested in a cash transaction. The prospect of such money being raised was almost laughable; a fact underscored by a candid admission from the Roker boss revealing that he had suggested to some Third and Fourth Division clubs that they could have certain players on loan for free (no match fees), but there had been no takers. It was a staggering indictment on the lack of in-depth quality at this top-flight outfit that such lowly clubs did not rate any of the fringe players. This only galvanised Durban's conviction that Sunderland's tomorrow needed to be nurtured at grass-root level, 'We turned out a reserve team that included only two players without first-team experience, but I would think by this time next year the side would contain six or seven apprentices.'

On the eve of the match at Old Trafford, Durban outlined the attributes he believed that Ursem brought to the fight, 'I will use him wide on the right as he is the type of player who will do more for us in the final third. He might not be as good as others in the other two-thirds but he is a natural finisher who scored seven goals in 24 starts last season. Perhaps where we have fallen down is asking the strikers to do too much work, and forget what they are in the side for.'

Manchester United were in a poor run of form, having scored only one goal and gained two points from their last three home games. Nevertheless, Sunderland were grateful to emerge with a point from a goalless draw. In the end, Ursem remained unused on the bench, but Arnott wore the number five jersey and put in a workmanlike display which did not go unnoticed in that night's *Match of the Day* analysis. His skills got little chance to shine in an attacking vein, but he twice scrambled the ball away in dangerous goalmouth situations. Midway through the second half, a Rowell flick had sent Pickering clear, but the chance was blazed over.

## In the Eye of the Storm, Hope is Born

Looking ahead to the 'six-pointer' against local relegation rivals Middlesbrough at Roker, Durban declared, 'If we are going to do it then we have got to do it now.' There was a general consensus that this was a 'must-win' match and that anything less would probably represent a deadly relegation hammer-blow.

Durban laid it on the line that there were wider implications, 'The north-east has been having a bad time. If Sunderland and

Newcastle are winning then all of a sudden there's no depression. If we can stay up it will lift a big cloud from the whole area.' The manager was looking for improvement, both short and long term, 'It was obvious at Old Trafford that the team is looking more concrete, and if we got into a good run it's the sort of side we wouldn't have to change for a couple of years. If we can string some results together I would have no worries about going in with the same set-up next season. I wouldn't change much – just add quality.'

Meanwhile, Boro boss Bobby Murdoch was sounding his own battle cry for this relegation showdown, 'We're going to Roker to win. There is no way that we can be satisfied with a draw.' The Teesside club had been experiencing its own dramas, and had been forced to call a clear-the-air meeting after David Hodgson accused some team-mates of not trying or caring. But, there were other more onerous issues which diverted anxious eyes away from sporting headaches – 'Crisis Alert in Falklands' read the front-page headline. This firmly put the Wear-Tees football 'crisis' in perspective – but did not mean that failure on the pitch would be mildly accepted.

Sunderland's list of remaining fixtures was dubbed 'the desperate dozen', and Durban was targeting six wins and two draws which, given previous form, looked well beyond his team. Nevertheless, that was the mountain that would somehow have to be scaled, 'We are in a desperate situation, and it's no secret why. The goals must start coming from somewhere unexpected to get us out of trouble. The full-backs have not scored this season. The longer the situation goes on, we start to rely on other sides and that's when the position becomes hopeless. We have got to win half of our matches to have a chance.'

In the capital, Mrs Thatcher called an emergency Cabinet meeting to discuss the escalating Falklands situation. That same

Friday morning, the local press were talking about the following day's 'Do or Die' clash at Roker. Durban issued a stark message, 'I don't think both clubs can survive and, logically, if we can't win this one then we are going to struggle to get out of trouble.'

Encouragement had been derived from their latest spirited showing and Durban hoped that it would mark a turnaround, 'We just can't afford to let our fans down again. Some of our home performances have produced so much effort and so little return but if we play as well as last week then we should have too much for them.' However, he acknowledged the unknown factor of whether the psychological make-up of his 'youngsters' included big-match temperaments, adding, 'It could depend on how they react and savour the big time.'

In the matchday *Roker Review*, Durban had recalled the disappointment of the game against Leeds, 'We failed that test – but we must not fail today', but fail they did in front of a disappointing crowd of 19,000. Arnott and McCoist missed chances, while Platt produced tremendous saves to deny Buckley drives in the first half and Rowell's diving header in the second. Middlesbrough took a 34th-minute lead when Hodgson broke on the left and his cross was forced in by Ashcroft. In a last throw of the dice, Ursem replaced McCoist when it might have seemed more logical to retain the forward who would be most likely to benefit from the service the substitute was expected to supply. As things transpired, the inept and nervy display of the team infected the new man too. The crowd waited for Ursem to deliver some quality crosses into the danger area, but none arrived, and it became obvious that Ursem was not the type of player who could take on and beat a man; he needed to receive the ball in sufficient space to allow him the time to measure his cross. In such a frenetic encounter, his fraught team-mates could not give him that luxury, and Sunderland eventually sank to a miserable 2-0 defeat.

Durban condemned his players' lack of character and courage, 'After the first goal, the side was unrecognisable from the one at Manchester, but it was the same pattern against Leeds after we had beaten Southampton. We did not have the players to react. We did well in the destructive part of the job against United but we couldn't even do that. At times like this you have to roll up your sleeves a bit further, tackle a bit harder, and run a bit harder.'

He refused to criticise the three fans who had staged a sit-down protest on the pitch nor the one who flung a scarf into the dugout, and did not seek to sidestep his portion of blame, but warned that players' egos and emotions would be ignored amid the plain talking that would take place, 'I have got to feel responsible for what happened, but there will be no keeping anyone happy at the club now. You judge people under pressure, and not when things are going right.' In front of the press glare, Durban bit his tongue, and signed off with a declaration loaded with an almost comical sense of decorum and understatement, 'I cannot say what I want to say. I feel like using adjectives which are uncomplimentary.'

Uncomplimentary adjectives aplenty rent the air in the dressing-room showdown that followed this latest debacle, and the brainstorming session would prove a pivotal point, both in the team's survival fight and for individual careers. In a 'no-holds-barred' exchange of views, players and management let rip in pointing fingers and airing opinions on what was wrong and what was required to remedy the situation. Players were given free rein to criticise their manager and team-mates, and Docherty later rated it as the biggest dressing-room inquest he had ever been involved in, revealing, 'Stan Cummins took more stick at the meeting than anyone else.'

While the egos of some 'stars' were taking a necessary bashing in order to, hopefully, provoke a dramatically positive reaction, one novice striker's mind was racing. Colin West had enough self-belief to think he could be part of the solution his manager desperately needed. Despite his relative inexperience, he sensed it was a moment for boldness. West recalls the scene, 'People were speaking out and although I was young I realised that I needed to speak up a bit more. I felt physically up to it, and I argued that I'd been scoring goals in the reserves and felt it was time to be given a shot at helping us climb out of trouble. Thankfully, the boss listened. I felt that it was a potential 'make or break' moment for my career, where I could grab my chance and be successful. The alternative might have been getting released.' His soon-to-be strike partner Rowell recalls that Durban challenged West whether he thought he 'could do the job', and that the big striker was not shy about declaring his readiness.

The Middlesbrough defeat was one of Durban's darkest hours but the immediate aftermath, in a crucible of 'frankly exchanged views', proved to be the starting point for that season's salvation.

## Young Guns Go for It

With Sunderland now planted at the bottom of the table, the *Echo* editorial, oblivious to the group catharsis that had taken place, ran the headline 'INEPT DISPLAY HAS THE LOOK OF DOOM', commenting, 'Another embarrassing home defeat must surely doom Sunderland to relegation.' Durban had taken the inevitable stick on the chin, but remained defiant, 'Nobody here is abandoning ship. Where there is hope there is a chance, but I don't want to see another 45 minutes like Saturday.'

Only 48 hours after toiling against Middlesbrough, Pickering and Venison played in the first leg of the FA Youth Cup semi-final at Old Trafford which ended in a 1-0 defeat. Durban was glad to take any crumbs of comfort available at present, 'Pickering had a magnificent half hour last night after looking jaded on Saturday. It could be that playing him in the youth team has given him a lift. Mark Prudhoe was magnificent, and kept us in it. Suddenly we have three first-team keepers and if the situation presents itself I would like to give him a match in the first-team this season.'

Despite his insistence that they would battle on, any intention to blood Prudhoe hinted that Durban was thinking that relegation might become a mathematical certainty before the climactic weekend. However, the manager quickly assured his squad there would be no radical overhaul, 'It is too early to abandon the side completely, and after Saturday's let-down I am hoping for an immediate reaction from the players.' Arnott had picked up a bruised ankle and would miss the midweek visit of Ipswich but, following the team's run of only three goals in 11 matches, it was a striker who would pay the short-term price, 'Ally needs a break, and the side an injection up front.' The press did not know that the injection Durban had been 'talked into' during the dressing-room dust-up would be the imposing frame of West.

Sunderland were now seven points from safety: Leeds had played 31 and reached 30 points; Wolves had 29 from 34; Middlesbrough 24 from 32; Sunderland 23 from 31. For the Ipswich match, Venison was also omitted as Hinnigan, Chisholm, and West came in. On Ursem, Durban candidly stated, 'I don't think we will be on top enough for Loek to be in the side.' Ipswich were still realistic title contenders, and had notched four successive wins. Durban ruefully reflected on that opening Saturday afternoon which saw a six-goal thriller in the Suffolk heat haze, 'It is amazing how the clubs have gone so far apart since that game.' Well, quite.

Almost 12,000 saw a gutsy Sunderland display. Munro upended Gates as he was set to break clear, and the booking took him over 20 disciplinary points. In the 64th minute, goalkeeper Paul Cooper blundered and presented West with the sort of gift not to be refused, the number eight blasting in his first senior goal from all of a yard. Unfortunately, the young man's landmark strike was not a winner as, five minutes from time, Kevin O'Callaghan beat Pickering to cross for Kevin Steggles to head in.

Although there were no injuries to come out of this gritty performance, Durban indicated that an unchanged side for the following Saturday's visit to Stoke was far from guaranteed, 'It has been proved that we play better when we make changes. I will be giving the side for the next three matches a lot of thought. I picked a side for the Ipswich match with more power and six-footers as I believe that is what we have been lacking.'

Durban's abrasive man-management style challenged players to 'do a job' for him but, as well as demanding commitment, he balanced the approach and strove to take the heat out of tense situations. Lately, however, the manager had doubted his motivational methods, 'It bothered me all weekend that I had lost my effect as I did not get the reaction on Saturday that I was looking for. But after two days with the players they responded magnificently.'

For Durban's return to the Victoria Ground, Clarke replaced Hindmarch, while Stoke included on-loan Everton striker Alan Biley. Durban had seen his team humbled at home precisely two months previously by his former club, but Sunderland battled and took the lead two minutes before half-time. Cummins had a shot palmed away by Fox, but Rowell retrieved the loose ball and crossed for Buckley to tuck the chance away. In a spirited showing, the team withstood the expected second-half pressure, which culminated in a brilliant double save from Turner as the keeper stopped Chapman's close-range header before keeping out O'Callaghan's follow-up. Surprisingly, Stoke had not blocked Ursem's participation in this fixture, and his fresh legs relieved Rowell for the final few minutes. On a personal note, this was a satisfying win for Durban; more importantly, it gave his team a glimmer of renewed hope as well as dragging Stoke into the relegation dogfight.

Two days later, an Easter Monday crowd of 14,821 were at Roker to witness the team's continued attempt to resurrect their tattered reputations. Cooke was drafted in to take the number five shirt in place of Chisholm, and the home team continued to 'treat' their supporters to a set-piece tactic that had emerged against Ipswich. On winning any dead-ball opportunity in a wide position, a 'heavy brigade' of Clarke, Hinnigan, and West lined up outside the area, and advanced in formation, timing their forward run to arrive as a pack. When Buckley curled a 29th-minute free kick to the far post it was Clarke who got up and, although his header hit the bar, West reacted smartly to nod the rebound in. Turner then saved from a spectacular-looking Alan Curbishley volley but, in first-half stoppage time, the red-and-white line of tall men advanced menacingly for Buckley's corner. This one was met powerfully by West and his downward header beat keeper Wealands and the covering Pat Van den Hauwe.

A 2-0 win was earned, and a satisfied Durban noted the significance, 'This is the first important game we have won at home involving one of the bottom clubs, and after our victory at Stoke it means that two other sides are pulled down into the fight.' The manager then focussed on West's contribution, 'It is always difficult to know when to throw someone in, but he has done well and given us something we have been missing. He is a big galoot who tends to over-elaborate a bit, and tries to impress with his control, which only holds things up. We will have to wait and see if he can sustain it; but he could well save us from going out looking for a big striker at the end of the season.'

Durban's charges were now off the bottom and only three points behind the safety positions occupied by Leeds and Stoke, but these teams had played fewer games, 'We are still relying on others as well as ourselves, but it looked as if there was no way we were going to get out of trouble after the Middlesbrough result. We have now gone three games undefeated and to stand any chance we must win our three remaining home games as it will be very tight.'

There was little time to bathe in the afterglow of a victory as the team had to travel to London for their third match in five days. Their opponents were Tottenham, who had outclassed them at Roker and were coming freshly buoyed by a 3-1 win at fierce rivals Arsenal. No one said the 'great escape' would be easy.

## A Miracle-Man After All?

Chisholm and Hindmarch returned to the team as Durban reverted from a 4-2-4 formation to 4-3-3 in an attempt to stifle Spurs's creative hub of Hoddle, Hazard, and Villa. It was hoped that Chisholm could replicate the shackling job he had performed on Alan Ball as he was handed a tight-marking mission on prime danger man Hoddle.

In a pre-match interview, Durban homed in on the vital unsung contribution Rowell had been making in the team's mini-revival, 'Gary has worked very hard, and it has shown in terms of the team's results. Players must be prepared to graft.' Focussing on his 'big galoot', Durban issued a mixture of encouragement and warning, 'West has everything in his favour to be a success and if he continues to develop then he should make it. He has given us a lifeline and his goals have given confidence to the rest of the side, but the minute he thinks he has done it then he will be blown out.'

There were almost 40,000 at White Hart Lane, and the majority were enjoying what looked like a routine win. Tony Galvin shot through the legs of Turner, and after the stuttering keeper failed to deal with Crooks's cross on the half hour, Hoddle applied the finish. At 2-0 down it appeared as if Sunderland's luck was completely out two minutes after the restart. Ray Clemence saved superbly from a Hindmarch header, but then appeared to claw out Rowell's follow-up from *behind* the goal line. This would not be the last time that the linesman failed to aid the visitors.

With less than a quarter of an hour remaining, Durban saw his team's prospects receive an unexpected boost. A hot-headed Galvin kicked Cummins in the box and among the general tumult and squaring-up, a penalty was rightly awarded. Galvin was booked and immediately substituted, while Durban sent on Ursem for Hinnigan. After enduring this lengthy delay, and also some 'gamesmanship' from Clemence, Rowell retained his composure and duly dispatched the kick. Five minutes later, the ball broke for Ursem and his shot was fumbled for Pickering to grab the equaliser. There was still time for Turner to pull off a crucial save from Villa, before the final moments saw Pickering burst clear and crack home what looked to be a dramatic winner only for the linesman to controversially signal offside.

Having been in a seemingly hopeless situation deep into the game, Durban realised it might be a little churlish to bemoan the fact that his side had been unjustly denied a winner at the death, but the team's disappointment marked their dramatic recent change in mentality, 'We have got a point from what I considered to be our most difficult game left, so I have to be pleased. But we are in this position because of the stupid points we lost. My biggest complaint of the night was that the linesmen tried to run the game. We had what I considered two perfectly good goals disallowed; yet we must have sickened one or two clubs at the bottom with this result.'

Next up were Everton. As always, Durban would be taking stock of the players' input to the Friday training session as they coped with a flurry of tough games, 'We are still the bookies' favourites to go down but we have a big advantage over other clubs at the bottom – we are playing with confidence. I want to see how the players react in training today. We will see who is sharp and who is jaded, and though I don't want to disrupt too much I will leave anyone out who is not in the right frame of mind.' McCoist's prolonged break from the first-team 'pressure pot' continued in the hope that his goalscoring exploits for the reserves would restore confidence.

On Thursday evening the band Simple Minds debuted on *Top of the Pops*, and as Jim Kerr sang 'Promised You a Miracle', it seemed ironic that Durban, the manager who had tried to play down the concept that he was a 'miracle worker' on his arrival, was in the throes of achieving what might be regarded as a miracle escape for his team. As 17 April dawned, remarkably, Sunderland had not won at Roker Park on a Saturday since a day short of 12 months when a Ritchie hat-trick against Birmingham had given Docherty a winning start to his short caretaker stint. Docherty was now identifying the fiery post-Middlesbrough exchanges as the constructive springboard for the revival, 'A few home truths came out; perhaps the meeting should have been held sooner.'

Seeking that elusive Saturday winning feeling, Sunderland led from Rowell's glancing header after 18 minutes, but disaster struck five minutes before half-time as Cummins attempted a pass across the face of his own box and Alan Irvine's shot just beat the despairing palms of Turner. Durban later praised Cummins's half-time resolution to make amends, 'Stan knew only too well what he had done, and he went out for the second half promising the lads he would get them a goal.'

Ten minutes into the second half, the overlapping Hinnigan's cross was handled by Billy Wright and Rowell confidently stroked the penalty kick past Neville Southall. Cummins then helped to set up the goal that gave his team a crucial third. Taking a pass from Buckley, the diminutive forward's cross found West, and though Southall parried his initial header, the striker reacted sharply to shoot in the rebound.

Despite Richardson's fierce drive hitting the upright, the 18,000-plus crowd saw the home team break the Saturday hoodoo. Later, Durban was pleased to report that Rowell was now in a more settled frame of mind and might be persuaded to stay, 'Gary will be offered a new contract. I have been on his back all season but his ice-cool goals under pressure in the last two matches have been very important. Gary's play over the last few months has been one of the more pleasing aspects, and playing up front he seems to be enjoying his game more.'

Rowell recalls Durban telling him, 'You're a good finisher, and could do a job for me up front.' The player considered himself a midfielder (and always would) but was happy to oblige his manager if it meant a place in the starting line-up.

Durban was keen to emphasise his opinion that positive results, while welcome, would never gloss over fundamental shortcomings in a player's attitude or character, 'Although we have been winning I am always looking at individual performances. To make an impact on the game, there should be no diversions. Your ambitions to succeed must override any greed.' Therefore, it was an extra-pleased manager who reported, 'Nick Pickering wants to be tied to the club, and I am considering offering him a longer contract.'

That was the future but, returning to the immediate task, Durban assessed the mood, 'We need at least another nine points, and as four of our last six games are away we must win at least one of them. I only wish we were playing tonight as nobody has had time to come down from what has happened in the last couple of weeks. Saturday's game was the only time we have recovered from making a major mistake, and as long as we look like scoring it gives us a chance.' Meanwhile, the team captain was travelling to London to appear before an FA disciplinary committee, but Durban was hopeful that leniency might be extended for Munro to escape a ban.

The second leg of the FA Youth Cup semi-final was played at Roker, and Manchester United finally put an end to Sunderland's encouraging run. Schoolboy Paul Lemon levelled things on aggregate before Norman Whiteside struck. The scorer of United's second would also become a 'star' name, Mark Hughes, and it was reported of his goal, 'With his back to goal and all options seemingly closed, he turned and lashed a shot into the top corner.' The away team also included future first-teamers Graeme Hogg and Clayton Blackmore. Durban hailed the crowd response, both in numbers and fervour, as 'unbelievable' after it was estimated that the attendance had been five or six times greater than the 1,541 at Old Trafford for the first leg. He felt that the level of support amply demonstrated the passion in the area for football.

Two Home International matches were scheduled for the following week, and Villa (who were to play a league game against Leeds) had agreed to release Withe and Morley for England duty. As Leeds were in the thick of the ongoing relegation battle, Durban voiced his dismay. The Home International tournament was usually held at the end of the season, but fixtures had been rescheduled as England, Scotland, and Northern Ireland would be travelling to the World Cup. Durban merely stated the same opinion as other interested parties, 'There has obviously been no thought for other clubs who had to face the best Villa could field. Really, this is a bit off.' However, some administrative decision-making went Sunderland's way when Munro escaped with a disciplinary warning.

When asked whether Ursem would be extending his stay at the club, Durban responded, 'He has settled in very well, but he hasn't had much of a chance to show what he can do. I have asked if we can have Loek for another month, but it is dependent on Alan Biley staying at Stoke.' Biley was one of ten players made available by Howard Kendall who, as Durban wished to at Roker, was committing himself to a rebuilding plan at Goodison Park. Only one of these talented managers would receive the necessary time to complete their grand scheme.

Durban travelled to The Hawthorns to see next opponents West Brom lose 1-0 against Manchester City. It was Albion's sixth successive defeat, and they had free-fallen slap into the relegation struggle. 'West Brom have too many good players to go down, but some of them are not playing to their potential.' Durban planned to field an unchanged line-up, 'A draw is no good; we will be going for a win. We have had no hidings away from home all season and fear no one.' The rhetoric was bullish, but a draw would surely have represented an acceptable outcome.

To Leeds's chagrin, the Football League upheld the appeal by other interested clubs to postpone their match at Villa. The same evening, Brian Clough was holding court at a forum held in the Roker Park Suite, and the great man spoke in his usual no-nonsense manner, spelling out the almost unique pressures and obstacles faced by his former player, 'Alan Durban has done quite well in the time he has been here, but he is faced with the same old problems of the fans demanding instant success. The trouble in this game is there are so few accolades to go around, and nowhere is there so much intensity as this place. I have no regrets in not taking the Sunderland job which was offered to me by Mr Cowie.'

By Saturday, news emerged that Everton had refused Stoke permission to extend Biley's loan, and the knock-on effect was that Stoke denied Sunderland the use of Ursem. McCoist would therefore rejoin the fray, taking the vacated place on the bench. There was an early blow when an Elliott miskick in front of goal allowed Ally Brown to give Albion the lead. Ten minutes later, Cummins interchanged passes with Buckley before cutting in and arrowing in a tremendous equaliser from 20 yards. The visitors soon motored ahead, Cummins setting up Pickering inside the penalty area to drill a low shot past Grew.

Six minutes into the second half, Turner failed to deal with a cross and Elliott handled the ball to prevent Romeo Zondervan heading in. Gary Owen sent Turner the wrong way from the penalty. In a pulsating affair, Sunderland regained the initiative when Hinnigan threaded the ball through for Rowell to slot in. There were still over 25 minutes remaining but Sunderland survived to earn an exciting win. The sight of the league table was something that had barely seemed possible only three weeks previously. The Middlesbrough defeat seemed a distant nightmare, and Sunderland had somehow climbed to seventh from bottom. But, the bunching was incredibly tight.

Durban assessed the situation, 'The players have suffered too much all season to be overconfident. The day you think you've cracked it is when football teaches you a lesson. I reckon we need 44 points to stay up.' The manager also remarked on the greater willingness of players to declare themselves fit when vying for places in a team playing with freedom and confidence, 'There is a difference when somebody is not 100 per cent fit when things are going well.' Durban picked out the recalled Hindmarch for praise, 'Rob was one player I could not understand when I came here; he was very disappointing; but since I brought him back, I can understand why people raved about him. Rob felt that I had to make a choice between him and Jeff Clarke, and now that he has got his nose in front he has maintained it.'

## There Will be Some Turbulence Before Landing

As Sunderland made a speedy return to the Midlands for the match at Coventry, Durban revealed that McCoist's temporary omission from the squad had attracted attention, 'Another club asked if we would play Ally in our reserve match, but McCoist is very much part of the future of this club.' Turning back to that evening's opposition, Durban was concerned about the physical presence posed by 'one of the biggest teams in the league.' The manager also talked about ongoing attempts to get individuals to adapt their preferred roles for the good of the team, 'I tried to convince Cummins that we would get better results if he operated on the right wing, as it would give Pickering more room. It acted as a dual purpose against West Brom as it stifled [left-back] Derek Statham.'

Durban's presentiment of Coventry's height advantage proved justified in devastating fashion. The aerial power of Thompson and Hateley was in evidence as they knocked in two goals apiece. A Cummins strike was scant consolation in a 6-1 defeat. While not excusing his players, Durban indicated there would be no knee-jerk reaction, 'The last thing I want to do is break the spirit of the side. We were undisciplined for the last 20 minutes when we should have made sure we didn't lose by more than 4-1. We could not match them physically when it mattered.' Munro had been booked for a wild kick at Thompson in the 79th minute, but received no rebuke from his boss, 'At least he was trying to do something about the situation.' The wheels had come off the Roker juggernaut, and there was unwelcome news the following evening when Leeds, bristling at a perceived injustice, romped to a 4-1 win in the enforced rearrangement at Villa Park, Worthington scoring twice.

Durban now rallied everyone for the final push, 'I am confident the lads will quickly get over what happened at Coventry. We are back in the ruck, and I would have settled for that a month ago, and I only hope the fans appreciate how well the lads have grafted to get us into the position.' Again, the manager reassured the disappointing performers that he would not be ringing the changes for the visit of Brighton, 'The goalkeeper should not carry the can for what happened. The players must get Tuesday out of their systems. The side have to attack like they have over the last few home games and go out and enjoy playing.'

Meanwhile, the reserve team had clinched the North Midlands League title, but Durban was determined to push for inclusion in the far more competitive Central League. In other news, Juventus signed Michel Platini from St Etienne, and British aircraft had attacked Port Stanley to deny the Argentine invaders use of the airstrip. There was a war on, but Durban hoped to give the locals something to temporarily take their minds off events in the South Atlantic and his *Roker Review* praise for the supporters was unstinting, 'I make no apology for stressing yet again the magnificent away support.' Durban was also delighted to have seen the return of the good feeling at home matches, 'The atmosphere during and after the Birmingham and Everton matches was something special which we have missed so often this season.'

1 May brought sunshine, rain, and sleet to Roker Park as Sunderland worked to banish memories of the Coventry thrashing. A first-half decision of handball against Sammy Nelson resulted in Rowell coolly trundling in the spot-kick with goalkeeper Graham Moseley outfoxed. As the sun broke through the clouds in the second half, a rapid interchange of passes pinged between Rowell and Pickering before Rowell played the ball to West about 40 yards from goal. An unmarked Cummins was free on the wing, and many fans were yelling for West to play the simple pass wide, but the big striker motored on as Brighton defenders retreated. From 25 yards, West ripped in a blistering drive that beat Moseley's despairing leap and nestled in the net for a 'wonder goal'.

With the wind in Sunderland's sails, Rowell surged forward and sprayed the ball to Cummins on the right. He ran at the defender, checked, and then delivered a simple but accurate cross for Rowell who had continued his run; the first header was palmed into the air by the keeper only for the persistent striker to gleefully direct his follow-up into the net.

A satisfying 3-0 victory, and one that was becoming an accustomed taste at Roker after months of frustration. Colin West has fond memories of his spectacular strike, 'I picked up the ball and started advancing towards goal. The boss was *screaming* for me to pass to Cummins who was free on the right. But, as I was running, their defenders backed off and I let fly a shot that thundered into the corner.' In the dressing room after the match, West recollected that he heard a gruff 'Hey!' from Durban who growled at his young striker, 'Next time I tell you to pass the f***ing ball to Stan Cummins, just f***ing ignore me.' It was a piece of Durban's typical brand of joviality, and everyone relaxed.

Three days later, the revived squad faced West Ham at Upton Park. In the 36th minute, Turner diverted a thunderous Brooking drive on to the post and palmed Cross's follow-up header behind. That save looked even more valuable when Chisholm won the ball and fed Pickering whose run finished with a cross that West slid in. With around 20 minutes remaining, however, Devonshire was brought down by Elliott and Ray Stewart blasted in his 13th spot-kick of the campaign in no-nonsense fashion. With thoughts of victory erased, Durban's team withstood a fierce onslaught, displaying far greater resilience than seven days previously, 'It was harder as they pulled us all over the place. We did extremely well. The goal was first class.'

His opposite number, John Lyall, was full of praise, 'They play with a lot of spirit and enthusiasm. They try to play football and are showing the sort of attitude which will get them out of trouble.' That was a verdict from a manager whose team tried to play entertaining, 'pure' football. It was not the first, or last, such compliment bestowed upon a Sunderland team under Durban's stewardship. Yet, even to this day, many associate Durban with 'defensive' tactics – or twitter on about 'clowns'.

Although having been pegged back, one point looked an even better return when other results filtered through. Birmingham, Wolves, and Leeds had all lost. The following night, a rare Paul Bracewell goal ensured that Stoke bucked that trend as they beat Villa. Durban was philosophical on the inevitable vagaries of mixed results, 'The bottom teams can't go on losing all the time.' He emphasised the difference of managing even one goal in a match, 'We played quite well in the games where we didn't score but that is no use. The whole side has taken strength from Rowell and West. Gary is good to play with as he never gets in the way of other players. He does things naturally, and that has given Colin more room.' Durban then looked ahead, 'I think we will now have enough points if we beat Manchester City [in the final match].' The value placed on nicking a solitary goal would be underscored in both of the remaining games.

In an episode that spoke volumes about the lacklustre performance of the region's teams, a 37-year-old, Carlisle player-coach Pop Robson, was voted North East Player of the Season by that branch of the Football Writers Association. But, the enthusiasm of Sunderland's away support still burned bright. Sunderland had sold their allocation of 1,000 tickets for their longest away trip of the season to Southampton, with Durban hoping that Elliott would make it after having a boil on his thigh lanced, 'His pace will be so vital against Keegan.'

In the end, it was another former England captain who became the topic of post-match deliberation. Alan Ball had hauled down Pickering as he was set to burst away and was booked. Even his own manager, McMenemy, condemned Ball's action, 'It's inexcusable. I support those who want to see that type of foul punished more severely.' There was to be a dismissal, however, as Hindmarch, already booked after retaliating to a Steve Williams lash-out, was shown the red card after tripping Channon.

Although Clarke came on for Cummins, and Chisholm dropped back too, David Armstrong was unmarked when he applied a simple finishing header to a Nick Holmes corner with ten minutes remaining. It was a body blow, but speaking to north-east radio after the game, McMenemy's affection for his native region was evident as he offered consoling words on how the league table did 'not look too bad' for Sunderland's chances, with a home match on the final day.

## Operation Houdini: Final Phase

Durban outlined the approach to be adopted for the build-up to the big game, 'We will be playing the week very much in a low key, so the players will be banned from speaking to the press and television. I just want to take the onus off them until one o'clock on Saturday afternoon, and carry on where we left off against Brighton. We will prepare exactly the same way as the last three home matches.'

As well as the opportunity to preserve First Division status, the manager handed out an extra incentive for Elliott to shackle whoever led the City attack, 'Saturday gives Shaun the opportunity to prove that he deserves to be in the England squad, and not Caton. He made Keegan look very ordinary for the second time this season.' Durban recognised that his players required a better platform from which to pursue their ambitions, 'Internationals are chosen from successful sides and in an area like this it is even more important that we are successful.'

That week, Pickering had picked up a couple of the local young player of the year awards, and Durban was effusive about his first find of the season, 'We virtually took him to Scotland, as one of our top apprentices, to look after the kit and help out, but he is getting rewarded for what he has put in. He has rarely had two indifferent games all season, and is a pleasure to work with.' Despite focussing on the vital match, Durban confirmed that he had inquired about Darlington's £100,000-rated striker Speedie. But, it was the future services of the young prospects already on Sunderland's books that the manager was more concerned about securing, and had offered improved contracts to Pickering, West, and Prudhoe.

Thankfully, in two of the outstanding midweek fixtures, fellow relegation rivals failed to win. West Bom crashed 3-0 at home to Manchester United, while Leeds and Birmingham shared six goals at Elland Road where Worthington and Harford notched two goals each. Although approaching the final Saturday of the league season, it was ominous that Leeds, Stoke, and West Brom all had matches to play the following midweek, and would know what was required after other teams had completed their programmes. Sunderland had infamously been on the receiving end the evening they were relegated in 1977. A late kick-off had allegedly been orchestrated in the game between Coventry and Bristol City and, when news of Sunderland's 2-0 defeat at Everton filtered through, the teams at Highfield Road played out the game sedately as they realised both would be safe if the 2-2 scoreline was preserved.

Durban had no intention of Sunderland's immediate future hanging on the following week's fixtures. The emphasis would be on attack, and McCoist was named substitute to an unchanged team, 'I want a striker as substitute. We have got to go out and get three points, and worry about the others after, but if we win I am sure we will stay up. Our lads are in good nick, and over the next couple of days will be having lots of shooting practice. We will be aiming to keep the mood of the troops happy, and having taken nine months to taste the pleasure of winning at home regularly, we are confident.' Regarding the final outcome, the permutations veered dramatically: defeat for Sunderland and remaining on 41 points – it was possible to stay up; a victory and finishing with 44 points – it was possible to go down.

Durban's exhortations extended to the supporters, 'The crowd can be worth a goal start, and I hope they will roll up and shout us to survival. There will be extra people back who had given up when we were on the floor. I hope they see an improvement and then add their support next season.' The Roker boss was also looking ahead at 'the big picture', 'We are all aiming for the same goal, as you have got to experience the traumas to be able to enjoy the comparative success.' Ultimately, long-term success tasted all the sweeter for any manager – provided he was allowed the time to finish the job he had started.

There was a doubt over whether star striker Trevor Francis would be fit to play at Roker, but Durban maintained the job in hand remained the same, 'I am not interested in what City's team is as all we've got to do to stay in the First Division is play as well as we have been, and take the chances when they come. The players started off this run looking relegated but it is a complete release valve the way we have played. The absence of tensions has kept it going.'

It became apparent that Durban had not enjoyed the resources he had been led to expect when joining the club, but that was an aspect that meant an escape from relegation would represent his finest managerial achievement yet, 'I thought I could have gone out and bought in the middle of the season but because of the financial situation did not, so it will give me far more pleasure if we do it this way.'

Saturday afternoon came, and Phil Boyer stood in for Francis. In the 14th minute, Pickering broke clear on the left and although his shot was blocked he regained position to find West. The young striker had the awareness to tee up Buckley whose low drive from 12 yards gave his team the precious breakthrough. Corrigan pulled off a spectacular save to deny Cummins as Sunderland sought some breathing space, but the forward was called into action in his own six-yard box as, with Turner beaten, he kicked away a goalbound header from Bond. It was an angst-ridden finale, and the full-time whistle was met with great relief and jubilation by the crowd.

An initial glance at the revised congested table did not seem conclusive for many. Were Sunderland still not sure of safety? A look at the remaining fixtures, however, revealed that West Brom had to play both Leeds and Stoke. Therefore, it was mathematically impossible for all three strugglers to obtain the points required to leapfrog the Wearsiders. Durban's team had achieved what had seemed like 'mission impossible'. When Durban had advised 'don't expect miracles' on his arrival, he was referring to unrealistic hopes of winning trophies and qualifying for Europe in his first season, but this escape did constitute a minor miracle.

Earlier in the week, Durban had spoken of the sense of satisfaction that seeing the team retain top-flight status would give him (not having enjoyed the benefit of being able to compete in the transfer market). In the immediate aftermath, however, the manager was more subdued, 'It wasn't an achievement, but it avoided embarrassment for me.' The boss, instead, focussed attention on the lesson some of his players had learned, 'You get in this game what you deserve. I am pleased that certain individuals have been rewarded. We have now got to keep our best players and add to it to win anything. Things will get better with a younger side, as some of them have spent part of the season learning the game.' Yes, Durban wished he had more financial resources at his disposal, but he recognised that it was not so simple, 'Wolves have gone down with the most expensive centre-forward in the league [Andy Gray], and we have thrown a kid in [West] who will get us goals.'

The press photographer allowed access to the jubilant home dressing room snapped Munro, Elliott, Buckley, McCoist, and Cummins toasting survival with lemonade. The scene was one that exuded unity and happiness, but only hours after victory, one of that 'happy few', one of that 'band of brothers', was saying he wanted to leave. With one year of his contract remaining, that player was Cummins. Durban adopted his usual phlegmatic demeanour when dealing with unsettled personnel; he'd had plenty of practice throughout the past few months, 'Provided the money was right, I would be prepared to let Stan Cummins go, but the only people leaving this football club under contract are those who suit us.'

Two days after the team had preserved top-flight status, Elliott, Rowell, Chisholm, and Buckley were offered new deals but Clarke, Siddall, McGinley, and Arnott were released. In a situation that would have seemed unthinkable 12 months previously, their departures would see no fees involved. Quite simply, Durban had to clear the decks, 'The assessing period is over, and we have now made room to bring one or two new faces in. I will only be bringing in people I feel are better than what we have already as it isn't a question of numbers. I am interested in one or two players who have been given free transfers, and therefore hope that our players will sign up as quickly as possible.'

Looking back on his most demanding season as a manager, Durban surprisingly picked out a 6-1 defeat as a defining episode, 'Coventry was the turning point. I was tempted to change the side, but that would have been silly. Basically, the honesty of the players has been good despite some very poor matches at home, but they have never really cheated.' Durban was also gratified that he had managed to remedy one of the club's past fundamental blunders, 'The players need a rest after a season like this, and it is a great relief that nobody is going to America. Now is the time for individuals to look to improve as players and not improve income.'

With safety achieved, Sunderland supporters could relax as three teams battled to avoid the third relegation berth. For their final match, Worthington would prove a big miss for Leeds. After accruing 20 disciplinary points, he had received the discretionary one-match ban, and Leeds assistant manager Martin Wilkinson complained about the unfairness of a system where some players (including Munro) had only received warnings. For West Brom, Owen and Regis could play despite recent dismissals as their bans did not start until the next season. To rub salt into the wounds, Regis scored the first goal in a 2-0 win, and Leeds 'fans' rioted in an insane attempt to get the game abandoned. Leeds were left to hope that their conquerors could go away to Stoke 48 hours later and frustrate the home team. There was little hope, the now-safe West Brom succumbed 3-0 as Stoke stayed up, aided by goals from Watson and Chapman. The irony of Leeds's relegation was not lost on Worthington who, recalling his winner at Roker, admitted, 'I really thought Sunderland would go down after that.'

The final league table showed Sunderland had fallen below Birmingham, West Brom, and Stoke as only goal difference separated the four teams. It mattered not; Leeds had two points fewer and were relegated despite having splashed out on expensive recruits. Sunderland had managed to score only 19 goals at home (the same total as they struck away), with Rowell finishing top scorer on nine.

## Changes: Youth and Experience

New freedom of contract regulations had been introduced, and it became apparent that one of Durban's prized assets would not be putting pen to paper without testing the water. At 25, Shaun Elliott felt he might benefit from a move, 'I owe it to myself to see what other offers come in. It's vital that I get it right because I desperately want to make an impression on the international scene.' Durban was relaxed about the situation and was not pressurising the player, 'He has nothing to lose by hanging on. Shaun knows my admiration for him. I still think he will sign with us.'

There was other legislation introduced by the Football League. In future, 50 per cent of a transfer fee would have to be paid immediately, and the balance within 12 months. This was in a bid to end the drawn-out arrangement that saw clubs able to eke out payments two years after a player had joined. Poorer clubs had been suffering from being drip-fed funds that were desperately needed to survive. The measure would prevent such glorified 'hire purchase' deals, and act as an artificial restraint on transfer fees.

It did not take long before the most highly rated of Durban's released players was negotiating with another club. Arnott spoke with former Sunderland FA Cup goalscoring hero Ian Porterfield who was now manager at newly crowned Fourth Division champions Sheffield United, 'I was very impressed with everything about the club. Ian knows what I am capable of, and he's the sort of man who can bring out the best in me.' Within a couple of days Arnott had signed for the Sheffield club on a free transfer, only months after Middlesbrough had been quoted a £350,000 fee.

That move was no shock, but other news released the same day was; 'Roker End Coming Down' ran the *Echo*'s headline and supporters learned that the 71-year-old uncovered terracing would be 'demolished in the summer because of its dangerous condition'. The crumbling concrete's deterioration had been hastened by the intense frosts, and the 'intention' was to provide permanent seating in 'a new stand'. But, the uncertainty of the word 'intention' was further fuelled by the club statement's wording on when this improvement would be in place, 'As soon as the money is available.' In a shift of onus frequently employed by Cowie, the chairman said it was impossible to say when a new stand would be built, but it 'obviously' depended upon the amount of support. There would be a temporary reduction in capacity, a fact that seemed purely academic unless money could also be found to enable the manager to bring in the quality players to attract fans through the turnstiles.

Durban wasted no time in assuring supporters that any work would not interfere with squad strengthening, 'Our aim is to be firmly established as a First Division club on the field before we start with ground improvements. Unfortunately, adding a valuable asset to the stadium should have been done before the game got into its present financial difficulties.' This constituted another rap on the knuckles for the club's executives. When asked about the prospect of Buckley and Rowell re-signing, Durban was cagey, 'I will issue a list of the players who have signed when the time is right; not in dribs and drabs.'

At present, the manager was more concerned that those assembled for an under-20 tournament in Holland would fare well. McCoist, Cooke, Pickering, Venison, and Mick Whitfield were included, 'The squad is going to be the backbone of the side for the future. It gives the lads a chance to play against continental opposition which hopefully, in the not-too-distant future, they will meet at first-team level.'

In late May, youth was still in the forefront of Durban's agenda as he presented the awards of the Sunderland Schools FA at Thornhill School. In his speech, he condemned the system which allowed clubs to sign boys at 14, 'Wait until you are 16 and ready to leave school, because at 14 you can make a big mistake. It may all seem rosy in the garden when clubs invite you during holidays, but it can all change. It is difficult enough leaving school and working with men whose jobs you are trying to take without leaving home at the same time. That is why boys have a better chance with their home club.' As if to illustrate the point, Durban's first find, Nick Pickering, signed his extended four-year contract.

Meanwhile, the club's directors were attempting to secure a blanket safety certificate which would allow Roker Park to host an array of money-spinning events, sporting and non-sporting, as more clubs looked to use grounds for lucrative crowd-pulling promotions. Newcastle's St James' Park was to host a Rolling Stones concert that June and archives revealed that, prior to staging its first football match, Victorian entrepreneurs had staged events such as the 'Roker Park Olympic Games' (13 August 1898) which featured a pole vault record from Richard Dickinson, and an appearance by world champion sprinter Charles Harper.

That was the past, but future prospects were ripening as Durban watched his young team triumph in Holland, beating Linfield 2-0 in the final. Their wins included a 4-0 beating of Feyenoord, and Prudhoe was voted keeper of the tournament. Speaking from Haarlam, Durban purred, 'The kids were magnificent, having to play five games in just three days. It proves this club is now on the right lines. This triumph underlines the performances we saw from the youngsters in the Youth Cup. It has been an exacting test for them, and they have come through it magnificently.'

On his return, the boss formulated contingency plans to cover Elliott's possible departure. One player being monitored was 33-year-old former Sunderland defender Colin Todd who had been freed by Birmingham. Durban had played with the former England international at Derby, 'Todd is a player I know all about, and he could do a job for us. I want Elliott to stay, but obviously I need a safeguard.'

Durban was also linked in the press with Leeds's former England man Brian Greenhoff who was keen to stay in the First

Division. The back-page news of Sunderland's latest mooted transfer activity was not the sort that sparked excitement for supporters, but these were mere early-day feelers; perhaps some 'big name' might emerge later.

While Elliott bided his time, Rowell edged closer to staying put and insisted that the club's current status made them as attractive a proposition as anywhere, 'An offer from a First Division club takes some beating, so I may not move. I must admit it was a tremendous relief that Sunderland stayed up.' As Durban awaited decisions from his out-of-contract senior players, the club's ace talent-spotter Charlie Ferguson had been snapping up some of the top local schoolboys: from Sunderland under-15s, striker Dale White; from Newcastle boys, midfielder Gordon Armstrong; and North Tyneside utility player John Cornforth.

That influx of youthful talent coincided with the departure of 30-year-old Tom Ritchie who had signed for a fee of £185,000 less than 18 months before. Ritchie had struggled on his return to the First Division scene, but his position as one of the top wage-earners was the primary reason he was being shunted out. So keen were the club to offload him from the payroll, that they were prepared to take a staggering loss. While the player was back in Bristol during the summer, City manager Terry Cooper asked him in for a chat as he suspected that Sunderland's financial position could lead them to releasing him for a smallish fee. Cooper then contacted Durban, and the wheels were put in motion. Ritchie met up with his Sunderland boss at a hotel in West Bromwich, and negotiations resulted in the player being granted a free transfer.

Although not unhappy in the north-east, Ritchie had no desire to sit on a fat contract, 'Alan Durban has been tremendous with me. I know I am stepping down from the First to the Fourth Division but I would rather do that than hang about for the next couple of years.' His new boss Cooper had hoped for a bargain price but seemed as surprised as the Sunderland public that no fee was involved, 'It is unbelievable that we are getting a First Division player with his goalscoring record for nothing.' Ritchie's career goals return was respectable, and at Roker he had notched eight in 32 appearances. His departure reportedly meant a saving of £30,000 on the wage bill.

Durban's travels that week also took in the Café Royal London to attend the Central League annual meeting. Fifteen clubs had applied for the ten vacancies created by the formation of a second tier. Sunderland were duly voted in, and this marked the improvement in competitive action that the manager believed imperative to prepare players for first-team duty.

Back in the north-east, Durban was keener than ever for his free agents to re-commit, suggesting that Sunderland had been more liberal than others in their wage-cutting exercise, 'I have made inquiries for players as cover, but I don't think any other club has let players go as good as the ones we did. There was a lot of talk of clubs releasing senior players but all that they have done is clear out the kids.' On the positive side, Durban envisaged new arrivals, 'We have trimmed our professional staff from more than 30 down to 19, so there is room for one or two signings.' However, the overall economic gloom that pervaded sent a message that the manager's team-strengthening options might be limited to free transfers or 'bargains.' Durban also planned to monitor Nicholl's status when the defender's North American season with Toronto Blizzard ended.

Now it was the middle of June, and there were diversions to occupy the collective attentions. In Spain, the World Cup had started and Argentina had lost 1-0 to Belgium in the opening match at the Camp Nou stadium Barcelona. That night's live match on TV would be Brazil v Russia. The following day, hostilities in the Falklands came to an end with the Argentina surrender sparking scenes of crowds singing in Downing Street.

## Planning a New Campaign

The fixtures were out! Sunderland had an attractive opening-day trip to new European champions Aston Villa, and Durban commented, 'It is when the fixtures come out that it really hits you how important it is to be in the First Division.' There was greater onus on a football manager in this period to undertake a number of organisational tasks, including suggesting date changes. Durban had looked into delaying the pre-Christmas match at Roker to the next day but reported, 'Arsenal are not keen on Sunday football.' He had also suggested to Notts County a switch of the second match of the season from a Wednesday to cash in attendance-wise on the Bank Holiday Monday, 'They say that to play in the afternoon would mean them travelling on the Sunday for an overnight stay, and they don't want to do that.' It seems Sunderland were not the only club employing economy measures!

It may have been a full two months before the Villa Park curtain-raiser, but the manager was already mulling over his starting line-up. As a result of his sending-off at Southampton, Hindmarch would be suspended, 'I will seriously consider playing West in defence against Villa, and he will certainly be used at centre-half in some of the pre-season games as I think he will give us the best balance.' Durban did have other options at his disposal before he deployed his centre-forward in a defensive role, Chisholm and Hinnigan appearing to be more natural alternatives. West himself, however, recalls that he was comfortable about switching, and that his experience up front prepared him for the role, 'I roughly knew what forward players were thinking and trying to do. Heading was one of my strengths. I could play with both feet, so I could cope if I got turned to the left side.'

At the start of July, Durban found himself a wanted man. Leeds United had dismissed Allan Clarke, and saw the Sunderland boss as the man capable of restoring their fortunes. Perhaps Leeds had been alerted to the faint possibility by the fact that Durban had still to sign a contract, but they were refused permission to make an approach and it would be eight long years before Howard Wilkinson led them out of the Second Division 'wilderness.' There was one major appointment, however, as Bobby Robson was named the new England manager.

The board may have resisted the overtures of other clubs trying to lure their manager, but they were implementing cost-cutting exercises and Durban found his backroom staff disappearing around him. Coach Jim Montgomery and scouting supremo Jimmy Greenhalgh did not have their contracts renewed and, by now well-versed in the club's parsimony, Durban was not surprised, 'Considering the cuts in the playing staff, it was inevitable there would be redundancies to the backroom staff too.' Durban had been full of praise for the quality of last season's crop of youngsters coached by Montgomery, but his hands were tied, 'Companies in the present situation have had to make unpleasant decisions like these.'

Meanwhile, there was some disturbing dithering on the planned stadium renovations. The Roker End demolition work had not commenced, with general manager Geoff Davidson vaguely stating, 'The money has to be spent wisely.' Deflecting attention away from lack of expenditure on stadium and personnel, the chairman decided he would be the spokesman to announce a piece of positive news. Rowell had signed a new two-year contract, and Cowie declared, 'What gives me special pleasure is that he is a local boy and we want as many local lads as we can get in the team. I look forward to the Sunderland of the future being made up of 11 Durham or Northumberland boys.' Mark those words!

As the Roker players reported back for training, their former captain Clarke was signing for Arthur Cox's Newcastle. It was time for Durban to make his own decisive move to strengthen a depleted squad, and the target was 25-year-old utility player Ian Atkins who had been used in a striker role the previous season, scoring 19 goals for Shrewsbury in the Second Division. Stoke had offered £50,000, but this fell short of the Shropshire club's valuation. Durban had played alongside Atkins in midfield when player-manager at Shrewsbury, and was confident he could pip Stoke for the signature.

Atkins motored north for talks with Durban, and Shrewsbury's latest player-boss, Graham Turner, revealed there was an exchange element to the prospective deal as Alan Brown was travelling down from Wearside. Brown had been valued at £150,000 when on the verge of joining Newcastle at Christmas, but with Sunderland paying £30,000 *plus* the striker for Atkins, his valuation had been slashed to £70,000.

Durban had handed the young Atkins his league debut, and Turner sang the praises of a player who had operated in every outfield position, 'Ian is as honest as the day is long. He is the most popular player with the fans.' A big favourite with his total commitment, strong running, and hard tackling, Atkins also boasted a powerful shot in his arsenal. This was a player who possessed the character and quality that Durban wanted to see more of at Sunderland. In Shrewsbury, Brown faced a stringent medical and satisfied an orthopaedic specialist of his fitness.

Atkins swiftly decided to sign for Sunderland, and Durban expressed his view that the new player's best position could be in the back four but, with a small squad, his versatility rendered him a particularly important acquisition, 'We have now got three or four players who can play in various positions. Last season, when we had to replace someone we had to shuffle the side too much. We had too many front players, and were having to accommodate five centre-forwards in the reserves. That is why we let Brown and Ritchie go on loan. Now the squad looks better balanced.'

Supporters did not realise that this was to be Sunderland's only close-season signing. The press picture featured the beaming Durban and Atkins (in his new Sunderland shirt) standing alongside one another, but *Daily Mail* journalist Doug Weatherall reflected on the changed times for the 'one-time Bank of England Club' who even the previous summer had broken their transfer record. Now, 'in difficult times for football generally, it is relatively little-known Atkins' who was presented as the key signing. Nevertheless, Atkins was a player Durban was highly satisfied to have on board, 'He's a bread-and-butter player who's very reliable. He wants to play every week. I won't have to teach him. He knows what I want.'

Atkins's enthusiasm for the challenge ahead was refreshing, 'At Sunderland, I will be just glad to get into the team, but I think my best qualities are as a defender. It would be a great feeling to make my Sunderland debut against Villa, but I have to prove I am worth a place.' The player also revealed an episode that convinced him he would feel wanted at Sunderland, 'I thought I would be heading for Stoke, but Alan Durban managed to trace me to my hotel in Majorca, and I must admit I got a tingle when I found out Sunderland wanted me.' Atkins also relished the prospect of competing at Roker Park on a regular basis. He had played there once, on a pre-Christmas Friday evening in 1979 when a Marangoni header had helped Sunderland to a 2-1 win, 'The crowd sticks in my memory, they were tremendous. I had never sampled an atmosphere like that.'

Durban's playing staff had been reduced and the wage bill eased considerably. This assumed greater importance considering that the club's average home gate had fallen from 26,479 (1980/81) to 19,608. However, it might be added that even Manchester United and European champions Aston Villa had experienced falls. The returning players were put through their paces at their temporary training base at Durham's Maiden Castle, and Durban reported, 'The players have come back in tremendous condition. The lads have quickly regained their appetite, and they know they will be pushed for their places.'

Plans were taking shape; Munro was named as club captain to add to his on-field responsibility, and Durban stated an intention to give 18-year-old keeper Prudhoe starts in the pre-season friendlies. Current number one Turner offered his understudy words of encouragement, 'Mark is 18, and when I was 17 I was a regular in Sheffield Wednesday's first team, keeping out Peter Fox, who was signed by Alan Durban at Stoke, and is still their number one. Mark has improved a lot under Monty over the last year.' Turner had been undertaking some extra physical training sessions alongside Rowell, Hinnigan, and Brown, all being regular visitors to the gymnasium run by South Shields boxing promoters Tommy Conroy and Frankie Deans. Turner commented, 'It is harder than the normal training in football.'

On Hindmarch's early suspension, the manager pointed out the long-term strategy, 'It's early days to be talking about the Villa match, but Ian Atkins is a noisy player, a good organiser, which should help Shaun.' However, Elliott's future was still uncertain, being retained on a week-to-week basis while holding out for a better deal (which reportedly included a possible testimonial and 'loyalty payment'). The arrival of Atkins could only weaken the bargaining power of the unsettled defender.

## Ammunition for the Doom-mongers

Participating in a pre-season Isle of Man tournament, the squad used the training facilities of one of the local amateur sides where Durban coached approximately 40 youngsters who would doubtless retain fond memories of their surprise opportunity. The threadbare nature of the squad was underscored when injuries were sustained in a 2-1 defeat against St Mirren. Frank McAvennie grabbed the Scottish side's winner, but Turner and Buckley joined West on the sidelines. New signing Atkins had debuted at number nine.

Turner's gashed knee meant that Prudhoe would get an early chance in the next match against Carlisle. It was not a happy debut for the young keeper, who was at fault for two Alan Shoulder goals, with former Roker forward Bob Lee getting the other in a 3-0 defeat. The 15 remaining fit professionals travelled to set up base at St Andrews before a mini Scottish tour comprising three games in four days. Durban planned to play Atkins in a midfield role but, with one eye on the Villa opener, give him at least one game in central defence. The player was not fazed by the prospect, 'I will play anywhere as I will be delighted to be in the side.'

McCoist scored an opening goal against former team St Johnstone but, although slumping to a 2-1 defeat, Durban saw no cause for alarm, 'Had we played with a full-strength side and lost the three matches then I would have been concerned. It would not matter if we lost all eight matches before the season starts as long as we can go to Villa and get a result. We have tried to push too much in to prepare, and I feel that certain players are playing for themselves rather than a unit like the end of last season.' Sunderland would not lose all eight friendly games – not quite.

The torrid time McCoist had suffered while acclimatising to life in the First Division had not diminished the number of clubs keeping tabs on the young talent, Durban revealing he had received several inquiries, 'He has loads of ability but, ideally, I would have liked to have seen him playing alongside Colin West as he has never played off a target man. Last season was very difficult for all of our strikers, but Ally seemed to lose that valuable natural asset.'

McCoist scored again in a 2-2 draw at Dundee's Dens Park, his 'favourite away ground', and Durban saw promising signs, 'Atkins looked more comfortable and it was encouraging to see Ally get another goal which was a real cracker.' The tour's final game brought a win at last, McCoist firing the only goal against Dunfermline. Overall, Durban felt that the mini Scottish tour had been 'an ideal way of preparing; better than a continental trip.'

Sunderland's lacklustre build-up did nothing to raise their esteem nationally, and bookmakers again quoted them at 100/1 for the championship; only three clubs were given longer odds. Despite being the principal goalscorer in Scotland, Durban suggested that McCoist's prospects of securing a place in the team for the opening Saturday remained slim, 'The players who proved themselves in the First Division have got to be regarded as being ahead in the queue.' While the striking line-up remained undecided, Atkins was earmarked to start, 'Ian had an effect on the players around him as he is a good shouter, and though he will play in central defence in the two remaining pre-season matches, it is very much a one-off situation against Villa.'

Before the year was out, and not for the first time, the boss would have to renege on a stated plan. As Durban discussed the merits of two of his all too few Roker signings, news emerged that their Tyneside neighbours were in the race to sign Kevin Keegan. The rumour mill was fuelled further by manager Cox's absence from the pre-season photocall. Sunderland were holding their own photoshoot, and the published picture of a 15-man first-team squad had a certain sparseness about it.

Of course, Keegan famously signed for Newcastle in one of the surprise moves of the decade. Before setting off to watch the season's first two opponents play friendlies (Villa v Dukla Prague, and Notts County v Leicester), Durban commented on the boost that Keegan's arrival would give to the area, 'It is tremendous for the north-east. It should capture the imagination of all soccer fans in the area.' Years later, a *Daily Mail* piece by Doug Weatherall stated that Keegan had been 'offered' to Sunderland ahead of Newcastle, but the 'short-term' nature of the deal, not to mention the financial package involved, had been off-putting (a reported fee of £100,000 plus wages of £3,000 per week). Another 'what if' episode perhaps?

Weatherall was with the squad on their pre-season tour, and recalls being present at a hotel in St Andrews when Durban took a phone call advising him of Keegan's availability. However, the revelatory nature of this episode should be tempered with an acknowledgement that agents were constantly alerting a whole host of managers about available players. In fact, it was later reported that 'over twenty' clubs were standing by ready to snatch Keegan away when a late hitch developed as Newcastle were ordered to stump up the instalments owed to West Brom for the purchase of John Trewick. It was at this point that several directors dug into their pockets to the tune of £7,000 apiece to ensure that the historic transfer went through.

Even if the scenario of Keegan swapping the red-and-white shirt of Southampton for that of Sunderland had come to pass, the club would not have been able to accommodate the deluge of spectators due to the Roker End being closed for pending work. General manager Davidson stated, 'The board of directors have decided to preserve 15 metres of existing terracing, which will accommodate 7,000 when finished. It will be slow progress because of the state of the concrete. It is not a ball and chain demolition, but work to be done by experts.'

No doubt those reading this somewhat condescending statement were gratified that the club had confirmed that the demolition would 'be done by experts'! For the immediate future, it meant the ground's capacity was reduced to 29,000. Davidson proceeded, 'There is no way in the present economic climate that we can go ahead with the proposed five-tier seated stand, which would cost a minimum of £2m.' The underwhelming facts for supporters were that there would no new stand – and no Keegan-esque signing.

A week before the start of the new season, Sunderland went down 1-0 at Derby. Already missing Hinnigan, Munro, and Atkins, they proceeded to lose Elliott and West. When Buckley went over on his ankle midway through second half he was replaced by Durban who received a warm reception from the Derby crowd. The manager's assessment of the casualty list groped for silver linings, 'Our plans have been completely disrupted. My overriding feeling at the moment is that things are not as bad as they could have been, but I didn't expect another three players to be injured.' Regardless of injuries, a gloomy picture was being painted by the media over the team's prospects for the new season. In contrast, Newcastle fans rushed for season tickets as the city went 'Keegan crazy'.

Amid continued predictions of relegation toil from the doom-mongers, Durban offered a rallying message, 'We will prove a lot of people wrong as we are in a better position now than 12 months ago. The side we have is no weaker than the one at Stoke two years ago that finished eleventh. What we have learnt to do is play as a team which sometimes when you have a big squad is difficult to do as players tend to play for their own positions.' The manager was even squeezing out the positives from having fewer personnel, 'The more options you have, the more mistakes you make, whereas with a smaller squad it has the reverse effect as players know if they have a bad game they are not walking on thin ice. We all want to get going again.'

The *Echo* report's consoling sentiment included a repeated refrain, 'Miracles don't happen overnight, but while local rivals Newcastle and Middlesbrough will be striving for promotion,

Roker fans will have the consolation that their favourites are already there competing with the best.'

## In Like Young Lions

In the days preceding the opening match, Sunderland's opponents were making overtures for Elliott who Villa manager Tony Barton viewed as a potential replacement for an unsettled Ken McNaught. In fact, the press forecast that Elliott was 'likely to make his debut for the European champions against Sunderland'. Far from feigning an air of indifference, Durban spoke candidly, 'Shaun knows that I don't want him to go, and with the other injuries to a small squad we could do without further disruption.' This wish did not prevent contingency enquiries being initiated, 'It was a big blow missing out on Todd, but I have made moves as cover; if Shaun goes I will have to decide whether to replace that feature of the side or go for somebody who can score goals.' Todd had been snapped up by his former boss Clough at Forest, but that was now history.

There were already restrictions on incoming transfer activity at Roker (deals to be conducted on a self-financing basis), and there had been an absence of any post-World Cup transfer frenzy to break the stagnation. Once again, Durban enquired about Mick Robinson and, although the initial asking price was £500,000, with Elliott on a weekly contract and not certain to join Villa, a possible exchange deal could not be ruled out, especially if Brighton sold transfer-listed central defender Steve Foster.

Meanwhile, midfielder Buckley had accepted new terms, although opting for a one-year deal only. That welcome news was supplemented by the knowledge that Durban could play Elliott against his prospective new employers, with Barton widely expected to sign the defender the following week and let the matter be settled by a tribunal, an aspect that displeased Durban,

'Villa are getting the best of both worlds, as they can back out if they don't like the fee set.'

If Durban was envious about the 'Keegan effect' further up the coast, he was not showing it, 'I hope that a lot of the people who are going to St James' Park will want to come here the next week, as *the Keegan thing* will help to keep us on our toes and stimulate more competition.' Newcastle were expecting a 38,000 capacity sell-out for Keegan's debut against QPR, and ITV's lunchtime magazine programme *On the Ball* was to be broadcast live from the Newcastle boardroom, for which privilege the club would receive 'a considerable fee'. The message appeared to be, if the Sunderland board chose to heed it, 'speculate to accumulate'.

As Saturday, 28 August dawned, long queues had already formed at St James' Park eager to witness Keegan's debut. Meanwhile, the effects of the stringent cost-cutting measures on Wearside continued to bite. The rash of departures from the backroom staff meant that Durban had sent two of his players, Cooke and Whitfield, to Meadow Lane to check up on next opponents Notts County, 'Footballers must accept more responsibility this season. They have been briefed on what to look for. I also expect them to make their own observations, and when we assemble for training on Monday one of the first things we will do is listen to their reports.' Durban named Elliott in his team, saying, 'I am confident that he will play out of his skin.'

Atkins and West shrugged off niggling injuries to play, and McCoist was preferred to Rowell. Villa led via a first-half Gordon Cowans goal, with Elliott and Atkins struggling with the aerial power of Withe. But, the England centre-forward had sustained a hamstring pull and did not emerge after the break. West soon equalised and this was followed by a McCoist close-range finish. As supporters tuned in to their radios hoping their team could hold on, hearts skipped a beat with the news that there had been some more action at Villa Park. Many were expecting to hear news of a home equaliser, but the local BBC reporter simply bellowed above the din, 'Sunderland's young lions have done it'! The match was in its dying embers and a fine goal from Pickering had given Sunderland the cushion that provoked such exultation.

A 3-1 win at the home of the newly crowned European champions was a marvellous result, and one that would normally have been hailed as performance of the day. However, this was no ordinary afternoon. On Tyneside, Keegan had scored the only goal against QPR, and Sunderland's magnificent win was undeservedly put in the shade amid the hullabaloo.

A couple of days later, Durban was distinctly disgruntled by the conduct of Villa who suddenly cooled their interest in Elliott after McNaught settled his differences. Durban said that there had merely been a terse 30-second conversation between the two managers, 'The whole thing has been messy and, at times, discourteous. There is always the danger of deals like this breaking down when they are conducted through the press, and have an unsettling effect on players.'

Elliott would have a different central-defensive partner for the midweek match as Hindmarch came in with Atkins switching to midfield at the expense of Chisholm. Durban's pre-game message signalled that a positive approach would be adopted, 'It is time we started looking at the entertainment value for the spectators, and what fans have *really wanted*. I want my players to go out and look as though they enjoy playing. It is all an attitude of mind, and to have any influence on maintaining our level of gates, or improving them, we must have an attacking policy home and away.'

Almost 19,000 spectators saw Sunderland's supposedly new bold approach malfunction in a stuttering performance. Pickering had to leave the field for several minutes while he received stitches to a gashed knee, and was eventually replaced by Rowell.

However, the first-choice penalty taker was still on the bench when a handball decision was given against Nigel Worthington. It was anticipated that Cummins would be on duty, and there was general surprise in the crowd when West stepped up to the mark, most being unaware that the striker had taken spot-kicks at youth and reserve-team level. Unfortunately, his low shot lacked conviction and Raddy Avramovic dived to make a comfortable save. Later, Durban refused to dwell on the decision, 'We discussed it before the match. It is no use crying.'

In the 54th minute, Turner spilled a cross while under pressure from the physical presence of Kilcline, and Christie was able to screw the ball in from an angle. As County held on, both Avramovic and Christie were booked for time wasting, but it was to no avail as, on 89 minutes, West found Buckley on the right and his low cross was steered home by Rowell. His manager was relieved, 'That's Gary to a tee. He has made virtually no impression in the pre-season games, then up he pops to get you a goal. It was a difficult decision to leave him out of the side, just as it was to leave Chisholm out after we had won at Villa, but that goal will have given him a tremendous lift.'

The *Echo* reporter criticised the performance, with one exception, 'Sunderland struggled to create openings but, to their credit, attempted to put it together rather than revert to the up-and-under play which the fans demanded.' Durban's analysis also spotlighted his players' refusal to resort to 'kick-and-rush' tactics, 'We learnt a lot as a side last night but will have to take a careful look at our back four when playing at home as we were so vulnerable on the break. We have to work to our maximum to get a result, and half of our side came out of it poorly. When you've missed a penalty and your goalkeeper has thrown one in, you have to be relieved when you get a point. It was disappointing, but at least we came back with a bit of football.'

On the transfer front, Durban revealed that Brighton had sent their chief scout to watch the game at Villa to see if there was any possibility of an exchange deal if Durban made another bid for Robinson. The manager had also opened negotiations with Nicholl's agent about the possibility of the defender plumping to rejoin them after his playing commitment in Toronto ended. In the meantime, Durban had to confront the blow of the temporary loss of his centre-forward. An X-ray confirmed that West had sustained a foot fracture that would rule him out for several weeks, 'If the goals dry up then we will have to look at the situation. We have not got much size up front so we may have to change the pattern.'

Twenty-four hours is a long time in football. Durban had reconsidered; not waiting to see if his side would struggle for goals without his big striker, he sought a solution in the same mould to retain the offensive pattern. A call to his former player Kendall had resulted in Durban offering Everton's out-of-favour centre-forward Mick Ferguson the opportunity to come to Roker on loan. Surprisingly, the 27-year-old shunned the arrangement, and a disappointed Durban commented, 'I felt that we needed a bit of a boost, and he would have given us more height up front.' Although Everton had dropped their asking price to £150,000, a permanent deal would have still been too expensive for Sunderland, and Durban had not desired one, 'It would be silly to go out and replace West already. Ferguson has not played much over the last couple of years, and I thought we had a chance of getting him.' Kendall declared, 'Mick feels he does not have to prove himself to anyone on a trial period.' However, as Durban had never sought a permanent arrangement, Kendall's reference to 'trial period' was a misrepresentation of the offer.

As they had the previous year, Sunderland would meet West Ham at Roker Park on the second Saturday of the season. The previous season's 2-0 defeat had exposed a gulf in quality and there was plenty of incentive to show that the team had developed in the intervening 12 months. Rowell rejoined the fray, and he supplied the sole breakthrough in the 14th minute. Elliott pushed forward and found Cummins who jinked inside and sent in a low drive which bounced and rebounded from Phil Parkes's chest, leaving Rowell with the golden opportunity to tuck the ball in.

A satisfied Durban crowed, 'Few sides will beat us through the middle when Elliott and Hindmarch are in that mood; we told Venison to play Devonshire, and he gave him no room. I regard the result as terribly significant. The amazing thing is we had seven of the team in the same fixture last year – but in name only. It just shows how much they have matured; we have improved in leaps and bounds.'

## Progress Report

Durban claimed that the team had matured and improved, and when he referenced a low-point a few months previously his assertion gained credence, 'That day early in April when we lost at home to Middlesbrough was just about as depressing as any I have experienced as a manager. There seemed no prospect of us staying up.' After surviving on the final day, Durban had vowed to himself, 'We'll not go through that kind of agony again.' But, he acknowledged that he was working with one of the smallest squads in the top flight, 'We're far from ready to challenge the likes of Liverpool, that's obvious. You only had to look at the strength they had on the bench for the Charity Shield to appreciate the talent they have available – David Hodgson and Craig Johnston to name just a couple – but I honestly can't see us being involved in a battle against relegation again.'

Durban did not absolve himself from blame for his tardiness in sorting out the squad he inherited, 'It took us far too long to get a settled team last season – and I accept responsibility. We kicked off with Cummins, Elliott, and Siddall all playing in America and Bowyer was injured. I took 20 players to Scotland and it was months before I knew what our best team was.' Ultimately, there had been immense satisfaction, 'I have never been so pleased as I was with that last-match win, not for myself but for all the Sunderland supporters who had supported us so loyally. They deserve First Division football; they deserve a team they can be proud of. After all they had suffered, over 26,000 turned up for that last match. It's for passion and loyalty like that that I came to Roker Park.'

The boss then turned his eyes towards the future, 'This club has survived by the skin of its teeth in the last two seasons. Now it's time we really consolidated. Pickering's form, for one so young and playing First Division football for the first time, was remarkably consistent. He and Buckley kept us going many a time when we were very flat. West demanded a second chance after that Middlesbrough fiasco, and he took it brilliantly. Venison came into the team when he was only 17 and he'll make a good player; I have no doubts. West is only 19, but he's a better player than Lee Chapman was at the same age when I was bringing him through at Stoke – and Arsenal have just paid half a million pounds for Lee. Getting Atkins from Shrewsbury is a step in the right direction. He's a good competitor wherever he plays, and I am as pleased to have him as he is at being here.'

Focussing once more on the potential of record-signing McCoist, Durban stated, 'All players take some time to settle when they come down from Scotland. A year ago he hadn't taken part in our pre-season training, and once he stops trying to justify the money we gave, relaxes and plays his natural game then I'm sure he'll give us the goals.' There was also the prospect of the return of Nicholl to swell the ranks, 'I have high hopes. He's a quality player and a quality person. Getting him back would give us all a lift. We will make progress, we will do better.'

A few days later, it emerged that any deal for Nicholl would mean him staying only until April before returning to the USA. Durban admitted it was not ideal, but, 'We are so short of international players who want to come to Sunderland. Nicholl *upmarkets* our club, and this is the only way I can get an international in our side. He really wants to come here, and I have never seen anyone so disappointed when I had to tell him that we could not afford to sign him.' Durban was swift to contrast Nicholl's attitude with Ferguson's, 'It is an insult for someone playing in the Central League to turn us down. Players think they are doing clubs a favour by turning out for them.' *Plus ça change*!

Next up was a trip to Coventry, 'We have got to learn to combat sides with height.' Yet, Durban had gleaned enough encouragement from his side's start, 'We have done nothing dramatic yet, but Saturday's performance was the most solid in the year I have been here. We cut out the basic errors and are now reaping the benefit of keeping a settled side together.' On Pickering's defensive attributes, his manager remarked, 'He gave a better all-round performance, more like a wing-half, and it will do him good to play with a bit of discomfort [due to his stitched-up knee].'

## Optimism Derailed

The crowd of 8,190 was the lowest attendance recorded at Coventry for a First Division match. Garry Thompson finished from close range after only six minutes, and another Highfield Road hammering was threatened as Elliott and Hindmarch were given a torrid time by the tall forward-line of Thompson, Hateley, and Whitton. Not for the first time, Durban bemoaned his lack of a creative midfielder with vision, 'You can't keep going down the same channel when things are not working. We just didn't have a Gerry Francis in our side. Everything they did revolved around him.'

It was not long before Sunderland had agreed terms with Nicholl, but Newcastle created a slight delay by making a counter-offer. No matter how much he wanted the player to rejoin, Durban was adamant he would not get involved in an 'auction'. As Nicholl arrived at Heathrow, it emerged that, despite the Keegan factor, he was content to stick to the agreement reached with Sunderland. However, Durban stated there was no guarantee that Venison would be ousted from the right-back slot, 'I will have no qualms playing Jimmy in midfield as he is the sort of player who has contagious enthusiasm, like Gerry Francis.'

Given the previous administrative track record surrounding Nicholl, it was almost predictable that there was a massive delay in receiving the required international clearance. Durban could have done with having the player available straight away as Elliott and Atkins had sustained injuries in training, and were ruled out of the long trip to Brighton who had beaten Arsenal 1-0 in midweek even without the transfer-seeking Foster and Robinson. For the second consecutive match involving Sunderland, the home club posted their lowest-ever attendance for a First Division game; there were 10,624 at the Goldstone Ground.

A clever through ball from McCoist set Cummins up to shoot Sunderland ahead and, a few minutes before half-time, Cummins returned the compliment as McCoist evaded the advancing Moseley and slotted home from an angle. But, with Hinnigan employed as a makeshift central defender, Sunderland's frailty was exposed. By the midway point in the second half Brighton had overturned the deficit, Gordon Smith grabbing the first a mere 25 seconds after the restart. Gerry Ryan equalised, before a Tony Grealish shot gave the home side what proved to be the winner. Durban stated the 'bleedin' obvious', 'We threw a winning position away by not withstanding any pressure.' By the evening, he had set up a swap deal involving Cummins and cash in return for Robinson, 'Stan was offered a new two-year contract in the summer, but he chose to ignore it and operate on his existing one. Robinson is keen to come here, and I think we can satisfy his personal terms.'

That week, Pickering and Venison were included in the England squad for the upcoming European Under-21 Championship game in Denmark. Durban expressed delight, 'I love it when the kids are selected for internationals. [Paul] Bracewell was not blessed with talent, but it shows what can be done with hard graft. It is tremendous to have recognition of what you are trying to do in terms of developing your own side rather than through the transfer market. Both have earned it, and it is important that they learn from the coaching staff, and not what wages other players are on. Venison's handling of Morley and Devonshire must have got back to headquarters.'

Back to domestic labours, and a major stumbling block in the proposed exchange deal had emerged; incredibly, Robinson was on a lucrative ten-year contract at Brighton. Sunderland then drew Wolves in the two-leg second round of the League Cup, and Durban emphasised the extra onus, 'We need a good cup run to set the place alight, as I do not think league form will bring the crowds back.' Durban was partially correct in the sense that the board and many fans attached excessive importance to early cup exits, and this misguided sense of priorities would ultimately prove catastrophic for him in the future.

Two days before Sunderland's home match against Tottenham, it was believed that there was 'still ample time' for Nicholl's international clearance forms to arrive before the deadline, Durban wishing to deploy him in central defence to stifle the threat of Archibald and Crooks. The 'comedy of errors' continued as it dawned on club officials that the relevant offices were closed on Saturdays; so the forms had to arrive on Friday.

Nicholl had been training since Tuesday and was keen to play, while the struggling Atkins exhibited the attitude that Durban admired, 'Ian wants to play and he asked for a further 24 hours.'

There was also a warning from the boss to his pair of England starlets not to duck out of challenges ahead of the international, 'Their commitment to Sunderland very much comes first. They know that I would know if they were soft-pedalling.'

A crowd topping 21,000 were disappointed at Nicholl's absence as Sunderland did not enjoy the strength in depth of their opponents who were able to absorb the loss of Hoddle, Roberts, and Hazard, and still completely dominate the afternoon. Turner's goal was bombarded, Durban conceding that his team was inferior. A number of Turner saves restricted Tottenham to a 1-0 margin, but Gary Brooke's close-range finish was quite sufficient. Argentinian Ricky Villa was booed throughout the game in a crassly counterproductive gesture from a section of fans.

This time, the *Echo* reporter complained about the home team's lack of finesse, saying, 'It was all huff and puff stuff compared with the patient and classy build-up of their opponents.' Durban, however, adopted a defensive stance, 'We are a lot better now. A year ago, I did not know what the best side was, but I do now.' The same day, departed striker Alan Brown had scored a 70th-minute winner as Shrewsbury had beaten Keegan's Newcastle 2-1. There was no bitterness from the former Roker man, 'It's a beautiful area, but I didn't want to leave Sunderland. Alan Durban treated me fairly, but after the way I've been treated here, I've got no regrets.'

## Asking Too Much Too Soon

Following the game, Durban drove Venison and Pickering to the airport. Venison had been named in the England team at right-back, 'It will be a great experience for the lads. Barry did not like playing at full-back, but when Hinnigan got injured he got a bit of a sniffing for it. He may be a bit short creatively, but he has defended really well. It is always harder in the second season as other players are more wary of you, but the trouble here is we ask too much too soon from our kids.'

Another player who would have to bear the weight of expectation was Nicholl, whose clearance had finally arrived, 'He has looked tremendous in training since he came back. If the players don't react to Jimmy then they must be barmy, after I see what he puts in. You don't play for your country the number of times he has by accident. He can only give us that bit more quality, and I expect others to take a lead from him.' Nicholl played left-back as the reserves drew 2-2 draw at Bradford, a game featuring Durban who 'cracked home a superb equaliser.' Meanwhile, England's under-21s won 4-1 in Denmark, with Pickering joining Venison on the pitch for the final 20 minutes. Their boss planned a debriefing on their return to 'see what they learnt'.

As Sunderland travelled to play newly promoted Watford (always newsworthy when under the chairmanship of Elton John), it became clear that Nicholl would be part of another makeshift defensive unit. Over three years earlier, BBC's *Sportsnight* had broadcast a feature focussing on the continuing progress of two prime up-and-coming managers: Stoke's Durban and Watford's Graham Taylor. At one point, John Motson put it to Durban that, in some ways, Taylor was getting more publicity than the Welshman even though Watford were 'only' going for promotion from the Third Division while Durban's team were 'on the verge' of returning to the First Division. Quite content to be making quiet progress, and without an ounce of irritation or jealousy, Durban good-humouredly retorted about the perceived imbalance of acclaim, 'Yes, but just wait 'til my chairman starts playing that piano!'

The Sunderland boss was not surprised by Watford's strong start which saw them sitting in third position, 'People keep bleating what is wrong with traditional English football, but there has been nothing wrong with the game at Watford for the last four years. If people stopped moaning about the state of the game, and went out and played it the way Watford do, gates would go up. Any manager who thinks of closing the game up ought to be hanged.' It is noteworthy that the media did not greedily snatch up Durban's advocacy of positive principles as they had the 'clowns' quote. The injustice of it all!

Before the match at Vicarage Road, Taylor observed, 'Sunderland have lost their last three games, but there are no easy games in the First Division.' Quite possibly, but Sunderland were torn apart 8-0, with seven of the goals stemming from crosses. Luther Blissett grabbed four and, although Rowell and McCoist missed decent chances, Watford also hit the woodwork four times. Trailing 4-0 at half-time, Durban knew there was no way back, telling substitute Cooke, 'You won't get on unless we get an injury.' There was another sort of demolition going on the following day as Durban assembled the squad for an 'inquest'; the reconstruction of the Roker End had finally got under way.

By Monday, the manager had drawn a line under the debacle, 'We had a talk about Saturday's game and trained as I felt we should get it out of our system as soon as possible. They realised they played badly but it is no use harping on about it, and I just hope that they react in the same way they did last season after the 6-1 defeat at Coventry. It was not a day of disaster as no player broke a leg, no one was sent off, and the fans did not run riot in the town. I only hope that we have not done too much damage with our fans as they were magnificent throughout, and I really felt sorry for them. The damage has been done though and we must forget it. I was on a short fuse but I am sure the players will react.'

## After-Eight Digestion

As Durban mobilised his troops to start afresh, he observed, 'It is no coincidence that Watford have used only 12 players this season, and that when we had our good run last season we used 12 or 13 players. If Westie and Elliott had been playing in the four matches we have lost then I would know we have got real problems.'

One manager certainly had real problems as bottom-of-the-table Middlesbrough lost 4-1 at home to Grimsby in the Second Division, and manager Bobby Murdoch resigned. No such trouble to the north as Arthur Cox was the envy of many when he signed Liverpool's Terry McDermott for £100,000, and swiftly recruited David McCreery to the Newcastle bandwagon from Tulsa Roughnecks. Durban had enquired about 30-year-old former England international McDermott in the summer, a player who had the pedigree and goalscoring nous that the Roker manager wished to acquire. But, once McDermott had a sniff of the chance to return to Tyneside and link up with former Anfield buddy Keegan there was only going to be one destination.

Wearside was preparing for the visit of another of the promoted teams, Norwich City, but Durban reported that Cummins and Atkins had missed training, 'Though they both want to play I don't think it is worth taking a chance.' In the build-up, Nick Pickering spoke to *Roker Review* about his rapid rise through the ranks, 'Last season, playing at places like Highbury, Maine Road, Old Trafford, and Anfield was a tremendous thrill. It was all so new, so exciting. I didn't really have time to think. I just went out and played.' Regarding the Watford defeat, he spoke of the determination within the dressing room, 'The boss had a good right to be angry and upset. The only thing we can do now is bounce back with a win; we've got to kick that losing habit.'

Four successive defeats had their effect as 8,000 was wiped off the previous attendance, but one extra spectator was new

England manager Bobby Robson. He saw Norwich goalkeeper Chris Woods dive to scoop away McCoist's downward header which ensured the first half stayed goalless; there was little hint of the dazzling display that would follow. Five minutes into the second half, a purposeful Rowell glided past a couple of defenders before unleashing a superb drive into the top corner from just inside the penalty area. In the 69th minute, Elliott lifted the ball down the line for Buckley to deftly head inside to McCoist who kept running at the retreating Norwich backline before sending in a low raking drive past Woods. Five minutes later, Venison opened up the Norwich rearguard, and Rowell finished well. Then Rowell turned provider as his pass set up the opportunity for Cooke to cap an encouraging wide-man display by sweeping the ball home.

Four goals up, but it was worrying that Nicholl seemed to be labouring in the final ten minutes. He escaped a booking after lazily handling the ball, before entering the referee's notebook when he clumsily brought down Bertschin. Dave Bennett curled the resultant free kick past Turner to take the gloss off the win.

Durban seemed satisfied enough, however, as he praised his forwards, 'I am pleased for Cooke, who has worked hard to get into the side. Rowell was upset last week, but he rolled his sleeves up and trained to his absolute maximum all week. He's never had a better day, and that in front of the England manager. His finishing was brilliant, and he played the ball of the game for Cooke's goal.' The manager was always eager to prioritise good preparation, 'Gary got his rewards for what he put in on the training ground, and his first goal was the best I have seen him score. I know what Gary is capable of but he has got to ally skill with hard work.'

Sunderland lay 15th in the table with ten points as Elliott finally signed a three-year contract. On Tyneside, in a proposed deal that, with hindsight, acquires an intriguing 'what if' aspect, Newcastle were reported to have offered Birmingham £100,000 plus Chris Waddle for their Wearside-born midfielder Kevin Dillon. Meanwhile, Durban indicated that he wished to see some incoming action, 'We have spent long enough on pruning the staff, and putting the club on a sound financial basis. We, the club, must now take one or two positive decisions in the transfer market. After nine games, we have had a good chance to assess the position and realise that the side cannot sustain the form of the last two months of last season.' The Sunderland manager was on record as saying 'the time to buy is not when you're in trouble', and his remark 'We, the club' indicated that he hoped his chairman and board would display some foresight.

A 1-1 draw was earned in the League Cup second round first leg at Second Division leaders Wolves. Rowell was upended early and sent Burridge the wrong way from the resultant spot-kick, but Eves equalised before half-time. Venison was disappointed by his omission, but his boss explained, 'He is only 18 and doesn't understand why, but I wanted Atkins's experience last night.' Durban then watched next opponents Southampton in their tie at Colchester, 'I thought Ball was their best player, and as there is the possibility that this may be his last game before he goes to Hong Kong I hope it may improve the gate a bit. Though we had a good half hour last week, I want the period extended to the full 90 minutes.'

Newcastle's tie at Elland Road was marred as a Leeds mob pelted nuts, bolts, and coins at players, staff, and photographers, one of whom remarked, 'Every home game this sort of thing happens.' Assistant manager Tommy Cavanagh had beer hurled at him when he went to treat the injured Jeff Clarke, and police and stewards had to erect a screen round an injured Keegan as he lay suffering from a gashed shin after a Kenny Burns tackle; no doubt Barry Venison would have empathised with the former England captain.

The eager Atkins had collected four stitches after a collision with Wolves goalkeeper Burridge, but would keep his place in the team for Saturday. Durban recognised that he should not have to rely on such conscientious players pushing themselves through the pain barrier. The squad needed to be strengthened, but he was not impressed by the list of players officially available. The feeling was, following the recent influx at Newcastle, the Sunderland boss was seeking a 'name' to lure back the fans who had gone missing.

A crowd of 15,635 saw McCoist score against Peter Shilton (now playing for Southampton) for the second successive season, and there was an element of the spectacular about his overhead kick following some penalty-area pinball. That goal had come just after the hour, but Williams swept in an equaliser to share the honours. Durban detected grounds for optimism as well as his side's deficiencies, 'We dominated a team who qualified for Europe but we are a bit short of quality and could do with an Alan Ball or David Armstrong.'

## Think Big, Be Big

Durban would certainly have liked to add a player in the mould of Armstrong or Gerry Francis, but the next potential target that he honed his sights on possessed more the stamp of McCoist – unlimited potential. Sunderland were on the trail of one of the hottest properties in Danish football, 18-year-old Michael Laudrup. Durban, Cowie, and new director Iain Fraser travelled to Denmark and saw Laudrup score twice for Brøndby in a 5-2 win over Aarhus. Durban tried to downplay the scouting mission, 'I was in Scandinavia to watch a number of recommended players. There are one or two irons in the fire.'

There appeared little need for subterfuge, however, as Laudrup's attributes had become widespread knowledge. Barcelona, Juventus, and Ajax had all stated an interest in the player, and if a move to Britain did appeal, then reigning league champions Liverpool were monitoring developments. Even the most partisan Sunderland follower realised that the chances of landing this target were slim to nil. They had been successful in landing the much-sought-after McCoist, but that was in competition with Middlesbrough and Wolves. True, Durban could offer the lad regular first-team football straight away, but that incentive seemed to pale into insignificance against clubs of such international status.

On his return to Roker, Durban refocussed attention on the players he did have at his disposal, 'Westie is raring to go but will need at least three matches before he is ready for the first team. Had the midfield cashed in with one or two goals we would be in a much better position, but Buckley has gone ten games without a goal, and Pickering and Cooke have scored when games were sewn up. When Westie comes back, I will not discount playing Rowell or McCoist in midfield.' This seemed a baffling intention considering that Rowell had been tried in that role the previous season with little reward, while McCoist was a 'natural' forward.

The next back-page headline to raise supporters' hopes was 'Durban in Moves to Sign Big Talent'. Thus it was that 29-year-old Swedish goalkeeper Jan Möller was met by the Roker boss at Newcastle airport shortly after midnight, 'We have agreed with Toronto for Möller to work with us while we sort out immigration formalities.' The stopper had won 11 caps for Sweden and played for Malmö in their European Cup final loss to Nottingham Forest in 1979. Durban said, 'Jan was rated one of the top goalkeepers in Europe, and could be with us for a few weeks with a view to signing.'

The authorities had tightened up rules relating to the recruitment of foreign players, but Durban reckoned Möller's arrival would serve a dual purpose, 'It is better for the club if there is competition for places, and if we get a goalkeeper of this standing then it can only do both our keepers good.' Durban himself was about to be rubbing shoulders with some 'big players' as he partnered fellow Welshman Doug Mountjoy against a pairing of Arthur Cox and Alex Higgins in a charity snooker event.

Aware that their manager was attempting to draft in an international player for a position that seemed to be well covered, the squad received a reminder from their boss about how things worked in business, 'I got all the lads together and told them while footballers are under contract we are the same as any other company. If the chairman could get a better manager he would, and if I can get better coaches and players I will.' After only two days training, however, and all the hype, Möller was told that the deal would not be pursued, 'There were just too many problems to overcome and there was also a slight medical doubt on a knee injury.' But the manager had sent a message to his players, and had provoked a positive reaction, 'In the couple of days that Möller was here I could detect a big difference in Chris Turner. The biggest rocket, however, was given to Mark Prudhoe, who should have been pushing him more.'

The next match was at Maine Road. Sunderland were twice in the lead, through McCoist and Buckley, but were pegged back by Kevin Reeves and new signing David Cross. Despite the draw, Durban was scathing about his team's performance, 'Pathetic – no better than we were at Watford.' The manager also missed his big man, 'I feel that had West been playing he would have given us that bit more as we were so innocuous on set-pieces. We looked to be enjoying ourselves getting the ball off them, but not when we had it, and that worries me.'

With Atkins in defence, the boss had given the midfield vacancy to Chisholm ahead of Cooke. Some newspapers had criticised this as unambitious, and this irked Durban, 'We have had a bad time of it since I came here, but at no stage would I say that we have been negative. With the goals we have conceded we can't afford to be negative.' In fact, Durban believed the match should have been won, and was bitterly disappointed, 'Twice in a week the game has been there for the taking. The points lost make all the difference to us not being in the top half of the table. Last season we could not even get into these positions, but three times we have blown it.' It was a case of: we must have improved, but there are problems.

Two days before Sunderland's trip to Everton, Craig Johnston was transfer-listed at his own request. It was time for Durban to try again, 'I will be making a formal inquiry to Liverpool. I am interested in any top-class player and Johnston is proven quality.' But Durban realised that his board would not be displaying the same attitude, 'If Liverpool want their money back, however, count us out, but I will be asking them if they will be interested in a player-exchange deal.' The contemplation of pulling off an audacious move was mouth-watering, and the *Echo* pointed out that such a signing would 'appease Roker fans who have been disillusioned at the lack of transfer activity while Newcastle have brought in three internationals'. There was a fundamental flaw in the plan however; who could Sunderland realistically offer to the all-conquering Liverpool, a team brimming over with internationals, in a player exchange – the mind boggled. Similar to the Laudrup interest, a deal for Johnston seemed to be simply wishful thinking.

West scored twice on his return to action in the reserves and, although initially veering towards caution about bringing the striker back 'too quickly', Durban backtracked, 'I want him back for two home games next week, and to do that I must play him.' At Goodison Park, McCoist dropped deeper and still managed to find the mark, but it was only a consolation as an Elliott blunder

*May 1969 – Never intimidated at the prospect of leading his team against top opposition, Alan Durban strides out ahead of the Wales team to take on reigning world champions England at Wembley. The presence of Moore, Charlton, and Ball accentuates the size of the task. England managed a 2-1 win.* **[Mirror Pix]**

*June 1981 – Having resigned as manager of Stoke City the previous day, Durban arrives at Roker Park to take up the challenge on Wearside.* **[Sunderland Echo]**

*August 1981 – Ally McCoist signs for Sunderland and his new boss Durban looks on with satisfaction alongside St Johnstone manager Alec Rennie.* **[Sunderland Echo]**

*August 1981 – Record-signing McCoist always enjoyed the full backing of Durban who envisaged the young Scot developing and achieving great success over a lengthy career at Roker Park.*
**[Sunderland Echo]**

*August 1981 – Opening day, and captain Jeff Clarke monitors the danger as Ipswich Town's Eric Gates takes a tumble during an enthralling 3-3 encounter at a sultry Portman Road.* **[Getty Images]**

*October 1981 – Tom Ritchie appeals as Barry Venison lies prostrate, the youngster having been crumpled by Kenny Burns' flying 'tackle'. The incident fuelled a controversial encounter at Elland Road amidst a depressingly barren run.* **[Mirror Pix]**

*November 1981 – An away victory arrived at Goodison Park. A gleeful Stan Cummins watches Shaun Elliott reel away after sweeping home a close-range winner. Despite the boost of the goal, Elliott harboured deep reservations about being deployed in midfield.* **[Mirror Pix]**

March 1982 – A pensive Mick Docherty and Durban patrol the Old Trafford sideline as their team edge towards a vital point at Ron Atkinson's multi-million pound Manchester United outfit. **[Mirror Pix]**

May 1982 – A final-day victory over Manchester City secured First-Division safety, the ever-consistent Buckley's low drive providing the precious breakthrough in the 14th minute. **[Sunderland Echo]**

October 1982 – In the midst of a mini scoring streak, McCoist fires home Sunderland's first in the 2-2 draw at Manchester City. **[Mirror Pix]**

*February 1983 – Dependable penalty-taker Gary Rowell rifles in a crucial 83rd-minute kick to give the home team breathing space as they extended their revival with a 3-2 win over Manchester City. Former Roker hero Dennis Tueart can only watch and hope.* **[Sunderland Echo]**

*March 1983 – Rowell struck a glorious winner at Stoke, but some sterling defensive work was needed to preserve the lead. Here, Chris Turner has superbly pushed away a close-range George Berry header; Jimmy Nicholl and Leighton James combine to clear the lines.* **[Mirror Pix]**

*March 1983 – Following victory at Stoke, Durban clinched the loan signing of Forest's Mark Proctor. Proctor went through his paces in his first training session alongside Colin West, McCoist, Venison, and Mick Whitfield, under the watchful eye of a fully-kitted Durban (out of picture).* **[Sunderland Echo]**

*April 1983 – The Upton Park match saw the final appearance of Jimmy Nicholl in a Sunderland shirt. The defender had provided the international class that Durban was determined to instil at the club. His untimely return to Toronto Blizzard contributed to an anxious final month of the season.* **[PA Images]**

*April 1983 – Frank Worthington attempts to outfox the West Ham defence during the 2-1 defeat at Upton Park. The talismanic striker's December arrival had galvanised the team to kick-start their climb to safety, but he started to attract criticism from the local press when the team's form slumped during a cruel April.* **[PA Images]**

August 1983 – Although this Sunderland squad was probably the strongest assembled for many years at Roker Park, Durban had been forced to make sacrifices by the board, reluctantly selling McCoist in order to be permitted to complete deals for Bracewell and Proctor. **[Sunderland Echo]**

August 1983 – Goalkeeper Turner encourages his defensive troops in the season's first away fixture at Villa Park. As well as his ability, Durban admired Turner's 'readiness to analyse his game'. **[Getty Images]**

*September 1983 – A James cross has been headed across goal by Rowell, and centre-forward West gets ahead of Coventry debutant Sam Allardyce to head home the only goal of the game.* **[Sunderland Echo]**

*October 1983 – Nick Pickering matches the pace of Forest winger Steve Wigley in the 1-1 draw at the City Ground. Pickering had recently become the first Sunderland player to win a full England cap since Tony Towers in 1976. An eternal dilemma for Durban was whether his pace was best deployed in midfield or at left-back.* **[Getty Images]**

*November 1983 – Arsenal were fresh from battering Villa and Forest (6-2 and 4-1 respectively) but a fine Sunderland performance defused the Gunners. West has just lashed a 25-yard drive past Pat Jennings in only the third minute. Pickering, James, and Rowell make up the buoyant group on the way to an impressive 2-1 victory.* **[PA Images]**

handed Everton the chance to go ahead in a 3-1 defeat. Durban conducted the post-mortem, 'I am very disappointed. We gave two goals away and have not got anybody who will get in the box and score. We are so pathetic in some games. We have too many players waiting for the odd individual to spark them off.'

Durban was already thinking about the midweek game against Wolves, 'I will be having a meeting with the players and we will pool ideas as I desperately want to get through this cup tie.' The manager was seeking improvement at both ends of the pitch, 'Though we will be looking for an attacking formation it's about time we had some clean sheets.'

Down the coast, struggling Middlesbrough appointed Malcolm Allison as manager. The charismatic boss declared his desire to turn around the prevailing atmosphere, 'These are depressed times both in the area and at the club. I want to see happy faces.' Allison also expressed his ideal wish to 'stay here and build a really good side', a sentiment his Sunderland counterpart would have echoed. Durban was pleased at the arrival of a man he recognised as a 'tremendous enthusiast who will add even more colour and interest to the area'. Asked if there had been any developments following his move for Johnston, Durban's response did not inspire optimism, 'I made a formal inquiry yesterday. If Liverpool are interested in any of our players then it is up to them to come back to me.' The silence was deafening.

Resigned to hitting a wall in the transfer market, Durban concentrated on getting his existing squad to fire, 'I think we are on the verge of starting to show something. There has been a lot of talk about us having a young team with a lot of potential, but it is about time they came of age. They have got to be physically and mentally more resilient.' The immediate task in hand was to overcome Wolves, 'We are competing with the Newcastle v Leeds tie and, though they could have a bigger gate than us, a win could lead to bigger gates in future. One big cup win can have a bigger overall effect than league results.'

If the cup was such a 'big thing' for fans, the attendance of just over 11,000 did not reflect it. Remarkably, Sunderland were 4-0 up after only 16 minutes. Two close-range Chisholm finishes (the first after only 75 seconds) sandwiched a diving header from Hindmarch. A horrendous mix-up between Burridge and Coy presented Rowell with a simple tap-in for the fourth and, after the break, McCoist stroked home the final goal of the night. The reward was a home tie against Norwich.

Durban was grateful for the win but bemused at the thought that it had taken a post-Everton 'inquest' to generate motivation, 'I have literally had face-to-face rows with a number of the squad this week, but don't ask me why I have to do it to get results. I think the aggravation showed in the first 20 minutes. I want the players to savour last night's performance and then come in on Friday morning realising that they have it all to do on Saturday. We have all got to raise our standards when we come in for training.' Now for some praise, 'That was a magnificent first half; it was pleasing to get two goals from set-pieces, and send 11,000 fans home pleased. I would rather win in front of 3,000 than lose in front of 19,000.'

His chairman might have disagreed. Sunderland had fared better on the pitch than their Tyneside rivals, but 13,000 more spectators had been at St James' Park to see Newcastle concede four against Leeds, including a fabulous header from Worthington.

Durban was hoping his team's attacking vein would continue against Stoke, 'I want to see how the training session goes first but I don't want to make any changes. It has taken us a long time to get a result like Wednesday. The side was as positive as it has ever been, and provided they go into tomorrow's match in the same manner, they will be alright. Psychologically, West gives us a big boost, and with McCoist now a bit more relaxed the goals are starting to come.' The young Scot had notched five goals from the last six matches.

Former Sunderland legend Raich Carter was guest of honour at Roker Park, and Bobby Robson was again present. They and the 16,406 crowd witnessed a 2-2 draw. Sunderland went 2-1 up when Rowell was handily placed to gobble up a chance after West's miscued shot hit the post, but the spoils were shared after Mark Chamberlain shot home a 70th-minute equaliser. The England boss had been running a rule over the form of Stoke's wide-man, but Durban pressed the claims of one of his own, 'Pickering was as exciting as Chamberlain was for them, but it is obvious that we have got to tighten up at the back.'

The team had slipped into a relegation position, and Durban had been alerted by the fact that Mick Mills had been left out of the Ipswich side that had thumped West Brom 6-1, 'I have spoken to Mills over the weekend. His omission from the side will accelerate his decision to leave.' A transfer fee of £50,000 had been mooted, but the player's lack of desire for the move would be the biggest obstacle to overcome. Chelsea were also interested and the 34-year-old declared, 'I must admit I don't fancy the north-east.' Mills did, however, offer crumbs of hope for Sunderland fans, 'The situation is different to a year ago when I decided against coming.'

Overall, Durban was endeavouring to improve the intrinsic quality of the playing set-up and personnel at Roker. Inroads had been made, but it often proved an uphill struggle to convince others to join him. They failed to see the big picture.

## Millsgate (Oh What a Circus)

Mick Mills eventually declared that he had spoken to all interested clubs and would 'certainly make a decision in the next 48 hours', claiming he was prepared to 'sign for the first club that make a firm acceptable offer'. Such a statement seemed to leave the player a convenient loophole over what he viewed as 'acceptable', but he was not interested in the loan arrangement offered by Howard Kendall who wanted him in time for an upcoming Merseyside derby. Durban delivered his own update, 'I am meeting Mick today for further talks and I will be testing his attitude. I have discussed the merits with him of playing in midfield and helping the younger lads in the team, and he likes the sound of the challenge.'

Ideally, Durban wished to have Mills in his team for the forthcoming match at Swansea, and set a 'take it or leave it' deadline, 'I have told Mick I want a decision by tonight, and I expect it will be *very* late before I know what he is going to do. I hope that his ambition outweighs convenience.'

Durban received the late phone call, but the player was hedging his bets and tested the Sunderland manager's resolution by requesting a further 48 hours to make up his mind. Durban decided to be flexible, 'I had hoped Mick would be in the side at Swansea, but I have waited a year to sign him so another couple of days won't make much difference.' It was abundantly apparent that a move to the north-east was not the player's preferred choice as he hung on to see whether Chelsea manager John Neal could persuade chairman Ken Bates to sanction the outlay to take him to the Second Division club. Mills's statement, 'If I can't join Chelsea I shall sign for Sunderland', was scarcely one of enthusiasm for the challenge on Wearside. By Friday, the deal appeared to be dead as a resigned Durban stated, 'I have withdrawn the offer. We have bent over backwards to accommodate Mick, but I am not happy in my own mind that he wants to come here.'

Maybe the withdrawal was a psychological ploy, or maybe it was simply because Chelsea backed out, but within hours Mills had phoned Durban to reignite the move, 'One or two problems have been overcome and, though Mick has to pass a medical, I expect him to sign on Monday.' Durban also expanded on the extent the club had 'bent over backwards' for the player, 'He is committed to coming here in the sense that he will be buying a house though does not expect his family to move up immediately. He has three boys at private schools so I will allow him to travel home each weekend to be with them. Mick will have Mondays off and though I do not expect any animosity from the players, anyone who objects will be told that when they have captained England they will be offered the same privileges.'

Durban had been prepared to compromise for what he felt would be another 'upmarketing' of the club. He recollected his Derby days to illustrate the viability of such an arrangement, 'Dave Mackay was the best skipper professional I ever played with and he travelled from London to Derby each week, and it never affected him on the playing field.'

Following a 3-0 defeat at the Vetch Field, Mills's arrival was anticipated with greater urgency. Defensive frailties were exposed as Swansea's Curtis was left with only Turner to beat following a defensive mix-up involving Hindmarch and Munro, and the lead was doubled when an unattended Robbie James tapped the ball in. Leighton James came on as a second-half substitute and caused problems down the flank before Curtis headed the final goal. Without Elliott, the defensive unit looked short of pace, but Durban lamented, 'We were so green at times and not doing the simple things we do in training, and though Mills can improve things, other players are going to have to accept responsibility. Mick is one of those players who can make others around him play. He should help the five lads under 21 in the side to mature more quickly as they need guiding.'

With everything seemingly in place, Sunderland arranged a press conference for 4.30pm on the Monday, but another fiasco was about to unfold. News was emerging of late interest from

Southampton, whose manager Lawrie McMenemy said, 'I have always been an admirer of Mills and I just hope that I am not too late to get him.' Durban's reaction was that it should be a 'done deal', 'It is Mick's prerogative but as far as I'm concerned he has given me his word he will sign for Sunderland.' For Durban, it was a question of honouring an agreement.

'JILTED' ran the *Echo*'s back-page headline after Durban had sat through a redundant press conference, musing on yet another setback. Mills had signed for Southampton, and Durban appeared nonplussed by the fact that the player's word had decidedly not been his bond. Reportedly, Mills phoned the Sunderland boss around 20 minutes before the media gathering that was intended as his grand unveiling. Mills later said that he was not surprised that Durban received his late bombshell angrily and hung up. In the glare of the assembled press, Durban said that the episode had been 'unethical', before moving on, 'That is the beauty of football; today is a fresh day. I will be patient and wait for the people I want to become available. I know what I am looking for – someone who can not only play but influence others around him. Situations at clubs change all the time. I am not panicking.'

There was little entertainment for under 11,000 to witness at Roker Park two days later as, in heavy winds and rain, Sunderland did not possess the imagination to break down a Norwich team set on forcing a League Cup replay. Durban's view was that a clean sheet was a good habit to get into, 'I am disappointed; but if you can't win games like this then you must make sure you don't lose. At this time last year we were out so this is our longest cup run for some time. Frustration eventually spread to everyone, but towards the end I was shouting to our defenders not to do anything stupid.'

Claims that a third-round replay constituted the club's longest cup run for some time might be interpreted as someone grasping at a technicality. In a bad-news week, the club revealed that, despite introducing a raft of strict economy measures, the annual accounts showed a loss of £156,148. It was stated that the deterioration was 'due entirely to the drop in attendances'.

## A Gloomy Grind

Durban was now looking to two consecutive home league matches to revive spirits. The first visitors would be newly promoted Luton Town, and the fractious Cummins was being considered for a recall despite being reported as blurting out that he 'would never play for the club again'. The player was frustrated after only one appearance in nine fixtures, but his manager claimed that any rift had been healed, 'I don't hold grudges with anyone, and once I have had my say it is finished with. Players at the club are not playing for me but for the club and the supporters.'

Durban adhered to the philosophy that a player did not necessarily have to like you in order to produce the goods on the pitch, but recognised that the onus was on him to 'pick up the players'. Mills was another he would not be harbouring a grudge against, 'The essence of good manners is to deal kindly with the bad, and I think that sums up my feelings on his decision and the way we tried to deal with it. We have more important things on our plate.' Another former international who would not be joining the fold was Scotland left-back Willie Donachie, who had been training at the club for a week. Durban explained, 'We were not in a position to offer him a contract and I understand he is now joining Burnley.'

For the matchday *Roker Review*, McCoist spoke about how he felt things were slowly progressing, 'Although Alan Durban went out of his way to tell the fans it would take time for me to settle and that they shouldn't expect fireworks in my first season, it still came as a big surprise when I went so long without scoring. When this season opened I was absolutely determined to get on target from the start.' McCoist refuted any suggestion that the 'record signing' label had proved a burden, 'That big fee never bothered me – except that I wanted to repay Alan Durban and Sunderland for their faith. I always believed I could score regularly and with a few behind me this season it's whetted my appetite.' Regardless of fee, McCoist was aware of the harsh realities of being an out-and-out striker, 'When you've been bought as a goalscorer you know what's expected.'

Specialist help had been recruited to expedite McCoist's general physical development. He had been working with Pop Robson's father-in-law Len Heppell (one of the country's leading experts on body movement, fitness, and balance), who had tutored Bobby Moore, Peter Shilton, and Trevor Brooking among others, 'Len has improved my balance and sharpness no end. In fact, I've so many people to thank for their patience. Alan Durban has been marvellous and so has Mick Docherty. I'm grateful to everybody and I want to repay them with goals.' Despite the growing confidence that their record signing was looking capable of maturing into the club's jewel in the crown for years to come, the heartbreaking reality was that McCoist's strike against Wolves at Roker three weeks before would prove to be his final competitive Sunderland goal.

Cummins replaced the injured Buckley against Luton, but the team struggled. In the 76th minute, a Paul Walsh cross was missed by Brian Stein only for David Moss to be on hand to shoot past Turner. With four minutes remaining, Nicholl sent over a corner and West's knock-back was headed past keeper Alan Judge by Atkins who had come up for the set-piece. Amid heated protests from Luton players that the ball had been headed off the line, a goal was signalled. After escaping with a point, Durban was swift to home in on the influence exerted by visiting captain Brian Horton, 'It was no coincidence that the ball kept coming his way.'

The Sunderland manager had envisaged Mills functioning in much the same manner for his team.

Since Nicholl had become the regular right-back, Venison had been wearing the number eleven shirt and operating in midfield. Although his form had been unconvincing, he was selected to start for England under-21s in Greece. Durban remarked upon the player's recent travails, 'Obviously I am delighted for Barry who is probably in the side on the strength of his performances in Norway and Denmark. I know that things have not gone well here for the last couple of weeks but how long is it since we had three internationals away together?' Midfield was not the only area that had been lacklustre, as the manager commented on his forward trio of Rowell, McCoist, and West, 'They are too inconsistent but they need games under their belt to learn the trade in the First Division.'

As England's injury-hit squad prepared for a European Championship qualifier in Greece, an idea was put forward of postponing league matches on Saturdays before internationals. Durban voiced his concern at such an extreme measure, 'That would mean postponing four or five games a season. Matches would have to be postponed for every international. Every manager is working for his own club even though it is nice to have players in the national side. Fortunately, in this country, there are enough players to drop in when injuries crop up.' Some might argue that the Sunderland manager's 1982 opinion still stands good; most supporters accord precedence to their club's fortunes rather than the international scene.

At Roker, Durban's theory (echoing his mentor Clough) that players should generally rest up in the summer was being borne out by the jaded performances of Nicholl who freely admitted, 'I feel so stale. I can't remember the last time I made an overlap, but it is not surprising when you consider how long I have been playing non-stop [for 15 months].' Having pinned high hopes on Nicholl's return, it was frustrating that the solution appeared to be rest, but the player was not canvassing to be given a breather – he wanted to play.

There would be an immediate injection of energy from the return of the effervescent midfielder Buckley to face Clough's Forest. Following the nail-biting finish in May, Durban had extolled the contribution of that day's match-winner as the *Roker Review* highlighted, 'Buckley's enthusiasm throughout the season has been something to marvel at. He has been far and away our most consistent performer and there are players in this club who would do well to look at Mick and model themselves on his approach.' The player himself commented, 'Funnily enough, Alan Durban's arrival coincided with my first really good run of consecutive matches – and it's no coincidence that last season was my best.'

Buckley was one player who adhered to one of his manager's guiding principles; he put everything into a training session, 'I enjoy the feeling of being really fit and sharp. I'm the restless type. I can't stand still. That's how I play the game.' The one slightly jarring fact was that Buckley had opted to sign only a one-year contract, despite the offer of a two-year deal, because he was reluctant to risk continued seasons 'with relegation always such a menacing threat.' Although a fully committed performer, Buckley had not been prepared to strap himself in for the long haul.

Durban was certainly seeking a speedy improvement, 'With everybody now fit, I am looking for some continuity and the main priority is to get the strikers back on the goal trail.' He also emphasised that the buck did not stop at the forwards, 'There are just not enough players doing anything about it. Apart from Venison's goal against Manchester City last season, we have not had a goal from a full-back in two seasons. It is everybody's responsibility to support. We have to be more positive.' The boss was trying to address the problem, 'Most of this week's training has been spent trying to encourage more players to get into our opponents' penalty area.'

The team faced a difficult task against high-flying Forest, 'I am not surprised that they are in a challenging position for the title. They have two £1m strikers [Garry Birtles and Ian Wallace] and the best left-winger in the country [John Robertson], but how positive the home side is holds the key to the performance.' Durban then recalled, when player-manager at Shrewsbury, the one time he had achieved a win against his former boss, 'It was a Third Division match when Cloughie was manager of Brighton and we beat them 1-0. The referee ended the match about seven minutes early and I was first in the bath, but we had to go out again and finish.'

The Forest boss had been in the national news after calling in police to eject the suspended £1m striker Justin Fashanu from the training ground. Far from criticising the move, Durban believed certain members of his own squad needed a blast to keep them on their toes, 'They need stimulating, and I wish I had somebody here I could bring the police in for, as you have to set standards and discipline.'

A few months later, a deteriorating relationship with Cummins may have made Durban consider a similarly drastic action. Conjecture aside, Durban rated a no-nonsense attitude, 'Cloughie does what he thinks, and to hell with what anybody else thinks.' To a certain extent, Durban believed that Clough could do little wrong, 'He has left a lasting impression on me when it comes to the basics of management. The one thing I learned more than any other was how to discipline players from the time they walk through the door as apprentices.' However, Durban's programme notes emphasised that Clough and Taylor had enjoyed the luxury of time, '[They] built a side at the foot of the Second Division; it is a lot easier doing that compared to building one in the lower reaches of the First Division at this impatient time.'

The Roker crowd was certainly impatient as they saw their team go down 1-0 to a Forest side captained by Bowyer. The goal came in the 52nd minute when the two pricey strikers combined, Birtles setting up Wallace to drive a shot high past Turner. Sunderland had now gone seven games without a win and were looking ragged. Venison had been barracked and, this time, the manager had also come in for criticism from the crowd. Durban appeared fully capable of absorbing any flak flying around, 'I can take all of that, and perhaps it will take the pressure off the players. No one better is going to come in here and do a better job than me. Someone might be able to come in and do it for a couple of weeks, but that's all. It's all about getting the best from the players. We are so predictable as a side and must attack better areas instead of hoofing the ball into the goalmouth.'

Although unperturbed at the stick directed his way, there was an almost immediate reaction as Durban demoted first-team coach Docherty who switched roles with Peter Eustace (reserve and youth-team coach). The manager tried to downplay the move, stating, 'It is only temporary.' The next battle would be the cup replay at Norwich and Durban resisted the temptation to give Atkins a whirl at number nine despite West being the butt of much recent criticism from the fans, 'I know Westie has been going through a lean spell but I am going to persist with him. He was the main reason we stayed up last season, and it was no coincidence that he got the flick-on for Atkins to score against Luton.' The manager maintained an optimistic tenor, 'If we get a couple of results to coincide with the reopening of the Roker End it will help to get the atmosphere back.'

Despite taking a 15th-minute lead through Cummins, Sunderland slumped out of the cup 3-1. 'We are struggling to find a blend' was Durban's brief assessment, but the *Echo* reporter was more fulsome, ' The side is simply not good enough and must be strengthened quickly if relegation is to be avoided ... Until cash is made available to Alan Durban there is no immediate prospect of any significant progress. The playing staff and alternatives in team selection have been exhausted and support has dwindled.'

The foot of the First Division table bore out a blunt message after 15 games played. Southampton had 15 points, Norwich and Sunderland both had 14, and Birmingham were on 13.

Three days later, the bottom two would clash at St Andrew's and, in a surprise move, Durban elevated 16-year-old wide player Paul Atkinson (a first-year apprentice) to the senior squad, but lamented the need for shuffling, 'That is one of the problems. We look for people to bring in to give us a spark and that's the wrong way round. It is the regulars who should be doing that. We have let in three goals in our last three away games, so until we put that right, Atkins stays at the back. It will be another tough match – they all are in our position. We have got to start winning – a draw is no good.' The manager persisted in undervaluing draws, but the fact remained that three draws would harvest three points and would be a welcome alternative to staring back at three consecutive defeats.

Prior to the Birmingham trip, Durban was linked with Leeds's Frank Worthington, who had been transfer-listed at his own request. The manager's response was typically enigmatic, 'I am always interested in quality players when they become available.' An infusion of quality could not come soon enough as the team suffered a dispiriting 2-1 defeat. Ironically, Birmingham were given the lead by the centre-forward who had rejected a loan move to Roker only to accept a similar arrangement at St Andrew's weeks later. In typical cruel fashion, it was Mick Ferguson's first goal in the five matches he had played. 'BOTTOM' ran the miserable headline in that evening's *Football Echo*.

The following day Durban held talks with Worthington, and later said, 'I have to weigh up whether the package deal is worth it.' The player was asked about his thoughts on the prospect of joining another relegation struggle, but was unfazed, 'The position is nothing new. It doesn't alter my thinking.' Durban had also made an approach for England under-21 defender/midfielder Nicky Reid and the prospect of the player being allowed to leave Manchester City in an exchange deal involving Cummins was to be discussed at a board meeting. It emerged that Cummins had also been offered as bait in another aborted deal earlier in the season when City had refused to release Corrigan or Hartford.

By Tuesday there was some progress for Durban to report, 'Frank is travelling up and I will be making him an offer.' Similar to the terms stipulated to Mills, buying a house in the north-east was regarded as a required fundamental commitment. Worthington currently resided in Halifax, but Durban commented, 'We would expect him to move here.' In a veritable flurry of activity, it was announced that former Newcastle midfielder Nigel Walker would be training at Roker after being released by San Diego Sockers, 'He has a First Division brain and two super feet, but he has stopped making progress.' As the Roker boss chased a £50,000-rated 34-year-old, and scavenged for free agents, impoverished Second Division Charlton Athletic somehow funded the capture of Danish star forward Allan Simonsen from Barcelona for £324,000. These were frustrating days for Sunderland supporters.

Bottom of the table was bad enough, but now the manager received the 'dreaded vote of confidence' from chairman Cowie, 'Alan Durban is not the sort of man who will stay at Roker Park if he is unsuccessful. If he sees the team is not going to get out of trouble we won't have to tell him to go. He is a man with a great deal of character; an honest man. There is no doubt that Alan has a lot of pressure on him at the present time, but that is coming from outside the boardroom. That pressure is not going to diminish. Alan's job is as safe as any manager's job in football.'

Once again, the chairman's statement included a well-worn refrain, 'There is a limit to what we can spend, and we ask for the support of the fans during this difficult period.'

## Stardust: Mr Worthington Takes the Stage

The move for Worthington had fuelled newspaper speculation that Rangers might renew their interest in McCoist. As far as Durban was concerned, however, that notion was a non-starter. Meanwhile, Manchester City directors rejected Sunderland's bid of around £100,000 plus Cummins for Reid, but the boss remained sanguine, 'I am not too disappointed as I was never very keen to lose Stan when City inquired about him.' Months later, Durban would doubtless have reappraised his reluctance to 'lose' Cummins. The main iron in the fire was still aglow as Durban set up an 18-month arrangement for Worthington, 'It has been a difficult deal but it will have been worthwhile if Frank does well for us.'

December arrived, and so did the player that would mark the advent of a Roker revival. Frank Worthington ambled into the Seaburn Hotel and completed the final paperwork. Casually attired, the laid-back veteran and Durban were pictured beaming in unison at this relaxed unveiling. Worthington was to make his debut in Saturday's home match against Ipswich which would also mark the reopening of the Roker End, freeing up room for 8,000 spectators.

The manager was bullish about the upcoming game, 'I want a couple of red-hot training sessions to get the spirit right for Saturday. We have the opening of the Roker End, a new signing, and attractive opposition.' It became evident that Durban's priority remained a midfield motivator in the mould of the players he had praised, Horton and Francis, but he also flagged up the multiple positives that Worthington's arrival would deliver, 'I was not desperate for a centre-forward, but I know the supporters want that type of player. It is difficult to influence a team from the centre-forward position, but the other strikers will benefit. I don't need to push West as much now and, along with McCoist and Rowell, he should improve with Frank here.'

Cowie felt it was time for another appeal for loyalty, pointing out that the club had spent £200,000 on the Roker End, £75,000 on toilets, and £80,000 on seating, 'For years we have been under criticism for not improving conditions for the fans. Now we have done something about it and I appeal personally to everyone who is proud that Sunderland should have a team in the First Division to give the players the support they deserve.' He was concerned that certain Second Division teams were generating bigger attendances. Neighbours Newcastle were the prime example, but their directors had thought big and acted boldly to bring in Keegan. Cowie, however, resumed his usual tone, 'We cannot buy big unless we have the revenue and the revenue must come through the turnstiles. We want the supporters behind us lock, stock and barrel. My appeal today is stop the carping criticism and get behind Sunderland.'

Cowie's statements often contained valid points amid the rhetoric, but these frequently suffered from being delivered in a seemingly condescending manner. Although probably unintentional, Cowie's mode of addressing supporters was often perceived as slightly pompous and insulting.

Durban was aware of his chairman's latest remarks, but had his own down-to-earth style of getting across similar sentiments, 'This is the only area in the country where if you are even only half successful there would be no recession in football.' He realised that supporters craved 'big' signings, but he had previously pointed out that such a strategy did not guarantee success and he used his programme notes to issue a reminder, 'It is also important to develop your own players. I feel it is essential that I stress the importance of everyone connected with the club pulling in the same direction. We have got problems, as the league table shows, but it won't help the players if people get on their backs. The one thing that got us out of trouble last season was our tremendous team spirit. I am happy to say that is being maintained, and is encouraging in view of the task we face.'

Durban recalled Hindmarch to the defence in an effort to combat the aerial threat of Ipswich's Mariner and Terry Butcher, while Atkins would play in midfield. Regarding his latest recruit, Durban exuded confidence, 'Frank is itching to do well, and I know he will have an immediate effect on other people. When the situation gets hectic, and the pressure is on, you want players who have played in big matches and are not going to get carried away. Frank has a lovely first touch and I think players like Cummins will benefit.' The new signing also bolstered the club's quota of men with international experience, and Durban continued, 'Frank is a character who, apart from the good I expect him to do for the team, will also have a marked impact on our young players.'

As he looked forward to playing alongside Worthington, Gary Rowell was recalling that it was not the team's struggle the previous season that had prompted his transfer request, but simply that he felt he should be in the team. In the *Roker Review*, he looked back at the spirit that had helped dig the club out of that dire position, 'By the end of the season we were a confident squad – and confidence is half the battle.'

That raised the question of whether that vital commodity had ebbed away as the side had again slid to the foot of the table, 'It follows. Losing becomes a habit and nags away at confidence. But, we've all got a lift this week from the arrival of Worthington, and nobody here is even thinking of going down. Frank has both class and experience, and I rate it a top-class signing. He's just the kind of player we need, and I'm sure the supporters will welcome a man of his calibre.'

A 15,000 crowd were at Roker on a grey December afternoon, the greyness accentuated by the team's Le Coq Sportif sweatshirts as they warmed up in front of the Fulwell End. With sleeves pulled down and shirt worn outside the shorts, Worthington flicked and juggled and exuded the aura of a man not overawed by many occasions. The Sunderland line-up had an air of attacking intent about it, with Durban also finding room for McCoist and Rowell. After eight minutes of a free-flowing encounter, the ball was played to Worthington on the edge of the penalty area; the wily striker made to advance but instead deftly back-heeled the ball into the path of Atkins who struck one of the sweetest power-drives to be seen at Roker for some time. The ball ripped past Cooper into the roof of the net.

So far, so good. As the half progressed Sunderland held their lead, but the game was open; too open. In a three-minute burst shortly before half-time, a 1-0 lead had degenerated into a 2-1 deficit as goals from Gates and Brazil broke the spell that Worthington had woven; that the crowd had hung on to. As Sunderland failed to convert possession into chances, Brazil broke on 67 minutes to increase the lead. Although Worthington subtly chipped the ball over Cooper for a debut goal, his team were constantly being carved open by rapier counter-attacks as passes were zipped past a lumbering rearguard. Ipswich simply bypassed Sunderland's theory of utilising Hindmarch's aerial strength by pinging the ball around on the deck, and Brazil missed another couple of chances. At one stage, Durban considered throwing West on – as an extra defender! His side's defensive frailty had been repeatedly exposed, and after four consecutive defeats, Durban was deliberating adopting a more defensive policy, 'It is blatantly obvious that we must tighten up, as we don't see trouble until it arrives. Though it is not pretty to watch, results are now more important. Last year, we managed to get out of trouble without going defensive and we owe it to the public to not do it at home.' Given that his team had just been outplayed at home, this seemed a strange statement to make. However, the manager's succeeding observations endorsed the need for a tightening up no matter where the venue, 'We are conceding two goals a game. The longer the game went on the more vulnerable our back four became, and yet it is three of the same defence from last season.'

Others offered their views, Worthington declaring, 'We are nothing like a relegation side.' But he had exhibited similar confidence in March when joining Leeds before they slipped into the Second Division. New first-team coach Eustace stated, 'For 85 minutes we looked a decent side, but then we were like a bunch of amateurs. You can't let Brazil have the chances he got.' Captain Munro maintained that there was 'still a long way to go', and pointed out that 'individual mistakes' had been getting punished by the opposition; the squad must 'just keep fighting.'

In midweek, Durban watched Nigel Walker play for the reserves at Bolton, 'The lad has certainly got something. He handles possession superbly, but has got to have the same enthusiasm for the hard part of the game as the easy part. It is hard to make a judgement at this stage because of his lack of match fitness.' Playing Walker in the upcoming fixture at West Brom would have smacked of desperation, but Prudhoe was being prepared to oust Turner in goal – despite being beaten from the kick-off at Bolton while still organising the back four!

At The Hawthorns, Pickering was fit to return, as did Venison. In all, there were five changes that produced an alien-looking line-up with Hinnigan coming in at number five, and Nicholl wearing seven. Durban invited Prudhoe's erstwhile mentor Jim Montgomery to be present to boost the young keeper's confidence ahead of his debut, but things did not go well. A misunderstanding between Venison and Prudhoe contributed to Ally Robertson grabbing the opener before, with Prudhoe yards off his line, Owen chipped the ball into the net.

After the game, the keeper refused to shoulder blame for that goal, 'I had my angles covered, but Owen should have been closed down before he had the chance to shoot.' Zondervan added a third and, generally, the debutant goal-minder was left cruelly exposed by the defence in front of him – as Turner had been the week before.

Despite extenuating circumstances, the manager had his cold-blooded head on, 'I think Mark will have been a bit disappointed with his debut. He is no better than Chris on that performance. People are tense and it is causing them to play below last season's level. There is too much anxiety which leads to loss of confidence. I want the players to stop all this talk about relegation, to take the lead from Frank, and enjoy playing.' There was also a reminder for the fans bleating for major transfer action, 'It is more important to get people to play well than to be continually talking about bringing in new players.'

Rather than contemplating any immediate acquisition, Durban now had to deal with the unpleasant surprise of a transfer request being submitted by the very player who he had recently praised so highly for his attitude. Mick Buckley cited 'private reasons' for his bombshell, but Durban was consistent in his reaction, 'I have never been one for holding on to dissatisfied players. I am disappointed at the timing of the request considering the situation that we are in, but I will be asking one or two more if they want to go.' Buckley's unrest reinforced rumours linking the club with another midfielder, Bolton's £60,000-rated Peter Reid.

Durban did not deny his interest, but insisted Reid was only 'one of a number of players we have had watched.'

The club's annual general meeting was held on Monday, 13 December. With the club rock bottom of the league, there was no prospect of an easy ride being had by those holding senior positions. Batey accused Cowie of 'making a mess' of the club's finances, and Durban of 'plunging the team headlong towards relegation'. The chairman claimed that, prior to the meeting, he had spent over an hour with Durban, who had offered to quit. Whether this was exaggeration for effect or not, Cowie insisted, 'You won't have to sack Alan Durban. He asked me "Do you want me to go? Just say the word and I will."' At this point of the debate, Batey exclaimed, 'It is just as well he was not sitting in my office.' When considering future developments, Batey's opinion stands out as being significantly ominous.

Talking to the press later, Cowie commented, 'Obviously, results cannot continue like this, and Alan has certainly not got a licence for the next 18 months.' Hardly a ringing endorsement, but his next statement about Durban appeared to be unequivocal, 'This guy is something special, and we have got to back him as a board. We have got to give him a chance.' That is indeed a declaration that should have been adhered to; Durban was the 'special one' but, ultimately, such fine words were not consistent with events a mere 15 months down the road.

Amid the conflicting rhetoric of the chairman and the most vociferous 'rebel shareholder', Durban was eager to focus on immediate priorities, 'My position is not that important. We are bottom of the league.' In an urgent search aimed at toughening up the rearguard, Durban had tried to recruit central defender Glen Keeley on loan. This latest move was not one that fired supporters' imaginations as Keeley had recently made one appearance on loan for Everton when he had been thrust into a red-hot Merseyside derby at Goodison (after Mick Mills declined a similar offer).

Keeley had been in dispute at Blackburn and training by himself, but Kendall informed the under-prepared defender he was playing. After 32 minutes, being somehow unaware of the new crackdown on 'professional fouls', he hauled back Dalglish who was breaking clear, and was promptly sent off. Everton went on to be demolished 5-0 as Rush bagged four goals. The game had been recorded for *Match of the Day* and Keeley's infamous role in the debacle was ruthlessly highlighted.

As the pre-Christmas match at home to Arsenal approached, Durban revealed the possibility of implementing a sweeper system in a bid to stem the tide. Eustace pointed out that the ploy should not be interpreted as negative, 'Playing five across the back is not defensive provided the full-backs are prepared to break.'

There would definitely be one change to the defensive unit as Prudhoe was demoted. Following his hard-line assessment the previous week, Durban offered soothing words for the young man, 'He has time on his side; the first-team have not. I don't believe he should have responsibility like this at present. He will get his chance again as I believe he is the best young goalkeeper produced in the north-east for a long time.'

## Weaving Some Shut-out Magic

There had been an inch of snow on the pitch the day before Arsenal arrived and, although now clear, the playing surface was very firm. The much-travelled Worthington had tested his footing, and advised 'the lads' that moulded studs might be a good choice. The value of these words of experience became increasingly evident as the afternoon progressed. Whether it was their league position, or the fact that it was 'last Saturday shopping day' before Christmas, the attendance was only 11,753.

Coping better with the frosty conditions underfoot, the home team got off to a good start after eight minutes when Venison battled to gain possession and fed Rowell who sidestepped a challenge before firing a drive beyond Jennings. Rowell and Cummins later missed wonderful chances to increase the lead, and some began to muse whether it would be another frustrating day as Jennings touched a fine Pickering shot against the post with Worthington in the process of hailing a goal before the keeper's fingertips intervened.

Shortly afterwards, another surge down the left appeared to have been halted, only for Brian Talbot to inexplicably attempt a back-heel that presented the ball back to Pickering who wasted no time in swinging over a cross. Chris Whyte muffed a clearing header that fell across the face of goal where the alert Rowell gratefully shot into the roof of the net. With quarter of an hour remaining, Munro won a 50-50 tackle and charged forward before supplying Pickering who capped a magnificent performance by angling the ball into the path of Rowell's run. The striker completed his triple-strike in composed fashion as he slid the ball under the oncoming keeper – 'a real hat-trick' purred Durban later.

The manager opted for cautious optimism, 'Once I saw the pitch I fancied we were better prepared than them. I am not getting carried away with one result, but the team proved they can play with confidence, and I think we got a bit of the rub of the green when it mattered.' The new signing was making his mark on those around him too, 'Frank is an education, and he had much to do with Pickering's performance. He gave him tremendous service. Technically, he is one of the best players I have had around.'

Rowell's previous hat-trick had been in a famous 4-1 demolition of Newcastle at St James' Park in 1979. His manager was pleased, but set the bar higher still, 'Gary certainly appears to have more appetite for the game and has accepted that his best position is up front.' Rowell himself was prepared to play in whichever role requested as long as he was a first-team starter. Overall, Durban took immense satisfaction from the team's improved shape, 'The most important aspect of the display was the balance. Our best permutation seems to be to have one player wide [it was Cummins here] and Chisholm in front of the back four.' It had been a good day, and the perfect way to galvanise team and supporters alike before a festive nine-day break from fixtures.

The lull in first-team action did not mean a holiday just yet for the manager; there were still five spending days left until Christmas. The first shopper to call on Durban was Preston's Gordon Lee and a fee was quickly agreed for defender Hinnigan who, with Nicholl and Venison capable of playing right-back, had not looked as versatile as Durban might have hoped when assuming central-defensive roles in bad away defeats. His boss was not forcing him out, but simply declared, 'It's up to Joe now.' With the writing on the wall, Hinnigan signed for Preston a few days later. The initial fee of £15,000 seemed a poor return for the man who Knighton had brought to Roker from Wigan for £135,000 and had proved a competent performer at full-back. But, football had since been affected by the national recession.

Undeterred by rejections from Mills in consecutive seasons, Durban now hoped to entice another experienced candidate to share the load in a player-assistant manager role. The man in question was 35-year-old West Brom captain John Wile and, the player appeared to favour the proposed switch, 'Opportunities like this are few and far between and I would hate to miss the chance of moving back to Sunderland.' Wile had been a Roker apprentice before being given a free transfer to Peterborough in 1967 without making a first-team bow, 'This would give me the chance to get into management with a top club, and I want to go on playing as long as possible.' Here was one player at least who still regarded Sunderland as a 'top club'.

As days went by, hopes of Wile joining the relegation fight receded. Durban was tight-lipped, but West Brom manager Ron Wylie stated, 'John is still one of the best defenders in the First Division and is very much part of our plans. I don't blame Sunderland, but I've told them that he is too valuable to lose.' Wylie may have been 'boxing clever' as it was suggested that a fee would persuade him to relinquish his captain. However, Sunderland were reluctant to spend money on a player just short of 36. Two doors shut; despite Nicky Reid submitting a written transfer request, and saying, 'I'm not being given a chance in any position', hopes of a move to Sunderland were soon quashed as the City board rejected the request. Aware that this double setback meant that there would be no new 'presents' for the club's loyal following, Durban's 'Christmas Message' to the supporters was conciliatory, 'Sorry for having such a trying year, but we will be doing our best to make 1983 much happier. I would like to thank our fans for their loyalty.'

The fixture list had once again handed Sunderland back-to-back games against Manchester United and Liverpool. Furthermore, they would be played on consecutive days at the start of the Christmas holiday week. With Munro diagnosed with a blood disorder, Nicholl took over the captaincy and Pickering operated at left-back. An Old Trafford crowd just short of 48,000 saw Sunderland face the following United line-up: Bailey, Duxbury, Albiston, Moses, Moran, McQueen, Robson, Muhren, Stapleton, Whiteside, Coppell.

Durban's team survived an onslaught but with 20 minutes remaining, and already booked for chopping down Worthington, McQueen dragged the forward back as he was about to break clear.

A mere free kick was the outcome, and Durban later commented, 'Frank should have gone down and McQueen would have been sent off. He owes Frank a handshake.' Although having a justifiable grievance, the truth was that it had taken a stellar rearguard action to preserve a point. Former United man Nicholl bestowed plentiful praise on Turner, 'That was the best display I have ever seen from a goalkeeper at Old Trafford. He made several point-blank saves and helped us soak up the early pressure. I got more satisfaction from that result than I have from winning some games three nil. That was our second clean sheet in a row and we know that if we could knock in a few goals there are 40,000 fans waiting to watch us every week.' Who said draws were 'no good'?

Just 24 hours later, champions Liverpool rolled into town having comprehensively beaten Sunderland at Roker on their previous three visits. Durban assessed the state of his troops, 'I think we need one or two new engines this afternoon, but the dressing room spirit is as good as all season.' The usual bigger Bank Holiday attendance was enhanced further by those attracted following two good results; the 35,000 barrier was broken. Cooke replaced West and, in a tightly fought affair, the prime talking point centred on a first-half incident that saw Elliott stretchered off following a crunching tackle from Souness who was booked and subsequently thunderously booed by an incensed crowd. A tough competitor himself, Durban neither condoned nor condemned the combative Scot, 'It was a bad tackle. You have to take the rough with the smooth and I thought the crowd got Souness booked.'

A 0-0 draw stretched the unbeaten run of clean sheets to three games, and Durban could see the green shoots of potential, 'It gives me heart to build a better side, as I know that if we are successful we could get gates like this more often. We have stopped leaking goals, and that leaves us with one thing to put right. All of a sudden Chris Turner has become international class, and the full-backs realise that they are not forwards. [Without Elliott] the centre-backs have not got a lot of pace so I have told players not to expose them.' The following day, it emerged that Celtic manager Billy McNeil had been an interested spectator at Roker to see McCoist given his early entrance as substitute.

Sunderland's New Year programme would start with a double-header in Nottingham against Forest and County, but Worthington would be missing after going over on an ankle. On the eve of the trip to the City Ground, Durban warned that last term's low haul of 44 points would not be sufficient to beat the drop, 'We will need more points than last season. I just want to keep the run going and get back into the pack. The priority for 1983 is to improve our league position and strengthen the side. I am putting the players on trust; I want them in bed before midnight.'

## The Dawn of Durban-Land '83

With Elliott out, the unsettled Buckley returned along with West to face second-placed Forest. Wallace went close before Pickering headed off the line. For the visitors, Buckley narrowly missed with a ninth-minute header, although Durban later commented that the midfielder should have brought the ball down with his chest. Nevertheless, another goalless draw was an achievement not to be sniffed at. Durban's game plan had been to block Forest's main supply line; in short, to snuff out the threat of their spellbinding left-winger as Cooke explained, 'The boss told me to drop back and get behind the ball to stop John Robertson from playing.' Turner spotlighted an upturn in other areas, 'It's all about confidence and getting the breaks. I am not doing anything different in training, but the back four players are grouping around me and letting me command the six-yard box.'

The team stayed in Nottingham for the Monday fixture at Meadow Lane, and Durban was looking for even more from his team, 'Logically, we should do better against inferior teams.' Hopefully, the Notts County camp would not get wind of Durban labelling them 'inferior', but the Sunderland manager finally acknowledged the tremendous value of picking up some one-point rewards, 'Three draws are better than one win and two losses as it helps to keep the run going.'

Worthington was resting his ankle, bathing it in the sea near his Seaburn-based hotel. His absence meant that Durban would continue to pursue the cagier on-field strategy a while longer, 'We have broken out of a rut and you have to do things at times you don't like to keep in the division. You have always got a chance when your goalkeeper is playing well and full-backs are not trying to be forwards.'

Again, Durban was indicating that his full-backs had been too gung-ho in the past, but he had previously complained about the lack of any goals from that position as well as praising the attacking instincts of Phil Neal and Kenny Sansom. This smacked of inconsistency, but when a microphone or reporter's notebook is constantly thrust near him, a football manager (or anyone else for that matter) might be excused a few self-contradictory remarks when continually harassed for comment.

Hindmarch replaced an unwell Rowell at Meadow Lane, and would attempt to counter the threat of Fashanu who had swapped one side of Nottingham for the other following his fallout with Clough. On a heavy pitch, Sunderland deployed five across the back with Atkins as sweeper, and withstood heavy pressure. In the 29th minute, Chisholm centred from the right and Cummins shot past Avramovic from close range. Late on, Chisholm was called into action at the other end as he cleared off the line from Fashanu. The 1-0 win epitomised the qualities that formed the bedrock of Durban's football philosophy ('It was a day for hard work') and, although acknowledging that it was always easier to defend in heavy conditions, he noted, 'We have now gone five unbeaten in what looked like a frightening fixture list. At times it has been done by sheer graft and filling holes.'

Another player whose determination reflected this mood was the striker who continued to contribute even when not getting on the scoresheet, and the manager said, 'Colin West got in two good headers when he had no right to even be in there, but that is the spirit in the camp at the moment. We are back in the ruck, and I still expect another side to be dragged into it.' He was not wrong.

There would be a respite from the league scrap as the following Saturday brought Manchester City to Roker in the FA Cup. Again, in a possibly self-harming degree of fervour, Durban relished the possibility of progressing to the latter stages, 'The ingredients are perfect for a special occasion; for I know as a player I feared coming here before a big crowd. The fans that came through the turnstiles for the Liverpool game came to help us and I would love to pack the ground for four cup games which would take us to the semi-finals.' In hindsight, this kind of talk went beyond enthusiastic optimism. It seemed foolhardy to raise expectation levels in cup competitions, and it was a 'failing' that Durban seemed to have a blind spot about amending, 'I would love to give the fans something special at home. The lads are in good nick and the spirit never better.' Nobody would expect the manager to undersell a forthcoming cup tie, but it was a dangerous game to stoke public expectations.

To reflect with pride on the recent upturn in league results was far more reasonable, 'What pleases me is that we have done it with more players than last season's run-in.' After being forced to continually shuffle his pack, there was now the possibility of another experienced arrival as Durban monitored the situation at Swansea where Welsh international winger Leighton James had been handed a shock free transfer.

For a change, events moved rapidly and Durban was impressed by the player's eagerness to travel up to the north-east to check on the form of his prospective new team. After gaining permission from boss Toshack, James and his wife travelled from South Wales to have talks with Durban, 'Leighton telephoned and asked if he could come and watch our game today. I know him reasonably well, and he is certainly a useful player, but it all depends on what he wants after being given a free. It is rather pleasing for a player to come and see me because he is interested in joining Sunderland rather than me having to go to the other end of the country.'

## Still Feeling Fascination (but not in the Cup)

After watching a sterile goalless draw, a game he recollects as 'dreadful', James could see how much the team were crying out for someone with his vision and crossing ability. However, he also recalls seeing 'enough in the young players, such as the raw Nick Pickering, to recognise that the future promised much'. Durban attracted criticism for persevering with the sweeper system that had been successful in stifling the opposition in recent matches. Some felt that while it may have been acceptable against Liverpool, applying it for other home matches was counterproductive. An unruffled manager stuck by his choice of formation, 'You can't go out of the cup if you don't concede goals. We could not change our plans for one match or we could have had an Ipswich and lost 3-2. I know our lot are not going to let goals in. Nick Pickering hasn't allowed Coppell, Chiedozie, or Bodak to be a goal threat.'

However, Durban was aware that the spark of the display against Arsenal had been absent, 'We are so predictable, but with five youngsters in the side playing to their maximum we are not a cup side.' So why had the boss recently chosen to raise expectations that the team, including these 'youngsters', were capable of a sustained cup run?

Disappointed after being omitted from the City game despite participating in the productive long weekend in Nottingham, Buckley had further talks which resulted in the 29-year-old midfielder being officially listed for transfer. This expedited Durban's quest to add reinforcements and the manager quickly followed up his interest in James who was seeking an 18-month contract, 'What I have to do now is consider what is best for the club.' The following day, Durban travelled to London to watch the player in a reserve match at Craven Cottage.

The boss did not envisage another scoring blank in the cup replay, 'There should be more space for people to attack into but we need pace to do that. We are, however, beginning to learn about counter-attacking. Frank trained alone today in an effort to get fit.' The manager also confirmed that the Eustace-Docherty role switch would be extended to the end of the season, 'We have done reasonably well recently and obviously Peter has to take some of the credit.'

Worthington returned to the team at Maine Road, but first-half goals from Hartford and Cross put City in command. Former Sunderland star Tueart had been aggrieved at his omission from the match at Roker and put in a livewire performance, hitting the woodwork twice. McCoist came on and, from his knock-back, Chisholm sent a 25-yard piledriver past Joe Corrigan to provide hope. But, it was the usual early cup exit, and Durban was left to pick through the remnants for succour, 'At least we got Frank through 90 minutes.' Tueart meanwhile was slightly baffled that Pickering had not started in the attacking midfield role that he felt maximised his abilities, 'I thought he was wasted at full-back as he caused us all sorts of problems when he switched positions with Venison.'

James had been at the game and Durban implied that his signature would not be long in arriving, 'We badly need to improve the quality of the final ball into the box and I saw enough of

Leighton on Tuesday to see that he can do it.' Durban and James had been room-mates in Czechoslovakia when the young winger made his international debut in 1971. James had seen much to admire in his future team, 'I am really looking forward to coming to Sunderland. They play with a lot of spirit, so there is no reason why they should not get out of trouble.' The signing was completed, and the 29-year-old commented, 'Sunderland's offer was the best financially and, as they are a First Division club, it was the best status-wise.'

Supporters would get the chance to see the new man make his bow against Aston Villa two days later. Durban was now experiencing the right sort of selection problems; James would certainly start, but in which position was 'a closely guarded secret'. The transfer negotiations between manager and player had included discussion of a possible midfield role rather than the wide attacking berth with which he was more accustomed, 'He is keen to do well, and is smarting a bit after being given a free.'

An injured ankle ruled out Rowell, but the competition for starting places was still hot, 'I may change one or two things, but it is coming to the stage more of who to leave out rather than pick. The squad is a lot stronger than the one which finished last year, and the main thing is to make players play with confidence.' The manager was eager to see his team consolidate their improvement, 'There are no diversions. We have got to get away from the bottom as quickly as possible.'

In the matchday *Roker Review*, Durban noted, 'One of the main things that has pleased me this season has been our much-improved disciplinary record.' One of the combative players who had channelled his aggression positively was Venison who had been moved into midfield following the arrival of Nicholl, 'I'm getting used to it now. You don't argue when you see your name on the team sheet.' When asked about the worry of the league position, Venison maintained the camp was buoyant, 'If our spirit was poor, if we really didn't believe in ourselves and the manager, then we would be in trouble. But I defy anybody to find a First Division dressing room with a better spirit. We turned the corner with that win over Arsenal and now we're really bubbling. We're not even thinking about relegation.'

Ironically, Venison had been set to make way for James, and only made it into the starting line-up following Elliott's late withdrawal. The player's optimism about the squad was not misplaced as Sunderland completed the double over the European champions, their 2-0 win watched by a crowd of just over 16,000. A 27th-minute free kick from James was turned into his own net by McNaught. After the break, the Villa defender powerfully met a Cowans cross only to see his header superbly saved by Turner and, amid the resultant scramble, Sunderland were awarded a free kick. The ball was pumped forward and West's determined knock-down was met on the half-volley by Worthington, displaying expert technique. His left-footed effort sizzled beyond the diving Spink and into the corner of the net, giving the home side much-needed breathing space.

Durban was understandably delighted, 'It is incredible to think that we have equalled the club record [six successive league clean sheets] when our central defenders were Atkins, who was playing centre-forward for a Second Division side last season, and Chisholm, who has played mainly in midfield. We needed the win badly. Now we are able to look at the teams above and look to catch them.' Always on his guard against complacency, the manager warned, 'The big danger is the players may think the rest is going to come easy. We have not cracked anything yet.' Durban also commented on his eventual team selection, 'Venison was disappointed at being left out on Friday but I think he came back and proved his point. People will say, logically, I should have played McCoist ahead of West, but Colin was responsible for others playing well.'

The foot of the league table (Durban's 'ruck') now made more palatable reading after 24 games. Swansea had 26 points, as did Sunderland and Norwich, while Brighton had 24 and Birmingham 23.

The prevailing spirit of 'new beginnings' continued with the recruitment of former Roker player George Herd, who had been dismissed as Darlington assistant manager in a cost-cutting exercise. Herd had made 247 appearances and scored 47 goals in his Sunderland career, and he would bolster the backroom staff on a part-time basis, helping to coach the schoolboys and apprentices. Durban welcomed the appointment, 'People in the game have tremendous respect for George as a coach and his infectious enthusiasm should be an incentive for the schoolboys who join.' The same day, Arthur Cox came a-calling on his Wearside counterpart yet again. With McCreery injured and McDermott suspended, Newcastle wanted to borrow Buckley. Although things were looking healthy, Durban was understandably reluctant to send experienced players out on loan, and he rejected the approach.

Next opponents Tottenham had surprisingly lost 4-1 in midweek at home to Second Division strugglers Burnley in the League Cup, and Durban was wary of a reaction, 'I expect they will start a lot quicker but if they fail to break us down the crowd will get frustrated.' Following the run of clean sheets, the boss discussed his defensive unit's renaissance, 'We have switched things around a bit at the back and it seems to have benefited all of us. When the side is playing badly the tension spreads to the younger players, and it even got to Jimmy Nicholl in the Ipswich game.' Durban was ebullient about the general transformation, 'There has been a big change since those results at United and Forest, and we don't fear going anywhere now.' There was no danger of underestimating the opposition's flair, however, 'Spurs are so well equipped, you don't know where and when their next attack is coming from.'

After 573 minutes without conceding, and on his 100th league appearance for the club, Turner was beaten by a first-half Terry Gibson shot. The run of shutouts had ended. As Sunderland battled to take something from White Hart Lane, McCoist came on for Worthington. In the 85th minute, James surged down the right and whipped in a cross which Graham Roberts handled. Unlike the fixture the previous season when Sunderland had been harshly denied a last-gasp winner, this linesman helpfully signalled the offence. With Rowell absent, and Worthington substituted, up stepped Cummins who competently dispatched the spot-kick.

The player later talked through the incident, 'Clemence messed me about by talking to his full-backs and then the referee' (the keeper had employed the same off-putting tactics against Rowell in April). Similarly, Cummins had retained his focus, 'I decided to keep him waiting. I kept looking at one corner of the goal and thought if I did it often enough he would be convinced that was where I was going to put the ball. It is all a matter of confidence.'

Another vital point had been bagged, and the squad was now off to the 'bright lights' of Blackpool. With a blank weekend due to their elimination from the FA Cup, Durban had arranged a couple of days training followed by a friendly at Bolton on the Friday evening. The boss emphasised that the trip was to be no holiday, 'Blackpool are providing us with some of their training areas, and we will be using the days to concentrate on set-pieces. We can't afford to relax and expect to be ready for Coventry without adding one or two things to our game.'

Despite having done little training recently, Worthington was eager to play in the friendly at his former Burnden Park stamping ground. Despite harbouring reservations, Durban yielded to his player's plea, and the Bolton line-up included Jim McDonagh, Steve Whitworth, and Neil Whatmore (now on loan at his former club after disappointing at Birmingham). A Mike Doyle own goal gave Sunderland victory.

As his squad limbered up to resume their attempts to scale the table, Durban reflected, 'At this stage I am only interested in getting everyone fit. Frank worked really hard and will have benefited from having 90 minutes.' Turning his attention to their forthcoming opponents, Durban indicated that the level of resolve had to be maintained against supposedly less-glamorous teams, 'It is not going to be easier. After Liverpool, Coventry must have as good a record as anyone over the last 40 matches.' Perversely, after seemingly safeguarding against various forms of complacency, Durban declared, 'We have dug ourselves out of trouble earlier than last season.' Had we indeed? Experienced Sunderland supporters suspected such statements were premature – end of season drama was almost invariably on the menu.

Elsewhere, in an episode that Durban observed with interest, Mark Proctor had turned down a loan move to former club Middlesbrough, and now Newcastle had enquired about borrowing the midfielder. Brian Clough declared he was only interested in such an arrangement if the club had the money to make the move permanent. A thought occurred – Clough's stance might soften if approached by a former loyal player; Durban might succeed where others had failed. Meanwhile, although he had not released Buckley, the manager had no such qualms about lending reserve forward Barry Wardrobe to Scottish Premier St Mirren for a couple of months to gain first-team experience.

Durban had been pleased with the immediate impact of his free-transfer bargain, 'Leighton is a vastly experienced international player and has got off to a good start. The fact that he has already found property in the area demonstrates his enthusiasm for the move.' House-hunting was one crucial area where Worthington would have been well advised to follow suit. The boss proceeded to add, 'Our squad is now stronger than at any time since I came to the club. An example of that is that Buckley has not been able to get into the side recently, yet last season he was one of our most consistent players.'

Despite past and future bitter fall-outs, Stan Cummins's *Roker Review* comments showed a player capable of demonstrating appreciable insight when 'singing from the same hymn sheet' as his manager, 'During our unbeaten run various players have dropped out for a game or two with injuries, and the team has done well. That's evidence that our system is right and we now have a good squad. Of course we'll lose matches – every team does – but the mood we're in, the confidence we've got, I can see us bouncing back immediately; we now feel that we can play any team and expect to get something. We have achieved this through really solid teamwork. I'm sure the future is getting brighter.'

This last statement was entirely out of kilter with the player's past and subsequent public airing of grievances, and his assertion that 'our system is right' is a salient remark from a player more associated with berating Durban and the running of the club.

Looking at this from different perspectives, Cummins might be categorised as one of those individuals who Durban had advised should be judged when the pressure was on and not when things were going well. But, there is also the invaluable view from within the dressing room, from one of Cummins's team-mates, as Colin West recalls, 'Stan had a moan, but so did others when things weren't going well.'

West posits the valid theory that certain creative players were more liable to attract criticism for not contributing their quota of covering, back-tracking, and general chore tasks when the team was on the back foot, 'Sometimes Stan might be labelled as a 'luxury player' in relation to his appetite for defensive duties, but he was capable of doing things that other players could not.'

The question was how much license such individuals should be granted; to what degree was a manager willing to cosset or placate the ego of any capricious potential 'match-winner'?

## Frank Says 'Relax'

For the visit of Coventry, West was ruled out but Durban had ready-made cover available, and he said, 'Rowell will replace West, and as Buckley has done very well lately [in training], he could be substitute.' In addition, Munro was restored at left-back, releasing Pickering into midfield. Significantly, the visitors' influential captain Gerry Francis had a damaged wrist in plaster and would be unavailable, but Durban was aware that they might react to a midweek cup loss, 'It is another big test but I have no doubt that we can handle it.'

Considering the recent encouraging run, an attendance of 14,356 was disappointing even allowing for the windswept day. James was in marauding form and goalkeeper Les Sealey kept out a couple of ferocious drives, but he was beaten in the 36th minute when a Paul Dyson clearing header fell to Cummins who smashed an instant drive into the net from the edge of the area. Early in the second half, Steve Whitton met a Hunt cross and his crisp finish levelled things. Not to be denied, Cummins's 57th-minute cross found Rowell whose subtle header sailed well wide of a helpless Sealey and inside the far post.

There was a surprising, but very welcome, novelty for Sunderland supporters in the final phase of the match. Instead of resorting to hoofing the ball downfield as they sought to cling on, the team displayed much greater composure to the extent that a few possession interchanges took place with the two 'old hands' centre stage. The fact was not lost on Durban, 'Worthington and James had a tremendous influence in the last quarter of an hour. There are periods in a match when you need older heads, and I was wanting to bring Buckley on to give us a spark but there was no way I could bring off either Frank or Leighton. They have added new dimensions to the side and we must be making progress as we have never played like that in the last ten minutes since I came here.'

James recalls the attitude of the pair of wily veterans, 'Our game wasn't about defending (the young players could do the running and ball-winning), but we had the know-how to recognise, in the heat of the action, anything that required immediate attention on the field. We could say, "Right, you do this, and I'll do that" to address any problems.'

Rowell remembers that Worthington and James were players 'oozing with quality', and observes that Durban had not been daunted about bringing in a couple of older men 'with baggage', and channelling their attributes.

Durban's post-match superlatives extended to the backline, 'When you look at the England set-up, they have nothing settled in the centre of defence [Thompson, Martin, Butcher, and Osman]. They are looking for stability and should look no further than Atkins. Had he been playing for a London club I believe he would have had a mention by now.' There had been a recent precedent set by players breaking into the England scene after playing for lower-league teams the previous season (Gary Mabbutt and Mark Chamberlain had been at Bristol Rovers and Port Vale respectively). Durban continued, 'Atkins was pressed into central defence quicker than I would have liked, and though I always knew that was where he would finish, I would have preferred it not to have happened for another year or two.'

Turning to the overall picture, Durban noted that Swansea had suffered a bad defeat at home to Watford, 'Other clubs' goal difference are now suffering while we have gone a long way to repairing the damage of the 8-0 defeat.' He also picked out Cummins, although his praise was tempered with the observation that this was a prickly player who thrived best in certain conditions, 'Stan wants to be successful, but he needs to be in a successful team to do that. The speculation of him leaving came when we were looking for a centre-forward. Now we have Frank, and Stan is playing with a freshness I have not seen in him.'

For the time being, relations were cordial.

## Setting the Bar Higher

The manager had intimated that his team had clawed their way out of trouble, and he was looking for a general upward curve in standards, 'For the last two and a half years everyone has been looking at survival, but I am now looking to get a bit of respect for the club. I am working on three or four ideas [in training]. Buckley has had a super fortnight and McCoist is breaking his neck to get back in.' Those new ideas would have to wait to be tried out in anger as an early pitch inspection led to the match at Norwich being postponed. Instead, a hastily arranged friendly was to be played at Hibernian, where Easter Road was equipped with undersoil heating, 'I am really pleased. I now feel that we may have an advantage over other sides that have not been able to play this weekend.'

At Hibernian, Sunderland won 2-1 with goals from two Scots, McCoist and Chisholm, in front of watching national manager Jock Stein. It was refreshing to see Sunderland players pushing claims for recognition, or to be welcomed back from the international wilderness. In the week of his 30th birthday, James's impact at Sunderland had earned him a recall to the Wales squad ahead of the following week's Home International at Wembley. Having missed the friendly, he rang Durban requesting an outing in the reserves, the manager reporting, 'I am delighted for Leighton and particularly pleased that his move to Sunderland has resurrected his international career. It is good for the standing of the club to have players in a full international squad.'

The reserve match was at Barnsley and Durban announced that James would be joined in the line-up by McCoist, 'I want Ally to have a few games and a few goals under his belt; another 90 minutes won't do him any harm.' Both men scored in a 4-0 win, with Eustace commenting, 'A super show. When the first-team is going well everyone at the club wants a bit of the action, and they will all be chasing the substitute's spot at Southampton.'

James had opened the scoring, and Eustace highlighted the influence exerted by the experienced character, 'Leighton told Paul Atkinson to leave the free kick to him and that he would bend the ball into the top corner – and that's exactly what he did. The kids are looking up to Leighton and he is responding to them. Everyone needs a new challenge, especially at Leighton's time of life. It has been said that he can only keep going for a few weeks at a time, and he is aware of that, but the change has certainly done him good.'

The praise was well merited but Eustace's remarks also contained an implication that the player was 'getting on' to the tail-end of his career. For a man who was just about to hit 30, talk of James winding down the playing side and concentrating on coaching seemed premature. The praise and encouragement of James's aptitude for guiding young players was well-founded but, considering the squad's shortage of 'know-how', it appeared that such influence would be best exerted in the first-team until the landmark of 35 was hovering into view.

Durban had watched next opponents Southampton win 2-1 at Notts County, and had been impressed with their midfield trio of Williams, Armstrong, and Holmes. Meanwhile, the healthy competition to be included for that away trip continued as the reserves beat Bradford City 5-0 at Roker, including goals for West and McCoist, 'The performance and attitude of the players in our reserve-team games this week has been top-class, and it is a clear indication of how desperate the lads out of the side are to get back.' Atkinson had also scored, and Durban was contemplating the unearthing of another starlet, 'For a kid of 16 his performance was tremendous.'

The Saints also demolished Norwich 4-0, and Durban mused, 'We treated Coventry as if they were Liverpool, and we must show the same respect to Southampton, though we don't fear any side.' There was no complacency at The Dell, but a 2-0 defeat was the outcome. To rub salt into the wounds, Mick Mills scored his first goal for his new club with a fierce drive to seal the win. Durban was not happy with the performance of the referee, 33-year old Dennis Brazier, who was officiating at a First Division match for the first time, 'It is not sour grapes – we got what we deserved, but it was not a particularly bright appointment by the League.' The Sunderland boss then poked fun at the regulations that meant he had to exercise restraint, 'I can come in and criticise the Queen but I can't have a go at the referee.' Brazier himself reported that Durban had been nothing but cordial after the match, and said, 'I may have made some mistakes but we all have to learn. The main thing is that we all enjoy the game.' Well, of course, those are admirable sentiments but ones that provided little consolation then, and would probably be thoroughly derided amid the snarling high-intensity of later eras.

Interviewed following the game, Mills commented, 'I knew I would get some stick from the Sunderland crowd, and just wish I could sit down with them and explain what happened. The Southampton offer appealed to me because I was born just 40 miles away and still had connections in the area. It was Bobby

Ferguson's first deal as a manager and though he wanted me out he did not help me one bit. I requested to let Alan Durban know that Southampton were in for me but he said that if he did that it would kill off Sunderland's interest.'

This version of events sounded ludicrous; surely the fact that other teams were competing for a player's signature could have only benefited Ipswich. Had Ferguson really been so silly, or was Mills embellishing the tale in an effort to mitigate his culpability for the late about-turn? Like Durban, Mills insisted that 'bygones were bygones', and he added, 'In the end I had to make the call and I dreaded it as I knew what Alan Durban's reaction would be. He put the phone down on me, but four weeks later I sat down and wrote him a letter.'

This had been the first league defeat for over two months, and Durban was looking to get back on track, 'I am disappointed that the run has been broken but we now have two home games and must make sure that we cash in.' He then revealed that he had rejected approaches from two Scottish clubs seeking to take McCoist on loan, 'I just can't see any benefit in it for him or us. Ally is happy enough here and I am happy as he is coming along nicely.'

Other personnel were departing, however, the club announcing the retirement of Johnny Watters (their long-serving physiotherapist since 1956), and youth development officer Charlie Ferguson (he had arrived from Burnley in 1970). Durban had George Herd to shoulder extra work with the youth set-up, but the manner in which the club failed to make an immediate appointment to provide temporary full-time cover in the vital physio role was disturbing.

With Durban and Eustace in attendance at Wembley, James came on as substitute to earn his 54th (and final) cap in Wales's 2-1 defeat. Back at Roker, the lack of adequate medical care had already been felt. Buckley had pulled a hamstring in the reserves, and Docherty's update made the club appear small-time and inefficient, 'As we have no physio at the moment, I sent him to the doctor's.' Elliott had also suffered a reaction and could have done with the expert ministrations of the departed Watters.

Next up at Roker was another visit from Manchester City. Durban indicated an unchanged side and, little knowing the 'bone of contention' it would become the following month, he remarked on the lack of any serious upturn in attendances despite the team's improved form, 'We still have people who come here for the special occasion rather than previously when they came out of habit.' He also found time to praise an unsung hero, groundsman Bill Pattinson, as he remarked upon the magnificent condition of Roker Park, 'It's remarkable; apart from our first-team and reserve matches, we also train on it quite a lot, and allow Sunderland Boys to play English Schools' trophy matches.'

Prior to the City game, Chisholm exemplified the attitude that generally predominates during a relatively successful run when, determined not to relinquish his place in the starting line-up, he had a pain-killing injection to a toe. The crowd became restless as another stalemate seemed to loom, with no indication of the second-half excitement to come.

The flurry started when Bond bundled over Worthington about 20 yards out. With Venison shaping to shoot, Worthington rolled the kick into the path of Atkins and a nick from one of the outrushing defensive wall helped the fierce drive veer over Corrigan. Then, following an innocuous-looking altercation on the flank, Bodak petulantly raced after Munro and chopped him down in full view of the referee who promptly sent him off. To compound City's woe, James floated the resultant free kick to the far post where Worthington intelligently nodded the ball across goal and Rowell ghosted in to head home. Caton halved the deficit from a flicked-on corner but, with eight minutes remaining, the defender brought down Rowell in the box, and the forward picked himself up to send Corrigan the wrong way from the spot.

On this afternoon, however, the home defence was looking porous, and Reeves was allowed yards of space to side-foot in from close range. The crowd had to endure another scare before the final whistle and were grateful to see a Tueart volley fly straight into the gloves of an ideally positioned Turner.

Five goals and a welcome three points, but the boss was critical, 'I sensed the danger last week of players attempting to do things beyond them. Labourers get paid to labour – not to be artists. I must nip it in the bud or we will be back where we were a couple of months ago.' It seemed that Durban would have much preferred a solid-looking 1-0 affair, but he had a point as, on another day, attacking efforts may not have been able to redeem the defensive shortcomings, 'All I did was to remind them what they are getting paid for in my team – and that is not for defenders to be drawing ripples of applause from the crowd.'

Gary Rowell recalls that Durban did indeed prefer a narrow win with a clean sheet as opposed to an end-to-end goal feast, and that it may have been easier playing as striker for a manager possessing a more cavalier approach. However, the club's record goalscorer emphasises his respect that Durban 'always had a plan', and that any team he sent out would usually be 'hard to beat'. Rowell relished the fact that, under Durban, he was 'never sitting in the dressing room feeling as if the team could not go out and win. We always had a chance.'

Guarding against complacency was one of Durban's constant refrains, 'The worst thing anyone at this club can do is for them to let it cross their minds that we are out of the wood. That would be crazy. Other teams are picking up points regularly; we have got to get pride back into defending as it upsets me the way we have started conceding goals again. The worst thing I could have them doing was to go home thinking everything was okay.' But, it had been the manager himself who had previously said 'we have dug ourselves out of trouble earlier than last season'! Again, it might be harsh to condemn a manager for isolated self-contradictions when his every utterance was being scribbled down.

Worthington's influence had again been a prime feature, but Durban's praise was seasoned with an implication that the striker would now be expected to get in some covering tackles, 'Frank is just getting back to full fitness. He has had to avoid physical contact before Saturday, and got his first tackle in then. He has got past the stage of going past people, but if he keeps his contribution to others going then I will be very happy.' The manager had observed some pleasing traits that were emerging, 'We are getting better habits as a team, and the main difference has been the strikers working as a pair. Frank's header for Rowell's first goal is the best example.'

Turning his attention to the following week's home match against Everton, Durban voiced hopes for an upturn in tangible interest from supporters, 'Even though we have won four of our last five home league games our gates have only gone up by about 1,000. We have got to try and get more people back into the ground.' It may be suggested that five-goal thrillers such as the one that had just taken place were precisely the sort of enticement that would increase attendance figures, yet Durban had been so dissatisfied with the (too) open nature of that performance.

## Forward March

A strong reserve line-up was named as Durban issued an incentive, 'I am not sure that I shall be keeping the same team on Saturday, so the players have every chance to make an impression.' The benefit of the revitalised competition for places was reinforced following a training-ground collision in which Atkins sustained an injured calf. The player's usual steely determination to be involved was given further impetus by the team's form, 'I'll be there, even if I have to be strapped up and have pain-killing injections. There is no way I can afford to go out of the side; I may not get back in.' McCoist hit a fine goal for the reserves, but West was sent off with a Derby defender. Durban was not happy about the manner of the dismissal and West was duly fined, 'He is the first player that I have had sent off for violent conduct in ten years and I feel that it reflects on me. I don't like my players raising their hands or feet.' Meanwhile, he noted that Brighton had won 2-1 at Swansea, 'It is up to us to keep collecting points so we can stop worrying about other clubs' games.'

Although Durban's mantra was one that exclaimed first-team spots were up for grabs to boost the goals output, coach Eustace underscored the dilemma of endeavouring to balance the twin objectives of safety and entertainment, 'You have to give the lads who have done the job a chance. I am sure the league position is more important to our fans and that they realise we must learn to walk before we run. Entertainment is an important factor to get people to come to our games, but I think over a short period it is better if we go back to the formula we set out to stop conceding goals and, though I have a lot of sympathy for supporters, the club's safety is very important.'

With an away game at Stoke in the offing, Durban travelled to see his former club beat Manchester United 1-0, while Eustace watched next opponents Everton draw 0-0 at Maine Road, 'It is going to be difficult breaking Everton down but we have got the players to do it.' On the eve of the match, Durban maintained his anti-complacency tone, 'I don't expect to make any changes, but if somebody upsets me they would soon be out. It is the fringe players who have kept the first-team going recently and the pressure is on for places.' By this time, the squad realised that the manager rarely acted on this threat, but they knew not to take liberties.

A crowd of just over 16,000 turned up at a windswept Roker Park, and should have seen their team go one down as Graeme Sharp blazed over a gilt-edged opportunity. At the other end, a Worthington effort was cleared off the line, before a penalty was awarded in the 32nd minute. As James tried to latch on to a return flick from Worthington, full-back John Bailey helped the ball over the touchline with his hand. The infringement was spotted immediately and, although Bailey and his team-mates protested vociferously, the guilt-laden complaints soon petered out. The kick was confidently despatched by Rowell, sending Arnold the wrong way.

Everton may still have headed for the break in front. Following another slick move, Heath clipped the ball across for the hovering Sharp to comfortably equalise with a close-range header. Shortly after, Kevin Sheedy met a weak clearance to send a first-time left-footer just inside Turner's near post, but his celebrations were swiftly snuffed out by a linesman's flag for what appeared an innocuous offside.

The away side continued to threaten, but Sunderland re-established their advantage in the 56th minute; Venison was barracked by the crowd as he halted his forward motion to play the ball back to Cummins on the right, but the forward released the overlapping Nicholl who forced a corner. In the swirling conditions, James placed the ball down and, as he did so, made a quick circling signal with his index finger. Alive to the fact that an inswinger was coming, Rowell thrust himself forward to meet James's wind-assisted kick and send a bullet header crashing into the net.

The home side had to withstand sustained pressure as they were often outplayed by sharp-passing, swift-moving opponents (the *Echo* reporter wrote that 'Everton's superior class and polish in midfield enabled them to dictate'), but they lost Andy King when he was sent flying by Munro as he raced on to a pass. The Sunderland captain's attempt at this 30-70 challenge resulted in a caution and saw King writhing on the ground. With his archetypal 'football-manager sheepskin' billowing in the north-east gale, a concerned Kendall came on to the pitch to ascertain the damage and offer words of comfort as his player was stretchered off. Kendall's restrained-yet-acerbic post-match comment on the incident compared the bookings Arnold and Kevin Ratcliffe picked up for dissent, 'They will pick up the same penalty points as Munro.' Late in the game, Heath shot narrowly wide, and an effort from free-kick specialist Sheedy was survived as Sunderland clung on.

Although it had been a slightly fortuitous victory, Durban talked up leading marksman Rowell's improvement, 'If he keeps scoring like that he is good enough to play for anybody. I don't think he has worked hard enough in the past from Monday to Friday. He genuinely felt that it was enough to be a goalscorer but he is now getting his rewards. One of Sir Alf Ramsey's sayings was that he distrusted genius a bit if it wasn't covered in sweat, but I have no complaints about Gary now as we have lifted our standards as a team and he has as an individual.' Perhaps Durban's use of a Ramsey aphorism risked tarring him with the same 'negative' connotations associated with the later days of the former England manager's reign. Durban also spotlighted Turner, 'His handling in the opening minutes gave the rest of the side confidence.'

The general mood of unwarranted crowd dissatisfaction was chronicled in the local *Echo*, 'Winning no longer appears sufficient for Roker fans. They voiced their frustration as Everton dictated play.' But, surely it was far better to win in such circumstances rather than enduring the frustration of seeing your team dominate but fail to deliver the end product? Durban acknowledged that the performance had been far from ideal, but justifiably reminded all concerned they had reasons to be grateful, 'We have been mediocre yet we have beaten one of the best sides in the First Division. Our supporters are moaning now we have won our last two matches – not long ago they would have given their right arms for that.' At present, the local press were onside, with Durban saying, 'It has taken months of hard toil to put the club in shape and, though there is still much to be done, progress is being made.'

As usual Durban was keen to think ahead, 'Our immediate target has to be three or four more wins to see us safe, then to continue the spell by adding a bit more flair to our play. There is a lot of room for improvement in our away performances, where we have scored only two goals in the last six matches. When we are safe we can always prepare for next year by bringing in one or two youngsters, but not at the expense of points. We have clawed our way out of a bit of a hole.' This message appeared clear enough, but would not assuage the premature ambitions of the vocal minority now thinking in terms of qualifying for Europe that term.

When dealing with his squad, Durban's approach was hard but fair, and he had benefited from having a good teacher, 'The standard of the staff and players in training is better than any other club I have been with as a manager. We have released a lot of people who were not only not performing particularly well for the side, but were not good in training either. I learnt a lot from Brian Clough that short and alert training sessions are best. What I ask for is concentration in training. One or two of them have walked back from Cleadon.'

The form of Rowell and Worthington had restricted the opportunities for McCoist, but Durban continued to be pleased with the young striker's development, 'We have tried to change him into a team player. This has taken a little bit from him but it has helped to make him a better all-round player.'

Sunderland travelled to Stoke whose home record boasted nine wins and three draws from 14 matches. Atkinson and Venison had returned from three days' training with the England youth squad at Lilleshall, and Durban declared, 'Venison has grit and determination. Atkinson has more quality.' But, the Sunderland manager had been dissatisfied with the recent training shifts, 'The main threat tomorrow comes from ourselves. The players have been a bit sloppy this week, but I have 24 hours to get them in the right mood. One or two think they have cracked it, but we are better when the pressure is on and I will remind the players that what we have achieved over the last couple of months has been done by hard work.' Naturally, as a returning manager, any positive result would acquire an extra sheen, 'I enjoy going back to Stoke, having enjoyed working there, and I would like us to go and play well.'

In an unexpected move, West replaced Worthington. It was the first time Durban had omitted the signing without injury being the cause, and he named Atkinson as substitute. Stoke had Bracewell at number four, and a young Steve Bould on the bench. In a tactical ploy, Durban switched Pickering to full-back to curb the threat of England winger Chamberlain and the Sunderland boss watched his side absorb sustained first-half pressure. Five minutes after the break his in-form striker made an impact; West found James and the ball was moved on to Rowell who evaded a desperate lunge from Watson before sending a fine left-foot shot high into the net. Later, as a long ball from Watson caused consternation, Atkins and Turner collided and Nicholl cleared the danger. The Stoke crowd heckled their former manager as Durban went to the touchline to check on Atkins who, although he had fallen heavily, was fit to continue after receiving treatment.

Durban was highly satisfied with the manner of the 1-0 victory, 'We won because we worked hard and earned the rub of the green. I think the players responded to the warning I gave this week. The way that West worked set the seal on our performance.' The gamble of leaving out Worthington had worked, 'That decision also shows that we are prepared to pick a side to do a specific job. West's determination spread through the side who battled throughout and were rewarded with a goal worthy of winning any match'. Stoke boss Barker acknowledged that the result was not a flash in the pan, 'Sunderland have now lost only one of their last 12 league games and they showed how well-disciplined they are.'

There was further encouraging news for supporters that evening as details emerged of a meeting that had been held in a Nottinghamshire hotel between Durban and 22-year-old midfielder Mark Proctor. The upshot was that the player had agreed to join on loan. Even amid the general sense of achieving a breakthrough, the Sunderland manager realised the 'financial handcuffs' the board encumbered him with meant he was in yet another potentially embarrassing situation. Forest were mooted to be seeking a modest fee of around £125,000, but Durban had to concede, 'We haven't got the money, but in a month's time the situation could be different.' However, working with a chairman and board who continued in a collectively unimaginative, parsimonious attitude, how could things be different in a month's time?

Nevertheless, it was a moment to look at the positives, 'I know a few other clubs were interested, but the fact that Mark wanted to return to the north-east was a big factor in our favour and, hopefully, we can work out something permanent.' Although Clough had recently signed Chesterfield midfielder Danny Wilson, it was apparent that the Forest supremo had relaxed his 'no loan' stance to help out former player Durban. Proctor was relishing a fresh start, 'I have not been happy playing wide on the right. I made a stand with Brian Clough. He was adamant, so I made a transfer request. I am a midfield player and not a winger.'

Sunderland's next match was at home to Swansea, and the manager was quizzed about whether a winning line-up would be changed, 'I don't pick teams on Monday, but we will see how well Mark fits into our system. A measure of his success will be how keen we are to sign him after his loan expires.' Durban was pleased to have acquired a player with 'pedigree' who was 'extremely keen to join', but angered by press gossip that he would have to sell players to make the move permanent and also at rumours of a rift with Worthington. Shifting focus, the manager reaffirmed his contentment with the contribution made by his freebie who, it had been remarked, was yet to chip in with any goals, 'Leighton has nothing to prove. He has made a tremendous impact, and I knew he was capable of producing five or six opportunities a game to deliver good-quality balls into the box.'

The on-field situation was looking relatively healthy, but, with a typically bewildering lack of subtlety and timing, the chairman was primed to deliver another verbal effusion guaranteed to alienate a large percentage of fans.

## Chant No. 1: 'Cowie Out'

'COWIE: "I WISH WE HAD NEWCASTLE'S FANS".' That was the brutal headline that adorned the *Sunderland Echo* as Durban was in the midst of preparing his squad for Saturday. The chairman's ill-advised outburst had formed only a small element of his economics 'lecture', but it was always going to be the aspect that would be seized on by the press. His primary point had been that he saw no reason why the bumper Christmas gate should not be a more frequent occurrence given the team's impressive run, 'The Liverpool game gave us a net profit of £35,000, whereas against Manchester City, when we had a crowd of over 15,000, our net profit was £6,800. We are 10,000 short on gates. To continue running three teams we must find another 10,000. The only way we can continue – as a major force in soccer – is if the people of Sunderland really support us.'

Even staunch supporters might have had a wry smile at claims of being 'a major force', but Cowie continued, 'It boils down to the missing 10,000 who would give us another £20,000 a game. Newcastle are averaging 25,000 a game – that is marvellous for a Second Division side. I wish we had Newcastle's supporters.' It was those six words that blazed in the eyes of Sunderland fans.

The chairman attempted to justify his ire at the lack of big crowds, 'At the moment we have a £500,000 overdraft. And make no mistake, the situation is deteriorating.' Cowie also hinted that club property and training facilities might have to be sold, before posing a somewhat irrational question, 'Would Sunderland supporters have rallied had Kevin Keegan came here? We have signed Leighton James and Frank Worthington, who are no slouches, and we have Gary Rowell who has scored more goals in the First Division than Keegan has in the Second. To finish, I can only repeat – it is up to the supporters, and I want to see 25,000 for the game against Swansea and a full house against Manchester United.'

Do you indeed, Mr Cowie? Well, judging by the incensed reaction of supporters to his poorly worded criticism, Cowie could not have adopted a worse tack. Yet again, he appeared to be telling fans that the responsibility fell on their shoulders and, by the way, that lot up the road are better than you. A further dispiriting element of the message was that supporters had to attend in large numbers otherwise there would be no prospect of seeing major signings. The statement had the feel of an ultimatum.

It was recalled in the press that it had been Cowie who had clamped down on the players receiving Christmas turkeys, advising previous manager Knighton that if he was unhappy about the tradition being discontinued then he could pay for the turkeys. Knighton had already dived into his own pocket to fund an overnight hotel stay for his squad prior to a pre-Christmas home game after the chairman bridled at the suggestion. Cowie had also been unyielding when Knighton broached the subject of the club granting the recently arrived Allardyce a bridging loan to enable the defender's family to complete the house purchase they had lined up while waiting to sell their existing property.

According to Allardyce, Cowie advised him that his car sales reps did not complain about frequently travelling away for long stretches. 'Big Sam' could only try and enlighten his paymaster that sales reps did not need to concentrate on maintaining peak physical fitness and mental alertness, and that Cowie was supposed to be catering for top-flight sportsmen, not his car salesmen.

Cowie's latest statement also demonstrated a lack of appreciation of the game; an ageing Worthington was past his prime and James was a free-transfer acquisition. They were fine players, but for their drawing power to be compared to that wielded by Keegan was ridiculous – the former England captain and European footballer of the year was a 'superstar.' The Newcastle board had shelved penny-pinching notions and displayed the vision and ambition to sign a player who was an iconic 'brand', whose arrival, despite the overall financial package, would not jeopardise the club's future existence; Keegan would be self-financing even in the unlikely event that he failed to fulfil expectations on the field. It appeared that the Sunderland chairman was guilty of misjudgement on a gargantuan scale – he had blundered.

Durban was swift to disassociate himself from Cowie's remarks, 'I disagree with the chairman over what he said as I think our fans are every bit as good, and even better. The Newcastle situation is more emotional than ours. They have hung their hat on a superstar which has been the pattern of their success.

Our lack of success in the cups has caused a lack of emotional involvement. Our away fans are the best I have known and they certainly helped us to get a result at Stoke. People are interested in winning something, and not fighting relegation battles. What I want now is for our fans to prove the chairman wrong.' There would always be a distinction between a club's home and away support; that is not an unusual fact of sport, but Durban realised the self-defeating nature of overtly criticising the home crowd.

Refocussing on the imminent clash with Swansea, Durban playfully stimulated his fellow Welshman to score against his former club, 'Leighton has contributed to half the goals we have scored since he came, but it's time he got one himself.' There were also expectation levels for the new loanee to fulfil, 'I am looking to Proctor to stabilise midfield and give us a better supply to the front people.' There had already been healthy competition for places before Proctor's arrival, but it was a welcome problem for Durban as he set out some immediate goals, 'It is a difficult decision who to leave out, but one or two may just benefit from a rest. We want to be in the top half of the table by tomorrow night. I hope to see a vast improvement in the gate with the introduction of a new player, but I am not setting any figure.' Unlike his chairman, Durban was astute enough not to rap out, 'I want to see 25,000.'

Coincidentally, the preamble to the previous season's home encounter with Swansea had been fraught with financial worries, with Durban dramatically listing all but four of his squad. This time, following the chairman's condescending 'ultimatum', it was no surprise to see the attendance fall well short of that demanded, and it was to be a frustrating afternoon for the 17,445 as struggling Swansea deployed five across the back. The mood darkened when Chris Marustik hit a 20-yarder into the top corner after 51 minutes. Pickering had been deployed at left-back at Munro's expense, and the team were missing his midfield runs. But, a draw was salvaged when James supplied the cross for Rowell to send in a header which the linesman adjudged had crossed the line despite Chris Sander clawing the ball away. The young keeper denied Rowell a winner at the death when he got his fingertips to another goalbound header.

The crowd had vented anger at the directors' box, but Cowie was unabashed and claimed the gate was satisfactory, 'That represents an extra £8,000, and I will take a lot of stick for that sort of money. What I want to emphasise is that I was not having a go at the hardcore of loyal supporters at Roker Park. They are wonderful. People can go on booing me; so long as they come through the turnstiles. We need bigger crowds to be able to buy the players we want.'

Durban was disappointed that Proctor had seemed withdrawn, and pondered whether it had been a mistake omitting Munro, 'I am angered that I left the skipper out and we were no better. There is a big danger of taking the tacklers out of the team. If I had been a little brighter I would have selected a different side. Once we took Pickering out of midfield we did not have a forward runner. We had trouble against Manchester City when they played with a sweeper, and though we had enough of the ball we could not dominate in the box. I didn't expect Mark to come and dictate but he has got out of the habit of looking for the ball. He played much of the game as if he had been transferred from a relegation outfit.'

The following Thursday was transfer deadline day, but a hamstrung Durban could only issue the same stark message, 'I will only be in the market if I can sell first.' Switching the focus to his form striker, Durban pushed for international recognition, 'When you pick England teams, you pick players with a proven goal record – and Rowell's got that.' But, his manager was concerned about the over-reliance on one man, 'I can't see us getting into trouble, but an injury to Rowell could change the picture completely. If Gary does not score I don't know where the next goal is coming from. Gary converts a higher percentage of chances than any other player I have managed [Crooks and Chapman among them]. His goals are generally spread out, with a surprising number of headers.'

Durban's attacking options were limited, and his repeated cajoling for others to make penetrating runs from deep had not borne fruit, 'Unless there is some return from other areas of the side, I will look to McCoist – it is as simple as that. Not a full-back has scored in general play since I have been here and that is frightening. Neal of Liverpool gets in three or four shots every match. And midfield is even more frightening an area as Venison has not scored in over a year.'

Using the league champions' full-back as an example was rather selective as Neal was part of a team that often dominated the opposition and permitted their defenders greater licence to rove. That day's equaliser had taken Rowell's tally up to 18, but Durban's fear would be realised, not due to an injury to his prime goalgetter but simply a dry patch – he would not score again that season.

The following week saw more fall-out from Cowie's 'Newcastle gaffe' as fans penned letters to the *Echo*. Typical extracts revealed supporters' disillusionment and suspicion both of the club's chairman and any capacity to learn from previous mistakes, 'Will extra revenue generated by larger attendances be used any more efficiently than in past'; 'it's madness to sell valuable assets. I am sure that it will serve only to alienate rather than attract those less committed'; 'insensitive remarks'; 'had the Sunderland board showed the foresight and courage of their Newcastle counterparts'; 'any good work accomplished by Alan Durban recently has been completely undermined by the chairman's outburst'; 'he should move to Newcastle and go and join those wonderful Newcastle supporters.'

## All Aboard the Rollercoaster

For the visit to struggling Luton, Durban declared that Munro would be reinstated to the starting line-up, 'Iain is more than just a full-back to the team. Even in the run like we have had you cannot just sit back. I was angered that we dropped two points last week as we were left with time and space to be more positive.' For Durban, the crux of the issue remained consistent, 'I am continually looking for blend.' The transfer deadline passed without any movement and the Sunderland boss was relaxed, 'This week is always a sign of desperation – and we are not desperate.'

Luton had been busy, signing striker Trevor Aylott from Millwall and goalkeeper Tony Godden on loan from West Brom. They would both play against Sunderland. Meanwhile, there was one choice that Durban would not have to make as Cummins was granted what amounted to compassionate leave, 'His wife is in the later stages of pregnancy and with another young child he has enough problems on his mind.' Durban emphasised how his team now harboured an increased level of ambition, 'Luton have brought in a couple of new players and have been labelled an attractive side. Last year I would have been happy to go and not be beaten, but it all depends on targets. This year we are setting our sights on finishing as high as possible, so we will be looking for another away success.'

On a boggy pitch, Pickering shot Sunderland into an early lead but, in the 27th minute, Moss went down under a Munro challenge and, despite the skipper being adamant no contact had taken place, the linesman signalled for a penalty, duly converted by Horton. A minute later, the Luton captain escaped with only a yellow card for a nasty-looking tackle on Proctor. After recovering, the on-loan midfielder forced Godden into a magnificent save.

Pickering had been dropping back to help curb the threat posed by Moss who had been alternating between flanks, but at the interval Durban decided to try and unleash the midfielder's attacking potential, sending the team out with the message 'give him the ball and he will win us the match.' On 59 minutes, Worthington was unfortunate to see his header bounce down from the underside of the bar, but Pickering was handily placed to force the ball home. Better was to come as Leighton James notched his 100th career league goal with an exquisite chip over Godden before racing over to the bench in celebration. James remarked that he had scored with a similar finish against the same keeper earlier in the season when Swansea played West Brom and said he had fancied his chances of repeating the feat.

Durban offered a thoughtful appraisal, 'In Luton I saw a lot of our side of last season, where frustration spreads to the crowd. It was a solid performance by us with everyone contributing and Turner making important saves. I was pleased with the graft Venison and Proctor got through in midfield.' Proctor had also been impressed, 'I would love to stay. It is great to play for fans like Sunderland's. I could not believe how many they had. They get far better support than Forest.' Proctor's comments are illuminating; Sunderland enjoyed superior support, in both quantity and passion, than a club that had won multiple major domestic and European trophies over the past five years. It underscored the latent potential at Sunderland that Durban had recognised and was battling to harness (despite the obstacles continually thrust in his path).

Cue Tom Cowie, who was not lying low, even cranking up the onus on the home support, 'We have something going now. I want to see a full house against Manchester United. I think the team have deserved it and there is no reason why we should not expect it.' Meanwhile, it emerged that his team manager, with no transfer funds to play with, had tried to coax Frans Thijssen to Roker after the 31-year-old midfielder had been released from his Ipswich contract. Thijssen had been voted Footballer of the Year in 1981 by the Football Writers Association, and Durban had spoken to the player's agent at the weekend. Unfortunately, he was advised that Thijssen had already agreed an 'unbelievable' deal to play for Vancouver Whitecaps and would also reject a last-ditch attempt by Chelsea to lure him to London, saying, 'I have given Vancouver my word.' Durban commented, 'I was at the stage of finding out what he wanted. He is about the same age and pedigree as Leighton.'

But for the disappointing home draw against Swansea, Durban would probably have walked off with March's Manager of the Month award, and Sunderland found themselves in 15th position in the table, ten points above the third-bottom spot. There was also welcome news that, as part of extra spending by the Sports Council, the club had been awarded a £200,000 grant towards improvements at their Washington training centre.

On the pitch, the team faced an onerous task away to Liverpool, but Durban was upbeat, 'You have to give Liverpool problems rather than accept you are going to defend for 90 minutes. We have just plodded on without many people taking much notice that we have lost only one of our last 14 league games. It is important that we keep the run going and we are looking for a win rather than a draw.' Perhaps this was over-enthusing, but it underlined the progress the manager felt had been made in the past 12 months.

Prior to the match at Anfield, the *Echo* printed a 'league table' compiled using 1983 results which positioned Sunderland second only to Liverpool. Unfortunately, the team were also second to Liverpool that afternoon as Souness hit the winner, a typically venomous strike after 71 minutes. Two days later, 31,486 gathered at Roker (not quite the 'full house' wanted by Cowie) for the Easter Monday clash against Manchester United. Rainfall had made the surface skiddy, and Nicholl was made captain for the day on his final home match before he returned to Toronto. Despite a spirited effort, United's stand-by goalkeeper Jeff Wealands frustrated the home side by brilliantly saving two point-blank efforts from former Birmingham team-mate Worthington. With around 15 minutes remaining, James magnificently weaved his way into a great position only for an unfortunate bobble to cause him to blaze his shot just too high. Earlier, Steve Coppell had left the pitch after suffering the knee injury that would ultimately lead to the premature end of his impressive playing career.

Durban noted the difference to the last encounter at Roker between the sides, 'We lost here 5-1 and never had a kick. That shows you just how far we have come.' Ron Atkinson's view differed, 'Sunderland had bits of flurry, but we had so much of the ball for an away side it was unbelievable.' Meanwhile, Durban admitted that he did not possess the cash to make the Proctor move permanent, 'As it stands, he will be playing his last game on Saturday, but I am going down to Nottingham to have further talks with Cloughie.' Durban would also need to convince his former mentor that the club was capable of raising the transfer fee – eventually.

The imminent loss of Proctor and Nicholl already represented a double blow, but problems started to multiply before the trip to West Ham. Venison was suspended and Durban erred on the side of caution by omitting an unwell Atkins, 'There was the danger of the infection spreading to the rest of the team and that was a risk I could not take.' Nevertheless, the boss was keen to focus on the opportunities, 'The attitude of the players in the squad has been first class. We are going to have to make changes in the next few weeks, but the players not in the side are bursting to get back and they could give us a boost.' He was still persisting with a 'best-case scenario' attitude, 'If we end up with 60 points that will give us an outside chance of Europe.'

No 'boost' was forthcoming, despite Pickering hitting home a first-time drive from a James corner to cancel out Alan Dickens's opener. As the game swung from end to -end, Parkes denied Worthington in a one-on-one situation, François Van der Elst hit the underside of the bar, and Goddard scooped over from only six yards. However, ten minutes from time, Goddard held off Elliott's challenge to shoot beyond Turner. A 2-1 defeat; momentum had been lost.

## Falling from Favour

Although not mentioning Worthington by name, the manager's post-match summary from Upton Park sounded ominous for the veteran, 'We made five or six reasonable chances, but lost because we settled for a draw. Pickering is the only one who looks like scoring from midfield, and when the goals dry up from Rowell we have nobody else to score.' Proctor returned to Forest, a disappointed Durban explaining, 'Brian Clough quoted me a fee which we could not afford, and though he offered that we could pay over a period of time, that would only set the fee higher. It is a decision I expected, but there is a chance that the deal could be resurrected in the summer.'

Next up was the rearranged fixture at Norwich and, with Nicholl gone, the boss decided to give 20-year-old reserve-team regular Mick Whitfield his chance. In addition, West would replace Worthington in attack after scoring all four goals for the reserves against Bolton. The *Echo* correspondent reported that Worthington was to be 'rested', but the wording describing the veteran striker's contribution thus far seemed damning, 'He has scored only two goals in 17 appearances.'

However, most observers would have argued that there was far more to Worthington's overall influence on the team than goals alone. Durban delivered his take on the situation but, while logical, hinted that he was not revealing the full picture, 'Frank and I have had a chat about it and we hope that the rest will do him good and get him right for the Brighton match. He is not happy about missing matches, but it is for his own good. He has been troubled by an ankle injury but I am not using that as an excuse as it is a combination of things.'

At Carrow Road, McCoist was the surprise inclusion in a midfield role, 'When Rowell's goals dry up, we have to look to fit Ally into the team. I don't think we are safe yet – we still need to win a game.' Despite his eagerness to get back to winning ways, the boss still felt it appropriate to hand Whitfield a debut at a ground where the team usually struggled. Durban implied that the defender's long-term future was at stake, 'Obviously it is a vital period for him. This is more about how he reacts mentally. I do not want to play Venison at right-back on a permanent basis, so this is an ideal opportunity for Mick to make the position his own.'

Prior to the match, one of Durban's prime concerns had been lack of goals, but it was a vital position at the other end of the pitch that took precedence following a horrid afternoon. Turner was stretchered off following a sickening collision with Keith Bertschin, the keeper sustaining a fractured skull. Pickering took over as custodian but could do little about John Deehan's two strikes. Despite the shattering injury blow, Durban was critical of his players, 'We have become too flippant. Confidence has turned into casualness and there is a thin dividing line between the two. It has affected the concentration of some players, and I will now be putting the pressure back on. It is not pressure of relegation, but reassuring our supporters that we have made progress. It rankles with me that I did not see it previously.'

Eustace was also critical of the team's attitude, but senior pro James stuck up for his colleagues, 'No one shirked; they all tried. It would have been magic to get a 0-0 draw after losing our goalkeeper like that, and I believe we would have had we been able to keep our concentration going for just that bit longer.'

Durban visited Turner in hospital and the keeper was alert enough to enquire about results involving teams in the relegation zone. Although discharged, a lengthy recuperation would be required, 'We have to accept it and get on with it. Mark Prudhoe came into a side under a lot of pressure, but this is a different environment.' Durban may have been maintaining that relegation was not an issue, but some supporters were concerned about the danger even before knowing that an inexperienced goalkeeper would have to be drafted in for the remainder of the season.

For the visit of FA Cup finalists Brighton, West and McCoist were replaced by Worthington and Cooke, 'We have had a good look at finding someone to fill the role wide on the right. It is a question of finding the right balance.' Durban also believed that two of his rookies should now be better equipped to handle first-team football, 'Prudhoe has a lot of ability, and that is why we have signed him on a long-term contract. Whitfield should feel the benefit of a game under his belt and I expect him to play with a lot more freedom.' Despite Brighton being firmly in the relegation zone, the manager warned, 'We have had them watched away from home and know that we are in for a hard game.'

In miserable weather, a disappointing attendance (13,414) saw another poor game with Brighton going ahead after only 27 seconds. A long punt by goalkeeper Perry Digweed was flicked on by former transfer target Robinson and the hapless Whitfield's slip permitted Smith the opportunity to drill the ball past the other home debutant Prudhoe. Thankfully, a scrambled equaliser arrived on 38 minutes when Cooke's cross was palmed out by Digweed and Pickering forced a scuffed shot through the flailing arms and legs in the six-yard box. As the team struggled in front of him, there was a relatively competent performance from Prudhoe, and Durban praised the keeper's attitude, 'We got a point because of the way Prudhoe picked the ball out of the net. He didn't drag his feet. He picked the ball out with the attitude "Let's get on with it.'"

Although a win had been the aim, Durban was feeling slightly relieved as he recalled the near-disastrous last minute goal conceded at home against Brighton in the final home match of the 1980/81 season (which he had seen on video), 'I sent a message out ten minutes from time – 'Make sure we don't lose it.' That was a very important point for us and I am grateful to get one after the way we played. We looked a very tired side. I have told them to go away and I don't want to see them until they get on the bus for Ipswich on Friday.' Durban was not feeling quite so tired as his labouring charges; that night he represented the north-east region at tennis in an International Club of Great Britain tournament.

Another trip to East Anglia was not what the doctor ordered for an ailing team, but the reserves had won 3-1 at Nottingham Forest with a double-strike from McCoist. As usual, Durban had been present and remarked, 'Ally took on Colin Todd in a ten-yard run and won – that was something I did not expect to see.' His boss neglected to mention that McCoist was about 14 years younger than the veteran defender. After four months out of the picture, Hindmarch was recalled in an effort to stymie the aerial threat posed by Mariner and D'Avray. This philosophy, while sound in principle, had not proved effective in December when Ipswich had destroyed the Sunderland defence on the ground. Whitfield was axed as Venison reverted to right-back, 'I am reluctant to move Barry as he has done a good job in midfield, but I feel it is the right move for this match as I expect Kevin O'Callaghan to play.'

It had been disclosed that Cooke and Turner were to be offered fresh deals, but it gave the manager particular pleasure to contemplate a future Sunderland squad containing star prospects Venison and Pickering, 'The two of them are the ideal blend. It's nice to know I don't have any worries over the next few years as far as their positions go. No one will be able to prise them away from here. They are Sunderland supporters through and through. No manager having his head screwed on would consider selling his best assets. If I had a blind choice between Ray Wilkins and Barry at the moment, I would choose Venison. I think the game is getting short of people who can do the hard part of getting the ball off opponents.'

The encouraging of home-grown young talent was an admirable approach that Durban was attempting to instil at the club. Young local players could see that, if they were good enough, they would be given a chance. It made perfect sense that a group of young players who were raised as part of an enlightened club culture, and believed in the ethos established by an encouraging manager and backroom staff, would flourish and ply their talents at that club for the long haul. They would be committed to the cause, to Durban's grand vision.

This prioritisation of youth was underscored in the manager's programme notes, 'We were more than happy to play hosts to the Sunderland Boys squad. They came to Roker Park for hot baths and a rub-down from our coaching staff prior to the English Schools' FA Trophy Final. [In addition] the recent excellent performances and results achieved by our reserves have virtually assured promotion to the First Division of the Central League – very much a step in the right direction for this club.'

There was hope for the future, but until those glorious days arrived, Durban's team had to lick their wounds following another disastrous outing in East Anglia where Wark and Mariner had put Ipswich 2-0 up before half-time. Three minutes after replacing Worthington, McCoist set up a goal for Pickering, but Prudhoe was slow to react as Wark's 77th-minute header crept past him. It ended in an abject 4-1 defeat, and Durban could only cite extenuating circumstances, 'We have had an imbalance of away games, but we have three of our remaining four matches at Roker. We will need another win, but I am not worrying.'

This marked the point where it became clear that the local press had fallen out of love with Worthington. In February, the *Echo* reporter had lauded the impact of the artful veteran, 'There is no doubting the value of the contributions of Worthington and James ... Their experience is already beginning to rub off on the rest of the side. Worthington will be around for another season at least – long enough for McCoist and West to learn a trick or two from the much-travelled striker who is revelling in his new surroundings. The Roker crowd have certainly taken to a player who is not afraid to bring a touch of humour as well as class to the game, and although his legs may have gone he is still a force to be reckoned with.'

Praise indeed, but contrast the same correspondent's disparaging tone just over two months later, 'Worthington was so ineffective that the former England striker was brought off, leaving question marks against his value. His contribution to the side of late has been negative to say the least.'

The censure of Worthington appears to have been grossly unfair. He was not the only contender to be substituted at Portman Road, and it needed to be remembered that the team's loss of form had coincided with the departures of Nicholl and Proctor, not to mention Turner's injury. The 'humour' that Worthington injected had also been a welcome feature. Yes, this was a man who liked a laugh on and off the pitch, a man who cited his favourite foreign stadium visited as 'Bradford City', his most difficult opponent 'my ex-wife', and worst injury 'graze to left wrist'.

But Worthington possessed a winning mentality and was always professionally focussed on the job in hand; he did not sacrifice the good of the team for a cheap laugh or to indulge in glitzy ball-juggling or flicks when inappropriate. Worthington's form had suffered, but it was merely a symptom of the team's plummeting form, not the cause.

Leighton James confirms Worthington's serious approach to business on the pitch, 'Forget all the stories of the high living. Frank was a class act; one of the best professionals I've ever had the pleasure of working with. Alan Durban spoke to the pair of us shortly after I arrived, saying, "I've got some good kids, but I need two players who know what they're doing." We added some know-how to the team, and the younger players joined in the revolution, became part of it and, I believe, improved because of it. Gary Rowell was one who improved as a result of playing alongside Frank.'

## End-of-Season Drama is Compulsory Here

Durban's team were now only five points above the relegation zone, and the May Day holiday fixtures presented them with home games against third-from-bottom Birmingham and high-flying Watford. Durban's revised assessment was, 'I feel we have no problems at present, but we will have next Tuesday morning if we lose these home games. We will face both with confidence, however, as I have sorted something out over the weekend by studying the Norwich game on video.'

That sounded a feasible notion, although it may have been difficult to garner a great deal of relevant insight for upcoming home fixtures from an away strategy. Far from remaining tight-lipped about the precise aspect that had been 'sorted', the Sunderland boss was happy to broadcast his theory, 'We have allowed the opposition to come too far with the ball before defending. Defending will start with the front men, restricting the opposition who have had an open invitation to attack us.'

Away from the league, England under-21 manager Howard Wilkinson named Pickering in the team to take on Hungary at St James' Park. Durban was pleased to see his player line up alongside Stoke's Bracewell to 'give England a nice blend in midfield', and was keen to find the right blend at Sunderland. He wanted Pickering to be one of at least a couple of his team's midfielders to regularly feature on the score sheet, 'There is such a dearth of midfield players who can score goals. John Wark has proved that if you gamble and get into the box you will get your return. Midfield players tend to stop on the edge of the box, but Nick got one from a yard out at Luton. We feel that he has had a consistent season for a 19-year-old, and five goals in seven matches is a real bonus.'

England edged a scrappy game, but Pickering seemed puzzled by events both on and off the pitch, 'I found England's formation strange to play in, and so used my own initiative to get into the game. The crowd gave me some stick, which surprised me as I am a Geordie, but I just smiled at them.'

Before the Birmingham game, Eustace commented further on the week's training sessions geared to resolve the flaws spotted on video, 'It is up to the players to discipline each other with the strikers leaving the midfield to do their work, and the midfield not interfering with the back four.' To supporters' disappointment, Worthington did not line up against his former club and, surprisingly, Whitfield got another chance. Durban was adamant, 'I think West and Rowell will be the better pair to give us what we need. Gary is the one who can always pull a goal out of the bag. Whitfield has the chance to stake his claim now or the right-back position becomes a priority in the close season. The lads know exactly what they have to do. We have worked hard on it during the week.'

There was a curt response from the manager when pressed about Worthington's immediate future, while the player himself also refused to comment on his likely future whereabouts, instead musing on the extent of his impact, 'The object was to inject some experience and confidence into the squad and I believe I've done that.'

Worthington's presence would not have gone amiss as less than 15,000 witnessed an awful home defeat. Sunderland had taken a first-half lead when a James cross flicked off a defender and West sent a header past the helpless Tony Coton. Clinging on, Durban saw his team suffer a double-whammy in the final ten minutes, beginning with Munro conceding a penalty which centre-half Noel Blake comfortably converted. Worryingly, a succession of crosses were being won in the air by Mick Harford; Prudhoe denied him brilliantly on one occasion but in the 86th minute the Sunderland-born target-man hovered above Atkins to meet a left-wing cross and arrow a header well wide of the keeper. It was a sickening blow, and not the last to be inflicted on Durban's hopes by the tall forward.

Two days later, there was no bumper Bank Holiday crowd at a rain-soaked Roker Park. Fewer than 14,000 watched as second-placed Watford took the lead after only three minutes through Blissett. John Barnes spurned an opportunity to increase the lead, but a tenth-minute James corner was headed on by West for Atkins to crack an equaliser past Steve Sherwood. On 34 minutes, Elliott won the ball and supplied Rowell, whose pass allowed James to try his luck with a low 'skidder' on the wet surface. Sherwood permitted the shot to squirm through his fingers and Sunderland were ahead.

Unfortunately, James had to limp off with a groin strain after the interval, and there would be two cruel late blows. Firstly, the home side were forced to play the last five minutes with ten men after Rowell landed heavily on his ankle after attempting an overhead kick, and then the resistance was broken in the 88th minute. Although Prudhoe did well to touch a Gerry Armstrong header past the post, the corner was flicked on for Blissett to apply a finish.

Sunderland had at least displayed character, but a one-point return from two home matches was depressing, and the foot of the table was uncomfortably bunched: Sunderland had 46 points from 40 matches; Luton 46 from 39; Coventry 45 from 40; Birmingham 44 from 40; Manchester City 44 from 40; Swansea 44 from 40; and Brighton 44 from 40. After the previous seasons' agonies, Durban had pledged there would be no last-game relegation cliffhanger but, with an away fixture at Highbury looming, that scenario was looking distinctly likely, 'I have never been pessimistic and we have proved that when the chips are down we will give it a go. I am just grateful for small mercies. I thought the crowd were superb and that helped temper the disappointment.'

The two Bank Holiday weekend games had attracted a combined attendance of only 28,789, but Durban offered one potential remedy, 'All managers should be made to play the game as Watford. If they did then football grounds would be full.'

To compound his problems, Durban would be without the key men who had limped off the sodden Roker pitch. James and Rowell would miss the match at Arsenal, Rowell reporting, 'I heard a crack and my ankle just went numb.' In such circumstances, it was all hands to the pump; McCoist and Cooke would be the replacements.

Durban informed Worthington he could leave but knew he could still rely on the player to provide cover, 'I had a word with Frank and told him I was going to play Colin for the remaining games, and that with all the goals Gary has got I could not leave him out. Westie has done well. He has good defensive qualities and wins a lot of balls. Frank will travel to Arsenal and is in line to be substitute.'

Although James's injury healed more rapidly than expected, the quagmire pitch at Highbury meant he was not risked. In fact,

Sunderland made an official complaint over the churned up surface after a London schoolboys' final was permitted to be played hours ahead of the crucial top-flight fixture. Although Sunderland's line-up was a little makeshift, the balance was somewhat redressed by Arsenal being without England internationals Woodcock and Rix. It was to be a dramatic afternoon.

The wet conditions helped to generate goalmouth incidents and scrambles aplenty. Talbot's header was cleared off the line by Munro, and Prudhoe was busy as Sunderland rode their luck. Understandably, the keeper's handling was not secure on the wet pitch, but he employed some unorthodox methods to frantically scoop the ball away on numerous occasions. Meanwhile, Jennings was a virtual spectator at the other end. In the 71st minute, there was a bolt from the blue-shirted away team; McCoist played the ball inside to West and the big front-man swiftly turned, throwing off the attentions of a couple of defenders, and sent a drive ripping past Jennings to give his team a vital lead.

In a desperate rearguard action, marshalled by Atkins, Prudhoe saved superbly from Talbot allowing Munro to clear off the line, and the keeper palmed the ball away from Vladimir Petrovic before the rebound was blazed wide of the gaping goal by Talbot. By this time, Hawley had come on as substitute as Arsenal strove to save the game, but Sunderland held on for an oh-so-crucial win that exemplified the qualities that delighted their manager, 'We couldn't have put any more effort in than that; it was a gritty performance and a perfect result for us. We got the rub of the green, and the people in vital positions had super games.'

That evening, a buoyant group of the squad queued up for the Stringfellows nightclub. As Munro struggled to negotiate the players' way past some wary doormen, an Arsenal-supporting bouncer recognised the big frame of West as the man who had delivered the devastating bolt into the Gunners' net that afternoon.

Not harbouring a grudge, admission was swiftly granted. Ahead of Monday evening's rearranged game between Manchester United and Luton, relegation remained a mathematical possibility if Luton pulled off a win.

Durban admired the way David Pleat's team had tried to play attacking football and was not anxious to see them lose, 'I want Luton to have a chance at Manchester City on Saturday. They have contributed a lot this season and their goals tally of 64 is the fourth highest.' Roker fans did not mind if Luton stayed up, but held their breath hoping they would not pull off a shock win at Old Trafford. By Tuesday morning, Sunderland were safe; United had won 3-0, thus setting up a straight contest between City and the Bedfordshire club as they stayed in Manchester for a memorable final Saturday that saw Pleat skipping on to the Maine Road pitch at the final whistle.

Leighton James recalls that, at one of the end-of-season awards ceremonies, local journalist Bob Cass had thanked Durban 'for securing top-flight safety before the last fixture. We hope to see similar boring results in the future!' Like Rowell, James maintains that the vast majority of football supporters simply wish 'to see their team win', even if it involves a shortage of end-to-end action. The 'boring' quip from Cass was very much a light-hearted swipe at critics of Durban's methods.

Although relieved that safety had been guaranteed before the final match, a minority of disgruntled fans vented their feelings in letters to the local press, including complaints over how the team had 'fallen apart since losing Turner, Nicholl, Proctor', and how the club's 'administrators flounder while 10,000 fans stay away sick of annual relegation scraps.' It was pointed out that while Tom Cowie may 'wish for Newcastle's fans', the Sunderland fans wished they had Newcastle United's directors who were 'prepared to dive into pockets.'

## Farewells and New Beginnings

There was one piece of news that would appease a big section of the fan base when it was announced that the club had ended their clothing sponsorship deal with French firm Le Coq Sportif one year early. There were rumours that USA giant Nike would be the new sponsor (a suggestion fuelled by fact that north-east former champion athlete Brendan Foster handled a significant part of their UK operations). Durban offered hope that there would be a return to the traditional broad red and white stripes and black shorts, 'All I know is that negotiations will possibly result in us having a new shirt next season, and hope that the supporters get their wish.'

National headlines were dominated by the announcement that a general election was to be held on 9 June, but the Sunderland premier was outlining his own manifesto for future prosperity, 'I feel we have a better future and solid base and any replacements will have to be better than we have already. We signed the most influential player [Atkins] in the last five years for a modest fee.'

Already, Durban was painfully aware that he would not be given anything like the funds necessary to compete in the market for top players unless he sold assets first. Nevertheless, the Roker boss was still setting high standards, 'The yardstick over the last 20 years is that we have not been able to break the barrier of finishing higher than 15th. If we do not achieve that next year I will class that as failure. I would have been very disappointed had I not known the reasons for the slump over the last few weeks, but we slowly got into trouble by having to constantly change the side.'

Durban's analysis highlighted on-field reasons for optimism, 'We are going into a fourth successive season in the First Division with a very young side. We saw the effect two experienced players gave us just after Christmas. Proctor added a bit of know-how to prove that it does not have to be an ageing player. Provided Atkins comes back in the same frame of mind and Chisholm continues to step up the ladder, suddenly we look very solid down the middle. Chis has got to maintain the will to prove that he is better than people say he is.'

The manager indicated that West's form had elevated him into pole position up front, 'Rowell and McCoist will have a real battle on now as we will get enough goals from the centre-forward position.' In addition, the reserves had comfortably won promotion to the First Division of the Central League and this would provide fringe players with better preparation for first-team duty. Elsewhere, it became evident that the club had, for a change, timed one piece of transfer business well. They had received £210,000 from Middlesbrough for Joe Bolton less than two years previously and, following the economic slump, he had now been given a free transfer, linking up with Porterfield and Arnott at Sheffield United.

In midweek, as Aberdeen beat Real Madrid 2-1 in Gothenburg to win the European Cup Winners' Cup, Worthington made his one and only appearance in Sunderland's reserve team. He notched two goals (one a penalty) as the team recovered from 2-0 down at Burnley to win 3-2. The coming Saturday, Sunderland would wind up their league programme at home to West Brom and, with their top-tier place secure, Durban briefly considered missing the match to check on a right-back in Scotland.

At this stage, the manager remained reluctant to switch Venison from midfield on a long-term basis. More immediately, the player would be missing after being released to captain the England youth team, managed by Graham Taylor, in the start of their European Championship campaign on the Friday evening. Taylor commented, 'He is a solid dependable lad. His strength of character will help us.' A gratified Durban added his own perspective, 'Barry has got the right temperament for the job. There are some aspects of his game which can be improved. But, for a lad who is not yet 19, he has got off to a tremendous start in his career.'

Prior to the final weekend, it was announced that Buckley and Whitfield were to be given free transfers, but Durban was wishing his experienced midfielder had remained settled, 'Mick's contribution was the main reason we stayed up last year, but once he opted out before Christmas I was reluctant to involve him. He will get a club and do well.' Buckley had made 119 appearances for Sunderland, scoring seven goals, but Durban's pointed opinion that Buckley had 'opted out' of a relegation fight was stinging. Terms had been offered to Cummins and, unaware of the tribulations this would spark, Durban provisionally declared his summer priorities, 'I will be looking for either a couple of midfield players, or a right-back and one midfielder.'

James returned to the team against West Brom in a game which marked the final appearance of the visitors' John Wile before he left to take up the post of player-manager at Peterborough. Durban was anticipating an entertaining affair, 'I think the crowd will see something different as I am going to experiment, with the emphasis on attack. I want to see what the effect is on certain players when there is no tension.'

A crowd of 16,375 came out in the May sun, but the 'new-look' attacking Sunderland failed to materialise in a disjointed display. West Brom's major signing from Coventry, Garry Thompson, scored after 15 minutes when his looping header beat Prudhoe, but a 53rd-minute Atkins centre resulted in an emphatic header from Chisholm to earn a draw. Durban had noted how his team had been outplayed in midfield, and cast envious eyes at the visiting number ten, 'I tried for two weeks shortly before

Christmas to sign Gary Owen. That is the calibre of player we are looking for – someone who knows what he is doing. We need a midfield artist – someone who can play and have an effect around him, but it's a case of what we can afford.' Regrettably, for manager and supporters alike, it was the same old story.

If he was to avoid scratching around for transfer 'bargains' Durban realised he might have to part with Elliott or Cummins, and he was certainly annoyed with both of his 'stars'. Cummins was left out after venting his grievances in a morning newspaper. The boss adopted an air of nonchalance ('he said what he thinks is the truth, and that's okay'), but was aggravated that Elliott had declared himself fit to play with a protective covering to his wrist only for it to become evident that it was restrictive. Durban waspishly remarked, 'Shaun's hand was hurting an awful lot and somehow stopped him tackling.'

The defender's non-appearance for the second half gave the formation an even greater imbalance but at least allowed 'Worthy' a farewell appearance, and the Roker faithful a final chance to see some trademark flicks and guile. However, this proved difficult as the home side laboured, and failed to deliver the hoped-for attacking 'emphasis'. The manager admitted that the plan had not worked, but bemoaned the officious refereeing that 'didn't help'.

The following day, a Sunderland team played against Celtic to raise cash for Berwick Rangers's Ian Cashmore who had been paralysed after breaking his neck while training. West hit a hat-trick as Sunderland won 3-1 and Charlie Nicholas, who had scored two in an Old Firm victory at Ibrox the previous day, netted a second-half consolation in his final Celtic appearance before he set off negotiating with the host of English clubs seeking to take him south of the border.

The Sunderland forward line that had finished the game against West Brom saw an all-too-rare pairing of Worthington and

McCoist but, off the pitch, the two roomed together on the squad's short break to Magaluf (a club reward for staying up). The senior man, well seasoned in the art of enjoying the high life, navigated the young Scot through the late-hour partying. Well versed in ministering to any next-morning hangovers, Worthington served up a decent breakfast and ran a bath to ensure that a rejuvenated McCoist was set to roll for a new day and night's revelries. Sadly, although a good nightclub partnership, it transpired that the May fixture at Roker had marked both players' final appearance as a Sunderland spearhead.

## Durban's Dossier (Shopping List)

Despite working with a distinct lack of funds, Durban would spend the summer poring over a transfer-target 'dossier' that he had compiled, 'I know some players who would like to come here, and they are the type I want. There is no chance of a quick signing. It is a matter of starting at the top of the list and working down – and we have scrubbed a few off already.' The much-admired Garry Thompson and Gary Owen were two who would undoubtedly have featured on Durban's wish list at one time, but it remained to be seen how many of the names remaining would prove to be realistic targets, or whether the Sunderland boss would merely find himself, like the supporters, playing 'fantasy football manager'.

In the meantime, there was the consoling thought that another Sunderland player's outstanding form had been recognised as Atkins joined Pickering to play for a Bobby Robson England XI at Middlesbrough as they beat the hosts 2-1 in a testimonial for Wilf Mannion and George Hardwick. Paul Walsh got the England goals, while Atkins cleared off the line after keeper Iain Hesford had been beaten. On a less positive note, the Sunderland under-20 squad in Holland, shorn of Venison and Atkinson, fell well short in the defence of the trophy they had lifted the previous year, only reaching the ninth/tenth-place play-off.

On 24 May, the *Echo*'s back-page headline pronounced 'Orient Sack Ken Knighton'. Orient had avoided dropping down into the Fourth Division on the last day of the season by beating Sheffield United 4-1. Knighton had appeared optimistic at the weekend, stating, 'It has taken me a couple of years to sort out the dead wood, but we have a good youth policy now and it is the kids who hold the future of the club.'

Such short-sighted decision-making from club directors was an inauspicious omen for the current Sunderland boss. Knighton had been regarded as a bright young progressive manager (younger than Durban), yet here was a man, setting his stall on the value of youth to reap future rewards, summarily dismissed by an executive hierarchy that failed to see the grand vision. Durban's zeal to accord precedence to young local talent still burned bright and, despite musing that the first-team that ended the season had been 'overloaded with youngsters', he continued to encourage a youth policy, 'We are going to try to scout more locally. There is enough talent in this area.'

The manager was still hoping to make sorties into the transfer market for more experienced players to enhance the squad, but he had to tow his chairman's line, 'If there is a serious decline in the demand for tickets we may not be in a position to go into the market.' The irony was that this represented a classic 'catch 22' situation as a portion of fans usually proved reluctant to commit without having their appetites whetted by the arrival of new signings. Durban knew the next few weeks were crucial, 'We were very lucky to get such a return on Atkins with a small outlay, and the chances of another gem like that are few. We have made a solid base but now must be seen to be making progress in the summer. Nicholl and Proctor showed what effect two quality players had on us.'

Towards the top of Durban's wish list of signings was a player formerly under his care. Paul Bracewell's contract was up for renewal, but Stoke had placed a £350,000 fee around his neck. It was already debatable whether the club would permit Durban to go ahead with the signing, risking a tribunal favouring Stoke's valuation, but hopes of having the necessary funds were about to be rocked.

## Rebel Rebel

'CUMMINS REBELS IN CONTRACT ROW' screamed the back page as the player viewed as one of Sunderland's most saleable assets, and regularly touted as the potential makeweight in proposed exchange deals, was determined to leave. Cummins stated that the new 12-month contract offered was worth less in cash than his previous deal.

The PFA's Gordon Taylor advised him to report it to the Football League, and the player was claiming a free transfer on 'a technicality', 'I am only doing what anyone else would. I am only interested in the best deal for myself, and not Sunderland Football Club. The club have written to me three times this week, but in rushing into it have only added another flaw to the contract. I am only going by the book and the club are now trying to get round me, but I am leaving.'

It was an amazing administrative blunder from a top-flight club as their penny-pinching approach was about to turn around and bite them. A frustrated Durban was well aware that an already difficult task in attracting quality players was in grave danger of being further undermined by this ineptitude. The boss could not afford to meekly surrender, and felt it was a question of integrity and principle, 'He knows that we had no intention of giving him a free transfer and is looking for a loophole to make more money. Stan Cummins is showing no moral obligation to Sunderland.

He is grasping at straws and I am surprised the PFA are even considering backing him.'

Cummins's bombshell deflected attention away from the positive news that Nick Pickering had been called up to the full England squad for their three-week tour of Australia (becoming the first Sunderland player to be selected since Tony Towers in 1976). Durban was delighted, 'It will be tremendous experience for the lad and good for the club. His call-up shows how far he has got in two years by being dedicated to the cause.' That sent out a message to other Sunderland players. England had just beaten Scotland 2-0 at Wembley with goals from Bryan Robson and Gordon Cowans, and the fact that both scorers were County Durham-born only served to underscore Durban's point about harnessing the cream of north-east talent.

Dismayed at the prospect of missing out on a possible £100,000 fee for Cummins, Durban was reduced to adopting a no-nonsense line in other financial matters. A Swedish club had shown interest in signing Worthington but were warned, 'There will be no free transfer as I am looking for cash to strengthen the squad.' Durban's cupboard was virtually bare, 'I have had one or two inquiries about players but nothing concrete.'

As Durban discussed arrangements with Malcolm Allison for a pre-season Wear-Tees friendly, it emerged that another club in need of regeneration had noticed the sterling job the Sunderland manager had been doing with limited resources (and amid trying off-field interference and discord). Following their dramatic last-gasp relegation, Manchester City had sacked John Benson and now ambitiously targeted Durban, Clough, and Jack Charlton (who had resigned as manager of Sheffield Wednesday).

While having no intention of leaving, Durban light-heartedly acknowledged that being associated with such a prestigious position was flattering, 'After seemingly struggling through two difficult seasons, I take it as a compliment that some people still think I can manage.' Durban had been wanted by another 'big name' club, Leeds United, the previous summer.

## Sacrifice: Tears Are Not Enough

Nationally, Thursday, 9 June was the day of the general election, but the gut-wrenching decision that Durban elected to take meant it was a heartbreaking day for many on Wearside. Ally McCoist, the young man who should have adorned a Sunderland shirt for well over a decade as their talismanic striker, was allowed to leave the club by a manager fast running out of viable options to generate cash to secure his priority midfield targets. McCoist signed for Glasgow Rangers for £205,000, which represented a financial loss (but not as great as that suffered when previous record-signing Marangoni departed).

McCoist's exit represented an emotional loss too, and the player himself had mixed feelings about signing for the team he had supported as a boy, 'I have been tremendously happy in my two years, and I am sick to be leaving. The fans at Roker were tremendous to me, and that saddens me most. I discussed the move with Alan Durban yesterday morning and we decided it would be in both our best interests if I joined Rangers.' McCoist had then travelled to Carlisle to meet manager John Greig.

A disappointed Durban had been forced into an unenviable decision. He had to sell to enable him to make any forays into the transfer market at all, but even as the deal was being set up Durban realised the Glasgow club would reap huge dividends when McCoist developed into the finished article, 'I felt the only way we could get moving was to accept Rangers's offer, but Ally was not the first one I would have chosen to take cash for. He has been a great ambassador for the club. But I have been waiting for someone to come in for our players, and we are now in a position to make positive moves.' Durban was now primed for 'a big push' for Bracewell and Proctor.

Fellow striker Colin West recalls McCoist as a 'really bubbly player' and felt that the Scot had a 'slightly rough ride' in the physicality of the First Division where he would have benefited from having a more experienced, bigger man playing alongside him. Following his subsequent illustrious career with Rangers, some people were still apt to trot out the theory that McCoist had not proven himself at the very top level (i.e. in England), but West counters such scepticism, 'Garbage! He proved he could score goals in European competitions, and at national level.'

Leighton James also recalls McCoist's departure, 'It was a massive shame, but I can understand it because he was the club's biggest saleable asset at the time.' Although it would take more than a couple of years, the Glasgow club had the patience to realise the rich rewards to be reaped when the striker blossomed into the dynamic goal-machine that served them for over a decade. This was the amount of time that Durban would have loved to have devoted to McCoist who also proved himself an inspiring and ebullient presence to have in the dressing room and training ground. His enthusiasm off the pitch complemented his on-field prowess. If only this potential had been fulfilled at Roker Park instead of Ibrox.

Had Cummins's pugnacious stance (depriving Durban of much-needed funds) directly resulted in the departure of McCoist? While the young Scot packed his bags, a Football League committee discussed Cummins's latest grievance and decided to convene a commission to sit in Manchester (comprising Liverpool chairman John Smith, and Dick Wragg). Sunderland were pleading 'human error' and attempted to make the necessary amendment, but Cummins refused to accept that offer and the PFA were backing his claim.

While Durban waited to pursue the 'double splash' that would revamp his midfield, Carlisle's former Sunderland defender Jack Ashurst was linked with a return, 'It would be a dream come true. I never wanted to leave, but Ken Knighton told me there would be no first-team place.' However, the top target was Bracewell, and the 20-year-old travelled to Roker Park with his father to hold talks with Durban. He had spoken to newly promoted Wolves the previous day, but his former boss held the advantage, 'I am confident that the lad wants to come here.' In a busy day, Durban also spoke to Clough about Proctor, before confirming his interest in acquiring defensive cover, 'I am interested in Ashurst as he can play all along the back four, but certainly not at £80,000.'

If necessary, Sunderland could ask the next transfer tribunal (due to sit at the month end) to stipulate the prospective fees before committing to any deals for Bracewell and Ashurst. The advantage would be that they then had an option to back out of any arrangement involving a figure they were not prepared to pay. However, a drawback was that any delay left the way open for another club (prepared to commit regardless of price) to hijack the player's signature. Bracewell's tone was encouraging, 'I am very impressed with what I have seen here. The potential is unbelievable, and I have played with Iain Munro, Nick Pickering, Barry Venison, and Ian Atkins, as well as holding manager Alan Durban in high regard.' The young midfielder recognised the rich commodity of 'potential' present at Sunderland, but Durban needed those who wielded power at the club to develop similar perception.

Worthington did not go to Sweden, but became the latest experienced former international to join Southampton, the fee being £25,000. Durban acknowledged the veteran's important contribution and now revealed the major gripe that had hastened his exit, 'Frank was always a short-term signing and he did a good job in revitalising us when we were bottom. But, his refusal to move to the north-east had a big bearing on our decision to sell.' The press had complained about Worthington's low goal tally at Roker but, although the striker's legs had lost their former zip, Saints boss McMenemy recognised the 'gold dust' that his latest addition brought to the table, 'I see Frank as the ideal foil; I am mainly looking to him to make our forwards click. He is a wily and experienced character.' In contrast to Worthington's reluctance to plant roots in the area, Leighton James had moved up from South Wales, and even signed to play Durham Senior League cricket for local team Whitburn during the summer.

Pickering won his first cap in England's match against Australia in Melbourne, and it was a period of important meetings. Durban and Clough met in Manchester and the Forest supremo granted his opposite number permission to open negotiations with Proctor. The player travelled to Roker, 'If it all goes through I will be delighted to be back home in the north-east.' Durban added, 'Proctor and Bracewell are the priorities. We can always use Cooke or James up front.' Following the departure of McCoist, Durban's last comment implied that the transfer war chest would be emptied in tying up his midfield department and that no forward-line reinforcements could be afforded.

In what had become an aggravating feature, a transfer deal that Durban tried to bring to a successful conclusion hit a snag beyond his control. Following a meeting with Cowie, Proctor revealed that a hitch had prevented him signing, 'The problem is between the two clubs, not me.' Meanwhile, Bracewell had held talks at Everton, 'It is a question of which club offers me the best chance to further my career.' But, Kendall's interest cooled after new Burnley manager John Bond accepted his offer of £300,000 to take Trevor Steven to Goodison. Meanwhile, Clough denied media speculation linking him with a late swoop for Durban's top transfer target, 'It is news to me if I have made an inquiry for Bracewell. I have not been in touch with Stoke.'

In the final week of June, the Stoke board met to discuss the inevitable departure, preferring not to let the matter go to a tribunal. Durban commented, 'I am reluctant to say too much as I have not made Stoke an offer, and they have not told me what their bottom price is.' Well, it would have been a major surprise if Stoke quoted anyone their *bottom* price for a player, but one thing in Durban's favour was that Wolves's offer included two players in part exchange and Stoke preferred cash. For their initial £350,000 valuation, Stoke had used the same recent fee commanded by Steve McMahon (when he moved from Everton to Aston Villa) as a yardstick. Another factor was the recently introduced regulation obliging buying clubs to stump up at least half the total fee immediately. That would certainly stymie Durban's hand if the figure was set high.

As Durban awaited the green light from Stoke, there was lousy news from the FA commission as they decided in favour of Cummins. Although the club intended to appeal (Cowie threatening to take the matter through the courts), Cummins was confident they were powerless, 'I am glad to be getting away from Alan Durban. He is the whole cause of this. I have never felt wanted since coming back from Seattle.' Durban refused to be drawn into an exchange of words, but it represented a bitter blow for the manager's transfer kitty. In stark contrast, Bracewell was excited about the prospect of linking up with Durban at Roker, 'I believe the place is just waiting to take off. I want to win an England cap and I think my chances are better at Sunderland than at Wolves.' Unintentionally, this represented a somewhat backhanded compliment.

On 29 June, Durban travelled to the Midlands and the signature of Bracewell was clinched for £225,000, 'Very rarely do you land your number-one target. I have felt all along that we needed strengthening in midfield. We have got a lad who has played 135 First Division games and not yet 21. We could well have the England under-21 midfield next season [Bracewell, Pickering, and Venison].' Bracewell commented, 'I have had five good years, but felt that I needed a new challenge.' Although this signing signalled the extent of Durban's ambition for the club, the sacrifice, the sale of McCoist, was too great – and the manager knew it.

## Favourites and Clangers

Durban was still on the look-out for a budget defensive signing, 'We have lost five of our first-team squad and only found three replacements, and I will feel a lot happier if we had a right-back before the start of the season.' Durban would have loved to have been in a position to bring 18-year-old David Bardsley to Roker from Blackpool. The Fourth Division outfit were seeking in excess of £100,000 for the England youth full-back, but the Sunderland boss knew that his board would not sanction such an investment, especially on another medium-term prospect.

The arrival of Bracewell also marked a departure from the club as reserve-team coach Docherty left to take up the managerial reins at Hartlepool United. He went with Durban's good wishes, 'I think the timing was right. If he puts as much into management as he did in coaching he should do well.' Within a couple of days Durban had lost his first-team coach too as Eustace moved to former club Sheffield Wednesday to become Howard Wilkinson's assistant. When asked about replacements, Durban declared his desire to kills two birds with one stone, 'I will be looking for someone who can play as well.'

In early July, 37-year-old Pop Robson (now at Chelsea) was touted as the man most likely to be offered the vacant first-team coaching role, and thus join the club for the third time in his career. But the former Roker favourite was in demand; John Neal was trying to cling on to his services or, failing that, ram home the message that 'compensation' would need to be paid, 'I wouldn't want to lose him. He is a tremendous pro, a good coach, and is still playing. That's why I signed him on a two-year contract.'

Malcolm Allison was also keen to nab Robson as player-coach, while Darlington eyed him as a successor to Billy Elliott. Durban was seeking striking cover, and also hoped that Pop's experience could be put to good effect turning out for the newly promoted reserves where his presence would benefit the young players. However, the fact that Chelsea were seeking a fee (rumoured to be £10,000) represented a problem to Durban's bosses, whereas 'something for nothing' was music to the board's ears and free agent Nigel Walker was handed a one-year deal.

Sunderland had one slender hope remaining to avoid Cummins leaving for nothing. An appeals board was set to declare their verdict, but Second Division Crystal Palace and Brighton had offered the player terms provided the 'free' nature of the deal was ratified. Cummins was still in plaintive mood, 'I have had three seasons in the First Division with Sunderland, and none of them has been particularly good.' He disclosed that a move to the capital was on the cards, 'Palace have made me a brilliant offer and I am virtually certain to accept it. By going out of the area I think I will improve my chances of winning international honours.' Interestingly, Palace boss Alan Mullery indicated that, as far as he was concerned, the player had committed himself to joining, 'He's already given his word.' Cummins cost Sunderland £300,000 in 1979 and his record had been 29 goals in 132 appearances.

The club's fears were confirmed when the appeals board upheld the ruling that Cummins was entitled to a free transfer. An unsympathetic Football League secretary Graham Kelly commented, 'Facts are facts. Sunderland did not offer the player a better deal.'

The *Echo* editorial castigated the club's 'amazing £100,000 clanger', 'How could a First Division club make such an elementary mistake with one of their biggest assets. At a time when the club have been cutting costs to the bone it seems inexplicable that a player who would have fetched close on £100,000 can walk out the door for nothing because of a "clerical error".'

Cummins meanwhile warned that the situation could degenerate further, 'Sunderland could stop me going to another club until 1 August, when my contract will have expired, but in that case they would have to pay my wages, and I would report for a week's training.' It was probably just as well that Durban was on holiday in Spain. The club and supporters may have been feeling hard done by, but the parlous financial state of fellow top-flight club Coventry had forced them to sell a clutch of talent to wipe out a £600,000 overdraft. Players leaving included: Gary Gillespie to Liverpool; Danny Thomas to Tottenham; Garry Thompson to West Brom; Mark Hateley to Portsmouth; Les Sealey to Luton; and Steve Whitton to West Ham.

## Optimism Resurrection

On his return from holiday, action-man Durban represented Durham & Cleveland in an inter-county tennis tournament at Felixstowe. The following day, he contacted Clough to resume negotiations over Proctor, 'We are short on numbers having lost players this summer. We have space for people to come in.' There was also definitely gaping space in the club's coffers which were almost drained. Two coaches had departed and, in a further economy, only Robson was lined up to come in. As the squad returned to training, Durban was being assisted by George Herd as well as senior players Munro and James, 'I would like to appoint two coaches, and badly want Bryan Robson to become our first-team coach.'

Durban was satisfied with the squad's physical condition, 'They look in fine shape. I had thought about starting earlier but there was no need to worry. They have looked after themselves.' However, the manager demanded improvement, 'I am fed up of us being involved in a continual scramble to avoid relegation. Such days will hopefully be banished. There is now a fresh mood of optimism. Our fans won't stand for anything less.' But, the arrival of Proctor was being jeopardised by board-level interference. While he had plenty of time for Durban, Clough was becoming tetchy about the labouring negotiations, and threatened to abort the deal, 'I don't even know whether I can let Proctor go now. Our squad is a bit thin.'

With the squad already back in harness, Robson finally travelled north clutching the paperwork as Sunderland and Chelsea agreed a compensation figure of £8,000. Durban was relieved, 'Even though the lads have done very well in training it is obvious we are very bare in terms of full-time coaching staff.' Although Forest upped their asking price for Proctor to £120,000, this was haggled down to £115,000 and the signing was completed. The player immediately trained with his new team-mates at their Durham base, the session overseen by the freshly appointed Robson. As ever, the coach was in excellent physical trim and still possessed a natural goalscoring instinct. Although Durban was insisting that Robson would 'only be used as a player in emergencies', common sense dictated that, following the departures of Worthington and McCoist, forward-line 'emergencies' were almost inevitable. Looking back, James rates the recruitment of such 'a very fine coach' as one of Durban's supreme masterstrokes.

For Rowell and West, or whoever lined up in attack, Durban was confident they could rely on the men behind, 'We now have a midfield that won't be outworked by any other in the division.' Pleasing for the supporters was that the team would again be proudly sporting the broad red-and-white shirts/black shorts combination synonymous with past glories. It was no coincidence that it was the England under-21 triumvirate of Pickering, Venison, and Bracewell who were the men pictured modelling the Nike kit on its official press unveiling. The return to the traditional design had the full approval of Durban who felt that the move mended some bridges, 'I am glad we have been able to give the supporters what they want. I know there has been a lot of animosity from them over the strip during the last two seasons.'

As the squad prepared to leave for the Isle of Man, Durban announced that James would be assuming responsibility for coaching the club's youngsters and would miss the trip, 'I have had a word with Leighton and he is happy about the idea. He has had a couple of weeks of physical training and therefore I have no worries about his fitness.' Durban also pondered the opportunities the mini-tour permitted for another young gem to emerge as a first-teamer, 'We took Pickering to Scotland in similar circumstances and I am hoping that Paul Atkinson develops in the same way.'

Durban then oversaw the return of keeper Turner as he played his first practice match since being stretchered off in April, 'There is always a danger when a player sustains such a nasty head injury, but Chris came through without any problems.' Despite signing a new contract, Elliott was again unsettled but early indications suggested that none of the top First Division clubs were biting as Durban reported, 'I have had an inquiry from West Brom, and a fee suggested by Newcastle was way short of our valuation.'

Again, there were a number of routine organisational tasks that fell under Durban's remit in a period before the advent of clubs being run as major corporate concerns with an array of administrative departments. The manager had organised the upcoming tour with the Isle of Man Tourist Board, and was wrestling with obtaining a satisfactory travel itinerary from an agent setting up a proposed trip to Greece (a plan ultimately abandoned). In addition, he had switched the date of the team's pre-Christmas home fixture against Leicester to the following day, 'I am against Sunday football but feel we must do what is in the best interests of the club. Traditionally, the last Saturday before Christmas is a disaster [competing against shopping]. Last season we had an attractive home fixture against Arsenal but only managed a crowd of just over 11,000.'

In light of the Cummins debacle, perhaps Durban should have assumed responsibility for drawing up the fresh contracts offered to his players too!

The report coming back from Sunderland's opener as they demolished an Isle of Man XI was that Atkinson had been 'a revelation', and his manager enthused, 'Pickering has had to work hard at his game, but Atkinson does things so instinctively it's frightening.' Durban was most enthralled with his new engine room, 'Without getting carried away, considering the level of opposition, we had something in midfield which has been missing for the last two years. Perhaps the most pleasing thing, however, is how hard everybody worked for each other.'

Although not a natural goalscoring midfielder, Durban expected new signing Bracewell to increase his output. The player remarked, 'Stoke had Sammy McIlroy and Mickey Thomas to score goals from midfield. But I know the boss is looking to me for more.' Durban was constantly urging his midfielders to make runs into scoring positions, as well as encouraging defenders to push up. Meanwhile, newly capped Pickering spoke about the prospect who hoped to follow the lead set by him two years previously, 'We had a cross-country run which I won and Paul Atkinson was second, and he was just behind me in a 100-yards race which proves just how quick he is.'

In the next game, Burnley were beaten 1-0, and Durban was now satisfied that Turner was fully recovered, both physically and mentally, 'I think it took him some time to get over the sacking of Ken Knighton. I rate Chris in the top five in the country. He is much more confident now that Atkins is in central defence – they have established a fine understanding.' Durban was keen to win the final match as the tournament winners were automatically invited back the following year, 'The timing of the competition and the set-up here is ideal.'

In another good public relations move, the squad held open training sessions in front of appreciative crowds of holidaymakers on the seafront. With Bracewell and Proctor both resting blistered feet, Robson put the remainder through their paces. He was assisted by his father-in-law, fitness expert Len Hepple, who had been drafted into the coaching ranks. The squad then took time to sign autographs and pose for photographs and were applauded for their efforts. Durban then expanded on the immediate ambitions, 'We must put some pride back into the club and, though we now have several players with international recognition, the supporters want to see us in a more commanding position in the league. The club is in a much more solid financial position than when I came. We now have several players who could attract attention in the transfer market.'

The team got their hands on some silverware after a 36th-minute Atkinson goal secured victory over St Mirren. Frank McAvennie was substituted on the insistence of the referee after the strangely vexed striker had been guilty of repeated misconduct. 'Obviously I would like to win something that really matters' was Durban's slightly tactless comment following the game, but he was pleased with the shape of his team, 'I believe we now look much more solid.' A bonus was that the island's central defender David Cole had impressed, and Durban handed the 20-year-old bank clerk a trial, knowing that his spending funds would not run to buying Jack Ashurst to provide the defensive cover he wanted. On the rave reviews attracted by 17-year-old Atkinson, Durban preached caution, 'It is important that we don't lose sight of the fact that he is still an apprentice.'

As well as the part-time involvement of Hepple, the coaching set-up was supplemented by the arrival of Ian Hughes, who had made one appearance for the club during the 1980 promotion year. Hughes was appointed part-time youth-team coach, but one player making an even swifter return to the club was the released Barry Wardrobe. In a worrying sign of their desperate lack of striking cover, and no money to address the problem, Durban had to resort to offering the reserve new terms to stay, which Wardrobe duly accepted after rejecting a rival offer from Sparta Rotterdam.

There was one unexpected addition when Sunderland became the first club to install an artist-in-residence as 27-year-old Chris Stevens moved up from Cheltenham to begin a one-year stint. It was no surprise to learn that the club would not be adding the artist to their payroll as the residency was being funded by the Arts Council. Nothing wrong with having an artist, but the appointment illustrated a lack of communication between the board and their manager. The directors congratulated themselves on gaining a small publicity coup at no expense, but the nature of Stevens's role was the subject of a host of misconceptions. Laughably, some fans had asked him if he would be responsible for designing the programme, or painting the terraces, while Durban imagined the artist would be hovering around the dressing room.

The manager's irritation at something he felt had been foisted upon him was evident in a news item recorded for *TV-am*. Durban dourly remarked, 'I wasn't consulted.' He envisaged that Stevens's presence could prove a nuisance, 'The dressing room tends to be a very private place; a place where emotions can run high. He might find he gets a paintbrush stuck somewhere if he's not careful.' Durban's tone had turned playful and he extended good wishes to 'the lad', before jesting, 'I've just spent the last couple of years getting rid of one or two artists.'

The players were equally ill-informed about Stevens's intentions as Turner jokingly voiced hopes that the artist would not be recreating scenes of the keeper picking the ball out of the net. Leighton James joined in the banter, declaring that Stevens should get a lot of good 'still life' scenes as the winger suggested his own level of speed had been somewhat lacking during that morning's training session.

The artist himself recalls that his spell at Sunderland was 'a fantastic experience' but was also 'quite challenging in some respects'. The chairman was one man whose expectations had been awry, as Stevens explains, 'I made paintings which focussed on the supporters rather than the players which is not what was expected of me by Mr Cowie.' Although given a no-nonsense welcome 'audience' by the team manager, Stevens appreciated Durban's candour as he discerned that there was no malice in the gruff joviality, 'Alan Durban was a bit prickly but I liked him. He called me into his office early on to get the rules straight. He threatened to stick my paintbrushes up where the sun doesn't shine if I got in the way, and I respected that.'

Durban and his players had no need to worry as the artist harboured no desire to impose on the sanctuary of the dressing room with a sketchbook in hand, his aim being to capture 'the spirit' of the club, 'The residency was more about my response to the importance of a football club to the local community.'

As on-field preparations continued, a West goal contributed to a 1-0 win at Port Vale. Chisholm was substituted after taking a nasty knock above the eye and suffering double vision. Durban commented on what he had gleaned, 'I wanted to have a look at the sweeper system again as we may have to use it in one or two matches next season. We were solid, but looked a defensive side and just did not get forward.' Despite urging his midfielders to make supporting surging runs, their reticence would continue to be frustrating. Meanwhile, West was relishing the challenge of justifying his manager's faith, 'My first priority is to establish myself in the side, and now that Frank and Ally have gone this is my big chance.'

A 2-0 win at Bishop Auckland included goals from James (penalty) and Robson. In stark contrast to later strict medical precautions applied to players sustaining blows to the head, Chisholm played in midfield 48 hours after his manager had asserted that his player would 'not be able to head the ball for a week or two.' It appears ludicrous that switching a player from central defence to midfield was viewed as some form of safety precaution! Although the outing was against non-league opposition, Durban had seen enough to convince him he had his 'emergency' striker option, 'I now know that I would have no qualms in playing Pop in the First Division for the odd game. He looked so fit and sharp and proved that he can still score goals.'

## New Season, New Dreams

A 16-man line-up posed for the official squad photograph, and eight days before the curtain was raised on the 1983/84 league season, Roker fans would have the chance to see the revamped team run out in the new Nike striped shirts in a Friday-evening friendly against Middlesbrough. The manager revealed one more thing that would be unveiled, 'We have been working on something in training. Pickering will switch to the right-hand side of midfield, with Atkinson on the left.'

Perhaps Atkinson's form had justified him being given an opportunity, but there were a couple of major reservations. Firstly, Durban indicated that Atkinson would keep James out of the starting line-up, at least initially, 'Atkinson's potential is as exciting as I have seen. It is difficult to accommodate Paul and Leighton in the same side, and the consensus of opinion is that the lad is ready. He has the ability and confidence and now he has to prove that he is capable of sustaining it. Leighton has been consulted and he is happy to develop the progress of the youngsters.'

It was also worrisome that Pickering was shifting position to accommodate Atkinson's left-sided role. At present, Durban was confident in his theorising of history repeating, 'Pickering found freshness in a new position. His development was helped by the fact the skipper [Munro] played behind him – the same as Atkinson.'

As for James, his skill and vision would be sorely missed and, to many, it seemed ridiculous to think of such a talent being prematurely 'manoeuvred' into a coaching role. However, James recollects the thinking at the time, and emphasises that the move was instigated completely 'at my behest'. Initially, Durban questioned the timing, reminding the international of his relatively young age, but his player's response was, 'Yes, but I made my debut when I was 17.' James now observes, 'I recognised that the crop of young players at the club had the talent to be very good, and my guidance and experience could assist them to make even greater progress.'

As the team romped to a 4-0 win against Middlesbrough, there was little sign of the tactical problems to come as the striking duo, West and Rowell (two), hit the mark. The opening goal had been notched by the redeployed Pickering who was bullish about his new role, 'The boss asked if I would give it a go on the right, but now I know that I can do it. I had scored two cracking goals when cutting in and letting fly with my left foot, and this gave me confidence.' Again, conclusions were being drawn before any top-level opposition had been faced.

In contrast to the disappointing results that had accompanied the previous year's build-up, Durban's team had racked up six consecutive victories, 'There is still a lot of work to be done, but it was pleasing that we did not disappoint our fans after building their hopes up.

'I am more optimistic now than I have ever been since I became manager of the club. I haven't got question marks about anybody.' Durban was reminded that the three-year contract he had eventually signed would expire at the end of the season, and he was not complacent, 'I know I have to do better for my own sake. The worst two words in football are patience and potential.' Perhaps not the worst in principle, but the words that most directors and fans seemed unable to accept. They wanted success, and they almost invariably wanted it now. Another hard-hitting reality was, despite the promising form, season ticket sales were down.

At Darlington's Feethams for a final friendly, Durban suggested (unconvincingly) that his team for Saturday was not finalised, 'Atkinson has a fairly good chance of making his debut provided he does not upset me during the week. He will be a crowd-pleaser.' Durban included defender Cole, and handed a trial to former Middlesbrough midfielder Graeme Hedley, 'He is out of work after returning from Hong Kong and I just want to look at him. We must make sure that the preparations are spot on this week, though I have been delighted by the standard of fitness.'

A seventh pre-season win was duly supplied, 3-2. There was a spectacular winner from Walker, which prompted Durban to quip, 'I have already seen the goal of the season.' Trialist Hedley disappointed, however, (and soon joined non-league Horden). Preparations were now almost complete, 'I had made up my mind to play Atkinson and Pickering in wide positions against Norwich but I just wanted another look at them. Atkinson frightens me at times with some of the things he does. I felt that we had been playing well but were not scoring enough goals. In these two matches, however, we have made goalscoring look easy.' Yes, but the standard of opposition was nowhere near the levels the team were about to confront.

As Saturday approached, Durban once again urged the team to spread the load, 'I have impressed to the players the importance of sharing goals; that they must not rely on Gary Rowell. I expect the two wide flank-men to get into scoring positions, and the two central midfield players to share at least ten goals. Perhaps it is a tall order but if we are to have a very successful season we will want double figures from the four front positions.'

Chisholm had a bruised foot, but his manager's tone exuded confidence, 'I expect him to play; anyone who drops out now could have to wait a couple of months for another chance. We have good players out of the side who are capable of staying in.' There had also been a slight surge in public interest following the recent display at Roker, 'It can be a bit of a gamble playing pre-season friendlies at home, but we have had a favourable reaction and this has been reflected in season ticket sales.'

The Sunderland manager set out his vision, 'To be really successful we must not be looking to make too many changes in personnel. That has been the problem here over the last 20 years, but hopefully we can develop as a team, and I hope we are judged over the season. It is an endurance race but we must be seen to be looking good in the early stages. We must get in the top half of the table then be looking to teams above, not below us.' On new prospect Atkinson, Durban pleaded for patience, 'I hope the fans do not expect too much from him. Paul has not had a game in the First Division before, and is now starting to learn his trade where it hurts most. We are still talking about potential and promise. We were lucky with Pickering and Venison.' The boss had used the words 'promise' and 'potential' again, and even as he spoke he suspected they would fall on stony ground.

On a damp afternoon an expectant crowd of 17,057 turned up to see the following team kick off the campaign: Turner, Venison, Munro, Atkins, Chisholm, Proctor, Bracewell, Rowell, West, Pickering, Atkinson. For Norwich, new defensive signings Willie Young and John Devine made their debuts. A fiercely contested, but unimaginative, encounter was played out. In the 56th minute, Bennett's cross was headed in by Bertschin. Thankfully, an equaliser arrived swiftly as a long punt from Turner skidded past Young, allowing West to burst through and beat Chris Woods with a rasping right-footed drive. There was to be no dream debut for Atkinson, who struggled to throw off the shackles that top-tier defenders were capable of imposing. He was left unattended once, but spurned a great chance by blazing a close-range opening off target following a Pickering cross. Bracewell was constantly in the thick of things, requiring lengthy treatment in a muscular contest.

## Impatience Rears its Head

Two days later, Durban saw his team go down to a Mark Walters goal at Aston Villa. A body-blow was suffered in the very first minute when Bracewell aggravated strained knee ligaments and had to come off. Although Nigel Spink pulled off good stops from Atkinson, Proctor, and Rowell in the first half, the Villa keeper was not seriously tested again. The manager had spotted positives and negatives, 'For an hour we looked like a team. That was our first defeat in 12 games, so we have not suddenly become a bad side, but I think we need a bit of experience; the first time they have got behind they looked a bit naïve. One or two of them lost their appetite when the going got tough, and that's when it counts.'

Those players were not the only ones who were prone to lose their nerve when the going got tough. Durban's squad could not get through even one week of the new season before the unwelcome distraction of boardroom controversy erupted. The press reported that Tom Cowie had 'stormed out of a board meeting called to discuss two motions to call an extraordinary general meeting'. The rebel shareholders had resurfaced and they had managed to accumulate the necessary ten per cent holding to make the demand. While this group may have had an axe to grind about the way the 60-year-old chairman ran the club's affairs, the timing of their action, before anyone could reliably assess the likely fortunes of the first-team, could only serve to unsettle the playing staff and supporters. A group of 16 shareholders hoped to force Cowie out and have Batey appointed a director.

Focussing on his duties, Durban watched next opponents Luton win 3-0 at Leicester, before trying to reassure supporters that any boardroom power struggle would not interfere with his team's determination. Drawing on recent history, Durban reminded them, 'Aston Villa were the last big club to be in turmoil in the opening week of the season, and they went on to win the league.' The *Echo* reporter endorsed the manager's optimism, adding, 'The signs of a fairly successful side are clearly visible.'

The battered Bracewell had missed only one league match in the previous two seasons at Stoke (and that because of suspension), but was now ruled out. Durban commented, 'The team did not perform against Norwich; they were too apprehensive, and I do not want the team coming back from Luton under pressure.' But, that pressure was not averted as the team slumped to a 4-1 defeat, a first-half penalty save from Turner merely delaying matters. Durban dismissed notions of concern, 'There are what

I would call six or seven early-season sides. There is no real problem. We have two home games and we must make sure that we cash in.'

The boss was confident that his side would prove capable of exhibiting endurance over a long-distance season and, unlike the rebel shareholders, saw no reason to hit panic buttons, 'I do not want to be disrupting the side, but I may have to look about bringing Leighton back. I have spotted something which has crept into our game again and it will be nipped in the bud. People are getting themselves into wrong areas. We had a good pre-season but they should now be stepping up a gear.'

Trouble rumbled on as the club announced the forced extraordinary meeting would simply be held prior to the AGM at the end of November. The 'rebels' were unhappy about the delay, believing they had the right to an earlier arrangement and now claimed to have the support of 25 per cent of shareholders. Another unsettled figure, Elliott, was informed the only firm offer that the club had received was from Burnley managed by long-time admirer John Bond. A fee of £120,000 had been agreed, and the defender was tempted, 'I don't fancy dropping down into the Third Division but I have been offered a fabulous deal, and how long do you wait for a big club to come in' (implying that he was not already at 'big club').

As Durban prepared his squad for the upcoming matches against Wolves and Southampton, he would have to plan around Bracewell's fitness, 'Badly as I want him to play it would be folly to risk him. He has been told to have four or five days rest.' Taking the Burnley bid into consideration, Durban omitted Elliott, and recalled James as he realised that such an influential player could not be allowed to enter quasi-retirement. Although Durban maintained his long-term strategy for the club, as boardroom ructions spluttered on and the realities of top-flight survival hit home, he was pursuing some short-term gains, 'A win will do us the power of good.'

In his programme notes, Durban had scornfully observed 'the "doubting Thomases" are already having a field day', and the level of attendance was not an encouraging sign as less than 13,000 turned up to witness an eventful match. After the linesman signalled for a handball offence, Rowell comfortably beat John Burridge from the spot. The second half saw Sunderland go 2-0 up when a James cross was headed into his own net by Peter Daniel. Better was to come in the 75th minute as Proctor's vision released Atkinson in space on the left, and the rookie went on to arrow a low drive into the far corner. So far, so good. However, from this seemingly comfortable position, a disturbing level of frantic disorganisation was ignited after Towner headed past Turner. Hindmarch was introduced into the action but, rather than shoring up the situation, the rearguard appeared even shakier. Eves was left unchallenged as he headed in on 87 minutes, and the crowd were relieved to hear the final whistle.

Durban admitted that it was 'not the most relaxed performance', but later highlighted the disproportionate onus that had been attached to this early-season game, 'Many people stressed the "vital" nature of the match. We kept hearing how crucial it was to get three points – as if it was a life or death matter. It just made me think about the fishing trawler which sank off the north-east coast this week with the loss of three men. It's times like this that you must keep things in perspective. When we were under so much pressure to beat Wolves, it was important not to panic and stick to our beliefs. Fortunately, we did that and got the right result.'

The next day, Durban decided to offer defender Cole the opportunity to spend a further three months at the club, and the bank clerk served his notice to accept the offer, 'People who have worked before becoming a professional footballer appreciate it more, and have more determination to succeed.' As Durban prepared to welcome one central defender, another's future was in the balance as Burnley's Bond announced, 'I will meet my board of directors tonight and press my case for buying Elliott. I consider it an honour that a player of his calibre wants to come here.'

Having already reintroduced James to the starting line-up, Durban now reappraised the Pickering tactical switch, 'Though Nick was happy enough to give it a go, we will destroy him if we are not careful. We have played him wide on the right and though he managed to get a couple of efforts on goal I must try to fit him in on the left.' This did not augur well for the first-team future of skipper Munro as Durban indicated that the latest young prospect would have to survive without the shelter of an on-field chaperone, 'In trying to bring on Atkinson we have neglected Pickering. Atkinson will have to look after himself. We were very patchy at times last night and the balance is not right.'

While pleased to have recorded a win, Durban knew that things needed to be tightened up, 'We must start keeping clean sheets. We have conceded eight goals in four games and the fact that five of them have come late on suggests that we have lost a bit of discipline. We have got to show the will to get out of defence quicker and better.'

There was a familiar face in the Southampton number nine shirt for the next fixture, Frank Worthington commenting, 'I am looking forward to the match. The fans gave me a great reception in the last game and I am sure they will be pleased to see me. Sunderland have the makings of a good side.' In the *Roker Review*, Durban gladly reciprocated the sentiment, 'Nice to see Frank back. He only had a short stay with us but he made a vital contribution to our revival at a time when we were in a lot of trouble.' Mick Mills would also be visiting for the first time since the circus of his non-signing, but Durban did not wish to dwell on the episode, 'Once I had said my piece – the matter was closed.'

Bracewell returned and James moved to the bench. Although the home team had plenty of possession, it was Steve Moran who displayed the cutting edge with two goals midway through either half, his second being set up by a typical Worthington flick. James did raise the attacking threat when coming on for the last quarter, replacing Atkinson who had been shackled by Mills. Durban was defiant, insisting that sound principles would see them through in the long run, 'One defeat does not change the overall picture. That was a solid team performance. I am more convinced than ever that we are on the right lines. We are a fraction out. I could have played a sweeper, like Southampton did, but it would have been at the expense of one of the kids and I don't want to do that. You get your rewards believing in what you are doing, and I told the lads that in the dressing room.'

The manager had to concede that his team needed the inventiveness James supplied, 'We looked like turning our possession into goals when Leighton came on as he got more crosses into the danger area.' It was pointed out that the crowd of 12,716 was the day's lowest in the First Division, to which Durban responded, 'It would be easy for us to get relegated and the crowds to come back when we were going for promotion, but I would rather do it the hard way in the First Division.' That was a message that would prove to be relevant for many years.

Meanwhile, Durban waited to hear from Burnley about Elliott as their board of directors were split about the wisdom of spending a six-figure sum on one player – they would have found some kindred spirits in the Roker boardroom! Durban had grown accustomed to Bond's failure to complete any of the deals that had been set up between the pair, and Elliott also became frustrated as the move collapsed, 'Having made the decision to leave, I am very disappointed they have backed out. No one from Burnley told me.' Durban once again was rankled by Bond's tendency to filter news through the media, 'I am disappointed that I did not get to know first, but that is typical of what happens in football. It is now up to Shaun to be physically and mentally prepared when his chance comes again.'

Durban was cheered by England under-21 call-ups for Pickering and Bracewell, 'I am pleased to see Sunderland players regularly mentioned for internationals, and I looked for Chisholm in Scotland's squads.' Meanwhile, Sunderland were drawn against Cambridge United in the newly christened Milk Cup but the immediate difficulty facing the team would be playing on QPR's artificial pitch. The manager made arrangements for his squad to train on the synthetic surfaces at Bisham Abbey, and sponsors Nike supplied the squad with astro boots. But problems emerged as James suffered a gash to his right foot which required five stitches, and an ill Proctor only travelled after starting a course of antibiotics. To round things off, Munro suffered an injury on the training pitch, forcing Pickering to play at left-back.

At Loftus Road, there was a crucial 38th-minute incident when John Gregory went down and a penalty was awarded. Terry Fenwick converted despite Turner getting his hand to the ball. It was a turning point, and West later complained, 'It was never a penalty. Gregory ran across me and when he went down he just laughed. I told him he was a con man.' Sunderland pressed for an equaliser but were caught on the break as Simon Stainrod headed home and, five minutes from time, Clive Allen turned and fired in a superb 25-yarder. Durban realised the futility of pleading injustice, 'If you lose 1-0 to a disputed penalty and say you were unlucky, they might believe you, but when it's 3-0 it is hard to convince people.'

The following week, the message was that if the rebels wanted the chairman out then he would not be going quietly.

It was reported that Cowie was offering some people £200 for each £1 share. The *Echo* commented, 'Neutral shareholders have been "tapped", and there is no doubt at £200 there will be some movement.' Meanwhile, responding to criticism following four defeats in six games, Durban resisted the usual calls to spend, 'Buying is not the answer to our problems. It has been done before at this club but what happens is that you end up buying players that are available and not those you want.'

Durban firmly believed that his squad was strong enough to at least improve on the previous season's position, 'It is up to Bryan Robson and myself to come up with the answers.' The manager could not provide supporters with exciting transfer activity, but did remark on the consistency of the travelling fans who had just endured the defeat in London, 'Their loyalty is incredible. I met four or five when we stopped at Wetherby and they were not flat.'

## Sweeping Changes

It was 'cruel to be kind' time as Durban decided to withdraw Atkinson from the front line, but he sweetened the news with the offer of a full-time professional contract, 'We are going to give him a breather. I feel he is very much part of the first-team squad, but he will not be relieved of his apprentice duties. There is no question of his ability, but we are taking him out now for his own protection. I don't expect Paul to be out of the side for more than two or three weeks.' However, the young forward would start only one more match that season – three weeks is a long time in football.

Things were becoming heated off the pitch as the club insisted that any independent meeting held by shareholders would be invalid. The rebels countered by issuing a High Court writ to force the club's directors to attend, but events took a dramatic and decisive turn when former chairman Keith Collings and fellow director Peter Heyward tendered their resignations and, critically, announced they had sold their shares (Collings 364, Heyward 200) to an unnamed buyer. They commented that they did not feel they could support the dissident group, nor offer the chairman their backing.

The immediate suspicion that the mystery buyer was Cowie was confirmed the following day, and this unexpected massive increase in his shareholding forced the rebel group to concede defeat, a club statement declaring, 'The matter involving the requisitioning shareholders has been amicably settled.' This prompted questions about the nature of such a settlement, suggesting that a policy of appeasement had been employed with Batey being offered one of the director vacancies.

As his team prepared to entertain Coventry, Durban tried to divert attention away from the boardroom, 'We must forget about directors and get on with the game. Our supporters were magnificent at QPR, and it was the best away support I have ever seen. All I am interested in tomorrow is that they come and support us again. We can't go on saying the side is playing well, and keep losing.' The manager revealed that a tight formation would be adopted, but that nobody should interpret it as a negative step, 'We will play with a sweeper, which is not necessarily defensive. A team attacks, and then defends, whatever the system.' To make the plan work, Durban had one crucial creative card to play – Leighton James, 'You can teach people what to do but not when to do it, and Leighton's timing is first-class.'

The lowest league gate for five years (11,612) saw a familiar face making his debut in the Coventry defence. Sam Allardyce had signed from Millwall and was pitched straight in against his former club. During the match, Venison in particular brought James into play with a series of raking cross-field passes. In the 53rd minute, a well-worked short corner saw the mercurial Welshman take a return pass from Proctor and cross to the far post for Rowell to head back across goal where West got clear of the attention of Allardyce to apply a finishing header from a couple of yards. A first clean sheet of the season was preserved when Turner rushed out to dive bravely at the feet of Gerry Daly as the midfielder broke through. The combative Bracewell added to his battle scars as he had two stitches applied to a leg wound and, still smarting from his gashed foot, James came off nursing a bruised cheekbone.

Durban focussed the spotlight on goalscorer West who had been on the receiving end of recent terrace criticism, 'We look as though we have found somebody else who will get us double figures apart from Rowell. Centre-forwards should be judged at the end of the season. He battles and gets goals, and that's what will win the fans over.'

West's tenacity helped Durban decide to drop out of the race for 32-year-old striker David Cross who was available following the end of the NASL season, 'I have been in touch, but there were one or two problems too many.' In a convoluted process, the club would have had to buy Cross for a fee then sell him back to Vancouver in March, 'I am hanging my hat on Westie. He is a typical old-fashioned centre-forward and his record of 12 goals in 39 matches is not too bad. It all depends on how ambitious he is and how hard he works. There is a history of centre-forwards getting goals and crowds not taking to them.' Durban might have added the conundrum of a manager eking out a series of good results and the fans not appreciating it – and not flocking to the stadium.

Although satisfied with a 1-0 victory, Durban acknowledged there was an imbalance when playing the sweeper system, and an over-reliance on James, 'There is no future in playing like that unless we play someone wide on the right.' Durban also complained about 'not enough players alert in the box and not enough gamblers.' So, why had James not been playing all along? Durban stressed that the player had not been railroaded into the coaching side, 'Leighton is responsible for the youth team through the week and is preparing for his future. I have never underestimated what he can do for us as a player. He crossed enough quality balls for us to win three games.'

Amid the manager's praise for Turner was a riposte at detractors, 'I think he is possibly the quickest reaction goalkeeper in the league and you can say what you like about not scoring goals, we must keep clean sheets if we are to be successful.'

## Treachery from the Top

Once again, another interview given by the chairman dominated the *Echo*'s back page. This time, Cowie speculated, 'There is no guarantee that if Kevin Keegan had come to Sunderland the crowds would have flocked back. We need new talent.' In a dramatically fresh tack, he intimated an awareness that flair players were necessary to attract crowds and that high wages would have to be paid. But, he insisted that he was not the bad guy and was actively looking for the manager to build a flair team, 'Very few people in football put money into the club themselves. I would only do it if it guaranteed success.'

It seemed remarkable, given the scrimping approach that had repeatedly reduced Durban to an embarrassing amount of haggling over relatively small fees, that Cowie claimed he was giving his manager the go-ahead to spend money on a player who would excite the fans. But, the hard-boiled businessman wanted assurances of success, and no manager in the world could give that type of 'guarantee' on a player's impact. What Cowie appeared to desire was to find a 'big-name' player available for no transfer fee allowing the club to lavish the requisite fat pay-packet. But players of that ilk, available on frees, were almost non-existent. Cowie had observed the 'Keegan effect', and now appeared to be speculating in hindsight – a case of 'look at what you could have won'!

The comments were put to the manager, who calmly reflected, 'We all love flair players but it is a question of getting them. We signed one last season in Frank, and gates did not improve appreciably. There are only three or four players in the country capable of making a big impact on attendances.' Durban had tried to secure the services of one that fitted the bill, Craig Johnston, but his bid to bring the all-action Keegan-style player to Roker had always appeared destined to fail.

The press conveyed that the general consensus among fans was that a striker was needed, and a cup run to lure back the missing thousands, 'It would make a marvellous break from another relegation fight.' Durban always placed onus on cup ties; his attitude on that score could not be called into question. As for a striker, it would take a massive fee to secure a forward of sufficient stature to satisfy the baying fans (and chairman). Durban urged doubters to keep faith and give West the time his level of commitment warranted, 'It is very hard up there; which is proved by the fact that all the big money is spent on front people.'

In one move beyond Durban's control, Batey was appointed to the board of directors. The 37-year-old property businessman, who was not averse to providing press fodder, stated, 'I feel I can give more to the club in the boardroom than standing in the Fulwell End.' Greater influence could be exerted that was for sure, and the fear was that there might be dire consequences for the manager before the season was out.

## Victory at Anfield: Is that Stylish Enough for You?

As the participants in the grand boardroom waltz paused for breath, Durban prepared his team to do a job at Anfield. The manager reflected on their previous visit which had been narrowly lost, 'The lads felt very badly done to last year, but having got so close it will give them a lot of confidence.' Tinkering was being considered, 'We lack pace in the side and I will be having a look at the reserves tonight. What we produced against Coventry will not be good enough and I expect to make a change.' The boss also mentioned an experiment that would be conducted in that reserve match, 'Munro will play at right-back as we have no cover for Venison.' The boss also acknowledged Elliott's determination to win a recall.

The reserves lost 5-4 at home to Stoke, thus stifling at birth the 'Munro at right-back' experiment. With no defender emerging with any great credit, Durban concentrated on other tactical options, 'We had a problem last week in that Pickering did not get forward enough, and a full-back has got to do that for the sweeper system to be effective.' The recent jibes from chairman and fans merely served to fire up the Sunderland boss, 'I am looking forward to going to Anfield. We have taken a bit of stick for not having any flair players, but when we are playing well we play with plenty of flair. Leighton James is a flair player; Nick Pickering is a flair player on his day, and Mark Proctor should be a flair player. He has got to go out and take more responsibility for 90 minutes.'

Saturday, 1 October was a landmark for Durban's managerial reign at Sunderland. He made one change to the team that had defeated Coventry as Elliott replaced Hindmarch. In the dressing room, Gary Rowell recalls that Durban jovially offered his troops one of his favourite extra incentives for gaining a superb result; that he would book an end-of-season trip to Spain for them (their boss required no encouragement where jetting off to the sun was concerned).

The Liverpool team they faced that day was: Grobbelaar, Nicol, Kennedy, Lawrenson, Johnston, Hansen, Dalglish, Lee,

Rush, Robinson, Souness, sub Hodgson. The breakthrough moment came in the 29th minute after a careless Hansen back-pass conceded a corner. When James drifted the ball to the far post, West headed it back into the danger area where Chisholm eventually got in a telling header that was prevented from going into the top corner by the diving Johnston's fist. After waiting for Johnston to be booked, Rowell coolly sent Grobbelaar the wrong way from the penalty spot.

Sunderland set about withstanding the intense Liverpool pressure that ensued. Atkins, adapting to the dual load of sweeper and captain, commanded his backline superbly, and the final whistle produced exhilaration and a sense of achievement for manager, players, and supporters. Durban led his players to salute the loyal fans who had encouraged them throughout, and then found their endeavour being applauded by home supporters too. It was a vindication of one of Durban's fundamental principles, 'We've an honest squad at Roker, and that honesty will get us more points.' New captain Atkins expressed the thoughts of the camp, 'We have been threatening to do it all season in patches. I just hope that the result takes some of the pressure off the younger lads.'

Rowell's only penalty miss had come at Orient in January 1978. Commenting on his fine record, the striker made it sound absurdly simple, 'I just concentrate hard, take my time, and I always believe that I will score.' Rowell possessed that indefinable temperament that kept him 'stepping up to the plate' for his team, 'You have got to be confident of scoring from the penalty spot. I would not hesitate to take another one should I miss. But that was a great team performance and the lads battled all the way.' His boss was confident that goals from free play would soon come for his prime striker, 'We'll be all right once Gary gets going but I thought he showed a lot of skill on Saturday. He has got an unusual technique but the only penalty kick I am concerned about is the next one.'

The back-up penalty taker, James, had again underscored his indispensability to the manager, 'We had hoped to be able to do without him but it showed we couldn't. He has proved that he has still got a lot to offer. It was premature to write himself off, but all sensible professionals start preparing for the future when they reach 30. He is so active and wants to be occupied all day.' The player recalls that Pop Robson was one person who recognised 'the method in my madness' and the potential benefits to be gleaned by the youngsters. Durban added that Atkinson's pre-season scoring form had seemed to promise 'just what we were looking for' but, for 'quality and experience', he asserted, 'I don't think there can have been a better free-transfer bargain than Leighton.' There were few who would have disagreed.

Prior to the Milk Cup first leg, Durban again stressed the importance he attached to providing some cup cheer, 'The match at Cambridge is more important to the club than last week's win at Liverpool. We have had them watched, and have to match their work rate first then hope class will tell.' The Cambridge line-up included former Roker midfielder Tom Finney and 17-year-old Andy Sinton. The boss saw his team build a 3-0 lead through Rowell (two) and West, but the home side scored two late goals which tarnished the performance, 'We were unprofessional to say the least. One or two of them just stopped running, and will be very lucky not to be playing in the reserves at Burnley; the back four got into an awful mess.'

There was time to work on ironing out some of the defensive follies as there would be no First Division matches that weekend due to England playing Hungary in a Euro qualifier in Budapest. England captain Bryan Robson had been canvassing for the return of an experienced game changer, 'Keegan could have a major influence on our chances. Kevin is the man for the job.' Voicing this opinion earned the player a stern rebuke from his fellow north-easterner, Bobby Robson issuing a terse 'I'll pick the team' message to his captain.

Durban's own top midfielder had also been expressing a firm opinion on being moved from his favoured central position, but Bracewell's comments were certainly not a sign of pique, 'I am not happy playing like an outside-right. It is not the position I was bought to play but am prepared to carry on as the most important thing is that we are winning. I just hope the boss can buy a winger as soon as possible; but I realise he is not in a position to spend much cash.' In fact, the statement constituted a plea from the loyal midfielder, applying some emotional pressure on the club's executives to help the team improve by backing the judgement of his manager.

Three consecutive victories had been earned, and Robson pondered whether this would prove to be a season turning point, 'A lot depends on where we go from here, but they have worked very hard and I felt that we were on the right wavelength and only needed the results to prove the point.' Robson went on to underline what, regrettably, would prove to be the crux of how their managerial regime would be prematurely judged, 'We are a young team and you have got to be patient, but I am afraid there is not much patience in football and that has spread to the players.' The coach's comments on the contribution expected from the squad had a familiar ring, 'I would like to see more goalscorers; other players should be getting goals, but we need Leighton's experience and crossing ability.'

## Trying to Consolidate

The team's improved run and promising blend had placed a question mark over the future of club captain Munro. Durban could not offer a great deal of hope for an early return to first-team duty, but made it plain that he was in no rush to usher a loyal lieutenant out of the door, emphasising the admirable standards that Munro maintained, 'Iain is not the sort of person to sit back and be inactive. He is prepared to take responsibilities that other players don't and still contributes greatly to the week-to-week running of the side. There are a lot of thankless jobs at a football club, especially when things are not going well, but Iain never ducks an issue.'

Following the unwelcome sale of McCoist, one thing that Durban would not be allowing was the loss of another of his prime young assets. He revealed that three clubs had made inquiries regarding Pickering's availability, 'I have nipped them in the bud. They really wanted to find out if I rate him as highly as they do – and I believe he is a major part of Sunderland's future.' On the subject of McCoist, Durban elaborated on his thinking, 'I didn't want to sell him, but he and Rowell duplicated the same position. I never felt they would gel together as a pair.' The bottom line, however, was that Durban would have gladly kept McCoist (no matter who he temporarily did not gel with) if he had been backed with the funds to sign Bracewell.

The next major development was one that appeared to promise the manager an influx of extra cash to spend as it was announced that the name of the chairman's auto company ('Cowies') would appear on the front of team shirts as part of a sponsorship deal. Yet, the financial details were not disclosed; so would the manager's transfer market bargaining power be increased or not? As far as many supporters were concerned, the club had just got rid of a generally unpopular home jersey, and now the new acceptable one would be 'adorned' with the name of an unpopular chairman.

Many wished to know the degree of expenditure that Cowie was committing himself to in return for enjoying the privilege. Nevertheless, it was a done deal and work had already commenced on embroidering the company emblem on to the shirts which would receive their first airing against Stoke. It seemed that no stone was being left unturned to generate extra income as several players undertook short stints at the ticket office, Durban indicating that every little helped, 'It could prove an incentive for a couple of hundred fans.'

Ever vigilant to strengthen the squad, Durban had sent James to check on the form of a former team-mate, out-of-favour Swansea forward Alan Curtis. However, a preliminary valuation of £150,000 for the Welsh international killed progress, 'I know what we want but at present there is no possibility of any business.' With no deals in the offing, Durban focussed on the visit of his former team with a familiar warning for his players, 'If anyone fails to pick up the importance of the match in training they will be in trouble.'

Durban's desire to field an unchanged line-up remained on despite Bracewell returning from England duty with heavy bruising, 'Looking at his leg he must have done all the tackling for the team. We have won our last three games and all I ask is the fans get behind the lads. It is imperative that we approach the game in identical fashion as we did Liverpool.'

Fewer than 12,000 were at Roker Park for the game. Steve Bould wore the Stoke number two shirt and Dennis Tueart was their unused substitute. In the 26th minute, a James shot took a heavy deflection to be recorded as a Thomas own goal, but Stoke's close-season signing Robbie James quickly hit home a fierce drive. On 49 minutes, Rowell notched one of the most spectacular goals of his career with a scorching half-volley into the roof of the net at the Fulwell End, but Sunderland were denied victory when James grabbed his second with a firm header.

Durban was left frustrated, 'It was unfortunate that Rowell's tremendous goal wasn't the match winner. We are still too inconsistent, even in 90 minutes. We have been through all this before. It was no consolation that it was the best game here this season. We were a bit dozy at the back which put us on edge. It is entirely due to lack of concentration which never happens when we are under constant pressure at places like Liverpool. That is something we are trying to put right.' But, Durban did push the merits of one of his defenders, 'Right-back is the position I can see an opening in the England side. Venison has done very well for us and though I feel he prefers to get further forward he has not utilised it as well as Pickering. He needs more belief in himself, and that would come if the side grew in confidence.'

Questioned about another low attendance, Durban diplomatically assumed the bulk of the responsibility on behalf of his team, 'We have got to earn the right to get the supporters back. We have not done enough. We are unbeaten in four games, but still only have the same number of points as at this stage last season. You are not given many things in football – you have to earn them. The fans will come back if they are getting value for money.' However, the manager was adamant that an overall improvement should be recognised, 'We are slowly losing the tag of continually fighting for survival and now have a more settled side, but we have got to make the young lads more ambitious. The side has to become more successful for the players to chase honours at international level.'

Next up were table-toppers Manchester United who had just played a midweek European Cup Winners' Cup tie in Belgium. This was the busy, successful agenda that Durban aspired to emulate, 'Let's hope we have the problem fairly soon, but the lads are looking forward to the chance.' The stakes would be raised by the inevitable larger attendance that accompanied such 'showpiece' games, 'There should be another 12–14,000 who have not been before this season and this is an opportunity to keep them. There can't now be any fear after winning the hardest fixture of the season at Liverpool. I have kept the same side and I am fairly happy. It is a big day for us as we have a super chance of exciting our missing fans.'

On the day, a BBC outside broadcast dispute meant that many were denied their first chance to see the team on TV that season as the planned *Match of the Day* broadcast had to be scrapped. Prior to the game, Durban offered solace to Steve Coppell who had retired from playing after failing to recover from the knee injury he had sustained at Roker in April, 'I played recently in a testimonial match at Derby alongside David Nish, whose career was also ended by a knee injury. David, after a long rest, now feels fine.'

An attendance of 26,826 represented an increase of almost 15,000 but they saw the team toil, and suffered further as Wilkins converted a controversial 19th-minute penalty, awarded against Elliott for an alleged push on Stapleton. Elliott later claimed it was the Eire international who had backed into him and conned the referee. Five minutes later, in the opposite penalty area, Macari's trip on James went unpunished. Speaking in the immediate aftermath of a sterile display, Durban acknowledged that his side had struggled to create opportunities, 'We were solid but unspectacular. We needed a break but didn't get one. We are now controlling games for longer periods but not converting that superiority into goals. In moving Pickering back we have lost a goalscorer, and the next signing has got to be a proven goalscorer.'

The conundrum of whether sacrificing the dynamic impact of Pickering's marauding midfield surges was an acceptable trade-off for the attributes he brought to the left-back berth had been deliberated many times. It was a question of which of Pickering's qualities Durban wished to prioritise, but the manager seemed torn and it was easy to regret the role deployed following a disappointing result.

An interested spectator at this match was Jimmy Nicholl who was pondering an offer to join Glasgow Rangers. Durban was not in the hunt for the international this season, partly put off by the fractured nature of deals involving players who insisted on continuing their contracts in the NASL. The player offered his impression of the current formation, 'Sunderland have lost a man up front by playing five at the back and there is a responsibility now for everyone to weigh in with goals.' Sunderland had boasted a lopsided corner-count and Durban was perturbed, 'We should have shown a better return from 13 corners. When you have one of the best in the country in Leighton taking most of them there must be something wrong when you can't make them count.'

The sweeper system would be temporarily shelved for the midweek cup tie as Pop Robson reported that Atkins would be ruled out with a hamstring strain, 'Ian has been so confident in doing the sweeper's job, he will be missed. I cannot see us bringing somebody else to do it as we would be too left-sided.' Expanding on Durban's lament over the failure to capitalise on a glut of corner kicks, Robson observed, 'Everyone is so much more professional these days. They have set-pieces off pat, so it is up to us to get some variation.' One message was constant, however, 'You can't expect two players to do all the scoring.'

Bracewell captained the team and Cooke was selected ahead of Atkinson. This seemed a strange move as Durban had stated that Atkinson would probably only be omitted for 'two or three weeks', and this game against Cambridge seemed to represent the ideal opportunity to give the young prospect a whirl. Instead, the boss focussed on Elliott's bid to win back a central defensive slot, but the incentive he issued also contained a barbed punchline, 'It gives Elliott the opportunity to show how good he is; or, just how much he and Chisholm have lived off Atkins.'

A paltry crowd of 9,059 saw an end-to-end game that resulted in Sunderland increasing their overall advantage with a 4-3 win. The Sheffield Wednesday management team of Wilkinson and

Eustace were in attendance, rumoured to be checking on Cooke. The following day, Durban expressed concern over the abundance of goalmouth incident, 'I have never seen so many efforts on goal from one of my sides in the first half. There were too many holes at the back. I enjoyed last night's match but Nottingham Forest will be a different proposition. Defence, in the long run, is best in the First Division.'

The team had looked vulnerable without Atkins and it appeared that the manager would be reimplementing the sweeper system at Forest. Durban also revealed that the players had spent three hours working on set-pieces in Monday's training sessions, but plans to continue the theme had to be postponed, 'I wanted the players in again today but Leighton, who can cross the ball just where he likes, has a problem on the back of the knee which keeps flaring up.' Being drawn away at Norwich in the next round of the cup was greeted grudgingly, 'I can think of better places; but if you want to make progress you have got to win ties like this.'

For the weekend, Durban would have to cope without two of his most influential players, Atkins and James, but still planned to revert to five at the back, 'We will be using the sweeper system, probably with Chisholm doing Atkins's job.' Durban was keen to boost the influence he felt Proctor was capable of wielding, and an apt time would be the midfielder's return to Forest, 'Despite Cloughie's disenchantment with the lad, he missed very few games. In the last two weeks, Mark has been playing with more freedom and confidence. Hopefully, he will get more goals. He is approaching 200 league appearances and still only 22. I believe players are nowhere near their prime until they are 25.'

On the eve of the match, news came from Scotland that, after a disappointing run, Rangers manager John Greig had stepped down from his post. McCoist had not been able to find his 'goalden' touch, and Greig was another man under pressure for instant results. It was a bad evening for high-profile casualties as John Toshack quit the Swansea hot seat.

At the City Ground, Durban's former transfer target Thijssen (another Vancouver player to be snapped up) gave Forest the lead on 28 minutes. Turner was also forced into crucial saves from Wallace and Steve Hodge. At this point, a disturbed Durban came down from his seat in the stand to join Robson in the dugout, later remarking, 'We were awful and never put three passes together. In fact, we looked as if we expected to go a goal down.'

Durban proceeded to deliver a half-time verbal lashing. There was a response, and Rowell squeaked in a 62nd-minute equaliser from an acute angle. A useful point was earned and, after his earlier anger, the manager was appreciative of his players, 'They worked very hard and I thought we battled well for our point.' The team had only had Friday to work on Chisholm's deployment as sweeper, but the defensive unit had performed a sterling job which Durban believed demonstrated squad solidarity, 'It would have been a disaster to have gambled on Atkins. We have got as much togetherness as anyone in the league and, what's more, we will retain it as the season gets longer while others crumble.'

## Fireworks ('Blockbusters')

A 5 November trip to Highbury beckoned, and the encounter would be given some extra spice by the fact it was Arsenal who were making overtures for Pickering, dangling a player-exchange possibility as bait to test Durban's resolve. After two years at Roker, Durban at last felt that the club had attained a position of strength, and his reaction to the speculation was dismissive, 'I am not looking for a deal, whether it is part exchange or not. We are not in a desperate situation to sell any of our better players.'

In fact, Sunderland seemed more likely to delve into the market as a straight-cash buyer. The departure of Toshack from

Swansea had highlighted the Welsh club's financial woes and the consequent need to unload their higher wage earners. This urgency meant that fees for their players would not be as inflated as previously quoted, 'If Rowell or West got injured we would have to look at contingency players. Latchford and Curtis are just two of a number we know we can go to.' It seemed remarkable, that Latchford could be rejected as too much of as an ageing 'gamble' at only 30 in the summer of 1981, but was considered a feasible option over two years later.

Any prospect of a transfer foray soon faded, however, as Durban re-emphasised his far-sighted ideal scenario for recruitment, 'There were only three players in the side at Nottingham for whom we paid money – the rest having come through the ranks.' The three in question were Turner, Bracewell, and Proctor with a combined fee of around £400,000. Durban hammered home his point, 'It is indicative that no matter how much money you spend you keep coming back to local lads for the basis of your side.' How this policy stacked up with his chairman's fluctuating stated desires was a moot point. Previously, Cowie had mused on a team comprising of eleven local-born players, but there was also his recent contradictory 'request' for his manager to sign 'flair players' – but only those who 'guaranteed success'!

The chairman and fans only had to look to their own club's history to see that their big-spending years in the 1950s may have provided some attractive play and high-profile signings but, amid all the glitz, the various line-ups achieved relatively little for the outlay. A couple of seasons that featured brief dalliances with the upper reaches of the league, and an FA Cup semi-final appearance; yes, that seemed quite desirable right now, but how long would it be before the vocal minority (in the boardroom and on the terraces) became dissatisfied with a lack of silverware? A couple of years?

In fact, for the approaching visit to Highbury, it was the fitness of a simple free-transfer signing that preoccupied the thoughts of the manager. The presence of Leighton James often set the keynote of the team's performance; X-rays to the player's knee had revealed no serious damage but it was responding only slowly to treatment, 'I am struggling. I think it must be wear and tear.' While his team-mates were earning a point at Forest, James had been on a watching brief at Villa Park as Arsenal had recorded a 6-2 win, 'It was the first time I had seen Arsenal this season and I was very impressed. They started with the sweeper system but became much more adventurous. Tony Woodcock only had five efforts all afternoon and he put them all away. Charlie Nicholas is a great player who has a lot of skill and it is only a matter of time before he starts scoring goals.' Ominously, Arsenal had also beaten Forest 4-1 in a recent home match.

Hot on the heels of being linked with Pickering, Arsenal boss Terry Neill inflamed matters as he boasted, 'Beware our double-edged sword [Woodcock and Nicholas]. The way we are playing we are easily capable of scoring six again on Saturday.' It was careless talk from Neill, and Durban calmly remarked, 'I am very interested to see that he feels it necessary to warn us. It has motivated me, and I am sure that it will have the same effect on the players. We have a good record in London, and Arsenal in particular, and when players are used to getting a result at certain grounds they look forward to going there.' After ten games, Sunderland sat in 17th position in the league with 12 points; behind Everton on goal difference, and with a six-point buffer between themselves and third-from-bottom Notts County.

That week saw the release of the club's annual accounts which revealed an overall loss for the year of £76,142 (this would have been a small profit but for the expenditure on the Roker End repairs). Meanwhile, Durban felt able to do Mick Docherty a favour as he permitted keeper Prudhoe to join Hartlepool on a month's loan, with 17-year-old Paul Thornton taking over in goal for the Roker reserves.

Before travelling to Arsenal, Durban was confident that his two kingpins, Atkins and James, would be available to enable him to field a 'full-strength' line-up. The manager was also trying to cajole one of his midfield recruits to find the higher gear he knew was there, 'Defensively, Proctor had his best game for us on Saturday, but has a lot more to offer. He did well at closing Forest down, but I want to see him surging forward more with the ball – he has got tremendous strength. We are continually working on him to play with the same freedom he expressed at Middlesbrough, but you can't expect him to do it all in a couple of months.'

The team that took to the field at Highbury were indeed boosted by the return of Atkins and James and, in only the third minute, James won the ball and laid it off to West; the big man astounded the crowd as he cut inside to lash a 25-yard drive wide of Jennings. Turner denied the home team's big-money signing Nicholas with a magnificent save before Sunderland gave themselves a little breathing space after 56 minutes when Atkins turned Chisholm's knock-down into the net. The extra advantage proved short-lived as Woodcock soon cracked home a fierce shot. Arsenal pressed, but it was the visitors who almost added a third when a West lay-off presented Rowell with an opportunity only for Jennings to thwart the striker.

The appraisal in the *Echo* report endorsed the manager's point about teamwork, 'What they may lack in flair is more than compensated with whole-hearted effort and application.' Durban pinpointed one other crucial factor to the team's critics, 'I would like us to play like Arsenal but we have not got their players. We have got to play to a system which suits us, and our results are proving it.'

Highbury had been a recent happy hunting-ground for Colin West, 'Leighton did well to win the ball and knock it to me. I saw that Jennings had left a big gap at the far post so I decided to have a go, although I had no idea I was that far out.' The centre-forward recalled the goal's similarity to the vital winner he had struck there in May, 'Last season's had to mean more because of the importance, but it is always a great feeling when you score goals like that.'

Retaining his combative tone, Durban rapped, 'You don't win three away matches and draw the fourth through luck alone. Our goalkeeper remarked that in the second half he only had two on-target shots to deal with as the back four block-tackled so well.' If the opening goal had been exquisite, the second represented a slice of fortune twice over. Atkins admitted he had been trying to get out of the way of Chisholm's header, 'but the ball hit me *on the arm* and went in'.

In a fine win against a form team, Pickering and James had shone, but the manager spotlighted Bracewell, 'There is not a better uncapped midfield player in the country. If 'star' players had his workrate and commitment they would become world-beaters.' Gary Rowell recalls his own early impression, 'Brace was excellent. As soon as he joined we knew he was going to be a good player.'

Durban's squad had to quickly refocus for their midweek Milk Cup tie, 'A win over Norwich would mean more to us than the result at Liverpool and Arsenal. We desperately need a good cup run – that is the one thing that will bring the crowds back.' At times, it appeared that Durban underestimated the general satisfaction and pleasure derived by a large section of loyal supporters from gaining impressive league victories and keeping clear of relegation bother. Unfortunately, the majority could be drowned out by the noisy minority who were fickle and required the transient glitter of cup progress.

While Durban glibly stated that the team was 'only three wins away from a semi-final', Rowell commented, 'when I heard we had to go to Norwich again I thought what a lousy draw. But we are a more solid side and are becoming very difficult to beat.' The striker's next remark showed that the squad's sentiments were attuned with their boss, 'I just wish people would start giving us some credit after our recent performances instead of comparing us with Newcastle.' Rowell also believed that he and West were 'settling down as a partnership', and he explicitly stated what many others were thinking, 'Leighton should have been in since the start. I think he made a mistake by putting too much emphasis on the coaching side when he still has so much to offer as a player. His crossing of the ball is still top class.'

On a foggy East Anglian night, a 0-0 draw was ground out at Carrow Road. Turner had been returning to the scene of the skull injury he suffered seven months earlier, 'They tested me in the first minute with a high ball and, after the match, Keith Bertschin said, "Well done."' His manager had noted the significance, 'Chris made a positive move which set the whole pattern.' Mick Channon had the temerity to accuse Sunderland of adopting negative tactics, and declared that Norwich 'would never go away and play like that'. The irony of the outburst was not lost on Durban; Channon had not been present the previous year when the teams met at the same stage and the boss enlightened the former England man, 'It was exactly what they did to us.' Following a discussion between Durban and Batey, the Sunderland party decided not to risk travelling in the fog-bound conditions, and overnight accommodation was hastily arranged.

Competition for places was now keen, and when press reports linked him with a move for Ipswich's £750,000-rated Wark, Durban coolly responded, 'We have lost only one game in the last eight and I am not interested in bringing anyone in.' Whatever his demeanour for the press, Durban was definitely keen if there was a chance of acquiring a player of Wark's proven quality. The midfielder had been transfer-listed along with Mariner, and was someone adept at fulfilling Durban's brief to be adventurous in the opposing penalty area.

As he prepared for the visit of Watford, Durban spoke about the vagaries of adopting a sweeper system, 'I don't think we have learnt to play with a lot of freedom and we must be looking for an improvement. The system suits us better in away games. Only Ian Atkins really comes out of defence.' The old 'one game at a time' philosophy would come into play, 'We must be careful not to mess about in the two home league games while thinking about the cup replay.'

Durban's team certainly did not 'mess about' as they gave their most dominant performance for years in a rousing 3-0 triumph. A crowd of 15,407 saw the following line-up do their manager proud: Turner, Venison, Pickering, Atkins, Chisholm, Hindmarch, Bracewell, Rowell, West, Proctor, James. Sunderland took the lead on 26 minutes with a finely worked effort. James whipped a telling cross past Pat Rice to pick out Rowell lurking at the far post and his intelligent header across the six-yard box was emphatically finished by the lunging West. The second half got off to an eventful start as Pickering headed off the line from George Reilly's flick to a Nigel Callaghan inswinging corner, and Sunderland's next foray brought them a second goal when James (yet again) marauded inside to cross for Proctor to head past Sherwood.

As the team purred into top gear, Chisholm got forward to crack a shot against the foot of the post. Minutes later, it was Proctor's turn to rue his luck as his piledriver hit the inside of the upright but stayed out. Much of this frustration was eased in the 72nd minute when a James corner was met powerfully by Chisholm who made sure of his first goal of the season with a thumping header. With about ten minutes remaining, James recalls seeing Nigel Walker preparing to come on as substitute and being dismayed to see the '11' board being hoisted. He ran over to where Durban stood in front of the Clock Stand, querying 'Why me?' His boss simply gestured towards the stands, saying, 'Do you hear that applause. It's for you. We would not be winning 3-0 if it wasn't for your contribution. If you stay on, you will be *part* of a standing ovation, but if you walk off now, you'll receive an ovation *devoted to you*.' James concedes that this 'stage-exit' philosophy had never previously occurred to him during his long career.

It had been an exhilaratingly cohesive team performance, with Chisholm and Proctor displaying the desire to push forward that their manager had long advocated. James had been instrumental in all the goals, 'If he gets enough of the ball he is a match winner.' West would be celebrating his 21st birthday on Sunday and he was one player whose steely determination had been evident from the outset. This was a mood that the crowd had responded to, 'I couldn't have wished for a better occasion – the supporters were terrific, the team won well, and I scored.' The centre-forward's impressive all-round show would stick in the mind of Watford boss Graham Taylor when he was hunting for a new striker a couple of years later.

Durban was pleased about a display that had oozed confidence and fluency, and had also detected the upsurge of emotion from the stands, 'If we are going to be any good then we must produce performances like that weekly, not annually. For the first time since I came to the club I felt genuine warmth for the players from all parts of the ground.' He elaborated on some of the tactical elements that were gelling, 'We have been working on Chisholm for set-pieces. I now want to see him getting forward more in general play. Bracewell and Proctor have a thankless task sharing the difficult role on the right-hand side, but they have compromised and it is working well.'

Stay-away or far-flung Sunderland fans had not enjoyed the chance to see the team's improvement on TV as the regional highlights programme *Shoot* had been discontinued that season. Armchair viewers tuning in to the Sunday afternoon sports broadcast now offered by Tyne Tees Television (*Extra Time* hosted by Derek Thompson) had to settle for an artistic impression of birthday-boy West's opening goal as studio guest Chris Stevens recreated the striker's header on canvas. The artist recalls that he 'attended all the home matches' but, as mentioned, portraits were kept to a minimum. He did strike up friendships with some players, however, and made an exception to the rule when requested to produce a painting of Chris Turner's young child.

Stevens also retains fond memories of another friendly character, 'Leighton James was good fun although he did write on one of my drawings I had made of him bending over. I didn't mind that at all, I think it increased the value.'

Sunderland were not the only squad to have been granted a couple of days off, and Ally McCoist spent a day back at Sunderland's training ground, keen to keep in trim and visit familiar haunts. Back in Scotland, the striker had toiled to amass 11 league and cup goals that term, and it would still be a couple of years before his potential would start to be fully realised. There was no disguising McCoist's affinity for what turned out to be his only English team, 'My two years at Sunderland were an important part of my career – the experience I gained here has proved invaluable. I am delighted that they are doing so well as I believed it was only a matter of time. I am pleased for the manager and the boys.'

McCoist then spoke candidly about the two leagues, 'The big difference between the [Scottish] Premier League and the

[English] First Division is that the players down here are better.' Now there was a blunt observation that would ignite contention if uttered in the wrong company!

Intriguingly, the mauling that Sunderland had inflicted on his team, sparked Watford to make a double swoop in the transfer market. Frustratingly for Durban, this 'unfashionable' club had the resources to meet Blackpool's valuation for right-back prospect Bardsley. Durban did not enjoy the benefit of a piano-playing chairman or, in fact, a chairman who retained faith that his manager was 'special'.

Of more spectacular impact for Watford was the £200,000 invested to bring striker Maurice Johnston from Partick Thistle. It only took Johnston a couple games before he started a prolific run, and a 20-goal haul helped his new team climb well away from the relegation zone as well as reaching that season's FA Cup Final (a game in which Bardsley also played). Unlike McCoist, Johnston hit the ground running after his move from Scotland, but it should be recalled that Johnston was a 20-year-old with a couple of season's experience, scoring 41 goals in 85 appearances in the Scottish First Division (a league higher than McCoist had been playing).

## Damp Squibs ('Blankety Blank')

In midweek, Wales had been beaten 1-0 in Bulgaria, and Durban pressed the claims of the player who had been contributing so much to his own team's revival, 'Get James back in the side to beat Yugoslavia even if it is only for half an hour. Since Steve Coppell finished there is not a more dangerous wide man in the country over a short period. If I wanted a sparkle I would look no further than Leighton. He can play in any area of the field, and his perception in playing balls inside the full-back is brilliant. Few have both qualities.'

Sunderland would stay at home for an attractive-looking encounter against West Ham, but Durban reported that there was a question mark hanging over Rowell, 'Gary has been a bit under the weather and if he fails to make it, I will have no qualms in bringing in Pop. He has not lost anything, and there are no problems concerning his level of fitness. Considering that he is playing, coaching, and scouting, it is remarkable.' The manager also hoped to encourage more followers, 'Our confidence has soared and I just want that confirming tomorrow, then the crowd will get behind us and we will take some beating.' However, his counterpart, John Lyall, planned to impede the home team's vigour, 'We will concentrate on a solid defensive display and rely on quick breaks.'

The attendance fell just short of the 20,000 mark, and they saw Rowell take his place against the league front-runners who lined up: Parkes, Stewart, Lampard, Walford, Martin, Devonshire, Whitton, Cottee, Swindlehurst, Brooking, Pike. One significant moment came in the 31st minute when the referee took no action when Ray Stewart brought down James only minutes after the Scottish international right-back had picked up a booking for another foul on Sunderland's danger man. Allowed to remain on the pitch, it was Stewart who launched the long throw in the 82nd minute from which Atkins's clearing header fell nicely for Swindlehurst, and his sweetly struck shot nestled high in the net.

Durban was naturally disappointed, 'It was a horrible goal from our point of view. We have been working on set-pieces. It is very difficult to criticise anyone, however, after a performance like that. There were one or two individual mistakes, but I hope the crowd have gone away appreciating what we did.' The boss articulated one of the fundamental ingredients still lacking in his team's make-up, 'We had enough chances to have won the game twice, but I think they had just a bit more know-how.' He also bemoaned the disappearance of the forward thrusts made by his team who had been in irresistible form seven days earlier, 'I have never known a side have so much possession and yet so few shots. We don't have shots from outside the penalty area.'

Despite being constantly chaperoned, James had conjured a number of decent crosses, and Durban remarked on the failure to capitalise, 'It's all about timing. The front men have got to arrive in the box when the ball arrives. Perhaps it's a bit of frustration, but you can come as late as you like on headers. This is the problem when you are playing at 100 miles an hour with the crowd firmly behind you – you fill the danger area too quickly.'

This underscored that Sunderland would have benefited from Robson's inclusion; Rowell had declared himself fit but was later diagnosed with a chest infection. With hindsight, the ailing Rowell could have afforded to stand down with little fear about regaining a starting place from a player-coach who was only ever going to be used in short bursts.

The following day, Durban was fuming over TV presenter Bob Wilson's announcement on *Match of the Day* that Sunderland were expected to complete the signing of Liverpool's out-of-favour forward David Hodgson. Durban had recently been present for Liverpool reserves' match at Burnley, but this, he asserted, had merely been a routine scouting sortie, 'I will be contacting the BBC today about the irresponsible statement. It puts totally unfair pressure on the front people with whom I am very happy.' It would not be the only time that season that the club would have grounds to be furious with the corporation and Wilson.

## A Man's Got to Know His Limitations

There was no chance of complacency ahead of the cup replay and Durban named Robson as substitute, saying, 'The good work done at Norwich will be undone if we don't take our chance. You are looking for someone to get you a goal, and have a steadying influence. Pop fits the bill. When the crowd sees Pop get on it will give us a lift; but there will be no sentiment in any decisions.' No sentiment was involved as Durban felt compelled to thrust Robson on as Sunderland sought to recover a 2-0 deficit inflicted by the lively Bertschin, but all they managed was a scrappy West effort a couple of minutes from time.

After the latest cup flop, Durban was contrite, 'We tried to be clever and let everyone down, and we all realise it. I want to apologise, and hope it does not destroy all the goodwill we have created over the last few weeks. It just proves that I dare not move away from the basics, and see that we play to our limitations as a side. We have moved away from our strengths – we were awful. We didn't play with any fire. From everyone wanting the ball, they lost the appetite for it. I must now analyse what happened and sleep on it.'

The manager's professional approach to addressing his team's shortcomings, as well as his apologetic tone, was admirable, but it should be highlighted that the attendance for this cup match was a disappointing 14,000. If the public laid so much store on achieving cup runs then it was not being borne out through the turnstiles for early rounds. In addition, opposition managers were beginning to get wise. Norwich boss Ken Brown said, 'We knew we could do it if we shut off the supply to James. We had wide-men who were not only a danger to Sunderland but dropped back to look after James and Pickering.'

The following day also failed to produce any 'cup magic' as several tired players travelled to Wembley Arena to compete in the annual *Daily Express* five-a-side tournament. Sunderland had famously won the inaugural event in 1979 but, on this occasion, a squad of Turner, Venison, Atkins, Pickering, Proctor, and Rowell fell at the first hurdle against QPR.

As an away trip to Birmingham loomed, James emphasised the resolve in the camp, 'We are determined to bounce back, but we will have to get back to grafting. We have got to get goals from other areas even if it means me having to switch over to the right for ten minutes, or drop just behind the front two. Teams are doing their homework on us after our recent good run so it is up to us to look for alternatives.' His manager also preached a 'clean slate' approach, 'Everything that needed to be said about the Norwich defeat was said on Tuesday. We kept off the subject yesterday and had a super training session. The players are raging with themselves, and they have high hopes of making Birmingham feel the backlash.'

The team's defence would have to steel themselves as Harford would be back to lead the City attack. The target man had endured 43 stitches inserted in a mouth wound sustained after colliding with Coventry's Allardyce (an uncompromising clash between two 'no prisoner' types). But, Durban knew it was not only Harford who would make his presence felt in Ron Saunders's team, 'We will have to match them physically.' The portents were not good as the previous nine visits to St Andrew's had yielded two draws and seven defeats.

Two of the squad's elder statesmen would not be involved. Firstly, the manager omitted Robson from playing duty and said, 'I don't want to involve Pop on a regular basis as I think that would be a retrograde step. One of the reasons he was substitute against Norwich was the fact that both Rowell and West had slight back injuries which I kept quiet.' Again, this prompts the question of why risk your two principal strikers when such a capable stand-in was at your disposal? It was not the first time that Durban had doggedly chosen to stick with a system for a cup tie with no reward. Munro then dropped out of the travelling party, 'The manager said if I get the chance to move to Scotland and the team isn't Aberdeen or Rangers he would let me go for nothing.' The club captain had never been popular with the bulk of the fans, a bald fact he did not duck, 'Yes, I have suffered with abuse from the crowd; but it is an extremely sad day for me. The club and manager have to look at the future.'

The clash at St Andrew's proved to be a tough, scrappy affair. Turner's confidence was given a severe test when he needed four stitches to a head wound after a typical Harford challenge, and Venison resolutely soldiered on after picking up a thigh injury. At half-time, Durban asked for more forward runs to unsettle the Birmingham rearguard. The breakthrough followed a determined challenge from Proctor; this enabled Rowell to lay the ball into the path of Bracewell whose 20-yard shot took a deflection on its way past Tony Coton. It proved to be the winner and Durban later remarked, 'Paul got the goal his performance deserved.'

The manager also revealed the tactical options that had been going through his head as he realised the game could be there for the taking if decisive action was taken, 'I told Pickering to get forward more to see if he could give us a spark. The game was dead, the ground was dead, but it was an important game for us after two successive defeats.'

Durban commended the efforts of Robson who had been devoting energy to 'lift the lads' spirits' in the wake of the Norwich loss and the 'heated exchanges' that followed. The boss also praised the controlled aggression of Venison, 'Being given the England youth captaincy has given him a bit of standing and increased his confidence. I hope to be able to give him some games in midfield before the end of the season.' Durban maintained that his right-back could and should be breaking forward more, 'He has matured playing in a side with a bit more movement and has got the ability to develop into a goalscorer, but at the moment he is not prepared to go all the way in a system that allows him.' Overall, the team had 'done a job' on Birmingham, and the manager added, 'I am a bit relieved. It was not an attractive game but we won it with a lot in hand when I look back.'

## Status Quo

Durban turned out with the youth squad as they gave a game to a team from HMS *Arrow* which was docked on Wearside. On his return to the office, the manager was questioned whether there had been any move for Hodgson, 'The only approach I have made to Liverpool was earlier in the season when I asked if I could have him on loan. I have watched him a couple of times and he is not playing with a lot of confidence.'

The forward's unrest had recently increased after new Liverpool manager Joe Fagan had preferred midfielder Ronnie Whelan as a replacement for injured striker Mick Robinson. Durban was certainly not desperate for Fagan to get in touch, 'League tables and managers should be judged at the end of the season, but you have to look at the players who you think are worth points to you, and I would say that Bracewell and Proctor have made the world of difference. Progress is there to be seen.' Unfortunately for Durban, that progress needed to be more widely recognised, and his advice about being judged at the end of the season would fall on deaf ears.

Elsewhere, there was an indication that even clubs rated as giants in European football had to tighten their belts. Forest and Glasgow Rangers had agreed a cut-price £100,000 deal to take million-pound striker Ian Wallace north of the border, but failure to agree personal terms killed the move. As well as not being prepared to meet the player's wage demands, it was significant that new Rangers manager Jock Wallace was thought to be seeking a striker to play *instead* of McCoist rather than alongside the young prospect.

Durban must have wondered what to expect as he headed for the club AGM, a meeting which had acquired pantomimic connotations in recent years.

This time, chairman Cowie insisted that there was cash available for team-strengthening, but former director Bill Martin urged caution, and for the directors to 'get back to the old days of scouting for local lads', claiming he knew of four or five youngsters 'who have left Lambton Street Boys Club but none of them have come to this club'.

Cowie retorted that offers of over £600,000 had been received (and rejected) for two of the current squad, and that north-east lads had not been neglected, 'Alan Durban has spotted local talent in West, Pickering, Venison, and Atkinson.' Cowie then proceeded to deliver a backhanded compliment to his team manager, 'Money is available to go out and spend but he is so resolute, he will not go out and spend a fortune. It calls for a degree of patience from spectators who, for a quarter of a century at least, have been bored out of their minds with years of non-performance.'

Cowie had both praised Durban's thriftiness and yet laid the blame on him for not compiling an exciting team. Cowie's next remark displayed greater reasoning, 'I think it will take another year to get the policy right as we need another player. We are on the right track.' He added that new director Batey had 'impressed me very much', and Batey joined in with this jarring newborn cosiness, 'Since joining the board, I have been very encouraged by working with the chairman. We will turn this football club into one of the greatest in the league, and I look to the future with *great expectations*.' Oh; but 'what larks' were to be suffered by the fans in the period under this incompatible duo's stewardship and their toxic working relationship.

Back on the pitch, the reserves took on Manchester United at Roker Park and, aided by the on-field presence of Durban, won 3-2. A tough tackle earned the boss a booking after only 14 minutes, and Atkinson scored the third goal from a penalty. Walker dislocated a collarbone, ruling him out for five weeks, but his manager maintained that the player could yet make an impact, 'The lad has so much talent. He did one or two things last night which were brilliant; then he does two or three things which pub teams would be annoyed at.' Walker would benefit from greater expert care during his rehabilitation as the club had finally moved to appoint a full-time physiotherapist. Twenty-five-year-old Steve Mason had been helping out on a part-time basis but would now leave his other position at Durham's Dryburn Hospital.

The *Match of the Day* cameras finally made it to Roker Park as the team took on Ipswich. Durban warned his charges, 'We must stop threatening to do it, and go out and do it. Ipswich's form has not been too good recently but you can't take away the fact that they still have several internationals.' Highlights were at a premium, and Sunderland toiled as Ipswich became the latest team to effectively adopt the plan 'stop James and you stop Sunderland as a creative force.' With James tightly marked, grit was not enough, and a 20-yard 'dipper' from that troublesome thorn Gates put the visitors ahead. But, just before the break, James curled a free kick into the area where Rowell plunged low to skew a header just inside Cooper's post.

The TV cameras had helped to spotlight some unpleasantness from Mariner as he lashed out petulantly at Atkins. With referee Keith Hackett taking no action, it was left to the home team's 'enforcer', James, to march across, jabbing his finger at the guilty striker while delivering a scathing verbal admonishment. Durban commented on Atkins's non-melodramatic nature, 'I know a lot of pros who would have gone down and made a lot of it. It is just as well for Mariner that we have no cheats here.'

The manager was pleased at the reintegration of Elliott to the fold, 'That was his best game for the club since I came here, and he knows any praise I give is fairly reluctant. When I came here Shaun was the only capped player [England B]; he was recognised as the club's biggest asset and was happy at that. However, we have raised the standards around him and he has had to raise his.' Durban's insightful analysis did not stop there, 'I liken him very much to Colin Todd who got better as he got older without winning the caps he merited. Shaun has so much pace it comes easily for him to put in a good performance without playing to his maximum. Complacency crept in. To defend and become a first-class performer you have to cut out unforced errors.'

In philosophical mood, Durban turned to an overall status check, 'We are making progress slowly and quietly, but we are not a Real Madrid. We are not going from a side that finished with 50 points last season to Europe this. You get better as you get older and what I am looking for now is for my players to add a bit of know-how to their experience. Ipswich had a bit too much know-how in certain positions.'

Days later, it emerged that Durban's transfer dossier had been refined, and there was a surprise but very welcome addition to his permutations, 'I have been in touch with Jock Wallace about the possible availability of McCoist as he was not in their side at the weekend.' But the Scot's name did not break into the top of the Durban charts, 'I have drawn up a list of five or six players I want, and I will not move from it. I want someone who will fit in on the right-hand side who can score goals.'

John Wark's name sprung to mind, but Durban also warned, 'Spending a lot of money does not guarantee success. Look at Arsenal; they spent more than anyone in the close season.' He had a valid point; at that stage of the season Sunderland stood in 14th position in the league, one place and one point above Arsenal.

It quickly became evident that Wark *was* one of Durban's 'chosen few' targets but, inevitably, the price was always going to be an insurmountable impediment, 'Ipswich will not move from the £750,000 mark. I would have thought that after a month they would have been prepared to come down. I am looking to strengthen our side with a natural goalscorer and he is one of the few who are officially on the transfer list.' To many supporters, this appeared to be a non-starter. Say Ipswich had lowered the asking price substantially; what good would that do Durban if his board were unwilling to match his ambition and surpass their transfer record layout of £355,000 by around another £100,000? And, talk of part-exchange deals was laughable unless the cream of the club's young assets were sacrificed.

Meanwhile, Hindmarch was permitted to join Second Division Portsmouth on a month's loan, 'I have no complaints with Rob. He has always put it in when he has been involved. He is a bit short of being a top First Division player; he is a very good cover player, but when you get an offer for one of them then you have to consider it.' Durban was making a plausible point, but the loss (albeit temporary) of the 23-year-old former captain did leave an already small squad looking decidedly vulnerable, a fact freely acknowledged by the manager, 'The chances of Munro leaving in the near future must now be limited. He is now our spare defender.'

What that admission failed to address was that he was not a central defender, and should injuries fall in that area, then Durban would be forced to either redeploy West or blood the triallist Cole.

The day before travelling to Notts County, Durban was sitting in his rain-lashed office. He revealed, 'We will now find the men for all seasons. It is easy to play when the sun is shining, but we will now see who earns their corn when it is wet, windy, and boggy. A year ago, when Arsenal came here, there was a bit of frost about and they did not like it.' But, the manager was still trying to improve the performance level, 'I want us to be more solid and keep our minds on the job. We won at Birmingham without really playing well, and I want us to be a bit more positive.'

That week, Durban's former assistant Richie Barker had been sacked by Stoke who lay second from bottom of the league. There had been transfer requests and general unrest from players over what were widely perceived as negative tactics. Barker had become a devotee of a system known as POMO that involved hoofing the ball upfield into his revered 'Positions of Optimum Maximum Opportunity'. Despite the objections of his senior pros who realised their creative players were being bypassed, Barker stubbornly persisted with the approach and paid the price. The sacked man attended the game in Nottingham as the guest of Durban who must have felt uncomfortable at the lack of resistance displayed by his team that afternoon. Martin O'Neill was in the County line-up as the home team ran out 6-1 winners on a surface that was described as 'a Meadow Lane gluepot.'

After Christie fired County into an early lead, Sunderland battled back and West laid the ball off for Bracewell to crack in a fierce drive past Ray McDonagh. At this stage, there was no inkling of the dramatic landslide that was to follow. Warning signs emerged as John Chiedozie passed up a couple of glorious openings, before the lowest First Division attendance of the season so far (7,123) witnessed the little winger net twice amid a five-goal flurry. Durban had called for greater positivity from his team, but the plan had backfired, 'We tried to control the game and push out early, and we were punished.' Still, there were no grounds for any knee-jerk reactions, 'If you are not too careful you start looking too deeply into things that are not there. You only get the same number of points for winning 6-0 or 1-0.'

A four-day trip to Guernsey had been arranged, and the squad would attempt to suppress thoughts of the debacle while preparing for the upcoming match against Leicester City which would mark the first Sunday fixture to be held at Roker Park. From their Channel Island base, Durban reported that the squad was confident of bouncing back, 'We are not shattered by this defeat. We have found reasons for it. If we had no idea why it happened, then we would have a problem.' Durban was wringing out the lessons to be learned and there was much logic to the reasoning, 'I sometimes think you are better getting a hiding than losing 1-0. Occasionally, you have to remind people of what they are capable of, and playing within their limits. The same thing has happened in the last two seasons at Coventry [6-1] and Watford [8-0], and we have got to learn from it and put it right.'

As well as setting out his immediate recovery plan, Durban dismissed media speculation linking him with Arsenal forward Alan Sunderland as 'garbage', and also quashed assumptions that his supportive gesture to Barker at the weekend meant that the two men would be linking up again. Meanwhile, the team were drawn away to Bolton Wanderers in the FA Cup third round, 'It is not a bad draw. There are more difficult Third Division grounds; at least at Bolton we have a big pitch to play on.'

A 9-0 win over a Guernsey XI, was followed by further media speculation linking Sunderland with 22-year-old Stoke and England wide-man Mark Chamberlain. The player's friendship with former team-mate Bracewell fuelled rumours that Durban had made a £300,000 bid. By this time, another right-sided forward that had come into the manager's radar, Swansea's Alan Curtis, had signed for Southampton in an £85,000 deal. This at least proved Durban's assessment that the £150,000 fee bandied about only a few weeks earlier had been unrealistic. It may also have taken all the persuasiveness of James to convince his buddy to move to the north-east when Southampton were currently involved at the top of the table.

## Festive Casualties and Shopping Setbacks

In the run-up to the Christmas period, there were managerial casualties. Mick Docherty's short reign as Hartlepool boss came to an end, his sacking cruelly coming in the very week that he had moved into a new house. A more high-profile exit came in the top flight as Terry Neill was shown the door at Arsenal.

At Sunderland, Rowell was looking to build up his fitness as he recovered from illness, earning praise from Robson, 'Gary wanted to come in today and work on his own, which says a lot for his attitude.' Meanwhile, Durban sought cover for the looming busy schedule, 'There is no question of any loan deal being completed in time for Sunday, but I expect to have somebody next week, preferably a utility player, but we will make sure that we don't drop our standards.'

Ironically, Swansea were now rumoured to be mulling over a move to appoint James as their player-manager following the departure of Toshack, but Durban made it clear he would take a dim view if Swansea thought they could do it on the cheap, 'Leighton is not a free-transfer player.' Well, he had been, but the Welsh international had increased his prestige since his January arrival.

The day before the visit of Leicester, Durban disclosed that he had made inquiries about taking Lee Chapman on loan from Arsenal only hours before Neill's sacking, and would be attempting to get hold of caretaker boss Don Howe to continue talks. He said, 'If there had been any chance of them letting us have Chapman I would have flown to London to beat the 5pm deadline. I am hoping to bring in someone on loan next week as we must have cover.' At this stage, Durban was still prioritising 'a utility First Division player'; presumably any Chapman deal would be a bonus. There was one prime target that Durban wished to add to the Roker ranks, and the upcoming match would afford him the opportunity to run a form-check on Leicester's 23-year-old striker Gary Lineker whose name was at the sharp end of the manager's shortlist.

The attendance of almost 17,000 represented an increase of over 5,000 compared to the pre-Christmas Saturday win over Arsenal the previous year. In that respect, it might be argued that the switch to Sunday had been justified. After a poor start to their season, Leicester had signed rugged defender Bob Hazel from QPR to add some steel to their rearguard but he made an impact at the other end of the pitch as he shot past Turner to put the visitors ahead on 63 minutes.

With the home crowd getting decidedly restless, and their plaintive attitude affecting the composure of the players, Sunderland relied again on a pinpoint James cross to dig them out of trouble. For the second successive home game it was Rowell who benefited as he ghosted away from his marker, inviting his wing-man to seek him out, before diving to head downwards past goalkeeper Mark Wallington to quell the moans and groans of an increasingly fractious crowd.

Nevertheless, it was just as well that Lineker had a day to forget. The highly rated striker had already failed to capitalise on a couple of presentable chances before he handed Sunderland an 85th-minute reprieve. Set up by Alan Smith, Lineker spurned the opportunity to hit a winner as his sliced right-foot shot sailed wide of the post and into the collective sighs of relief in the Fulwell End. Durban was fairly scathing about aspects of the performance, 'We had three at the back who for quarter of an hour played like schoolchildren.'

He revealed that James had pulled a muscle and had been given an injection at half-time, 'He did well to stay on, but the last thing I wanted to do was put young Atkinson on. When a team is struggling it is not fair to ask a 17-year-old to pull through.' His team were not mired in the relegation zone, and Durban's reluctance to send on a seemingly ready-made substitute underscored the extent of the pressure, and volume, of vocal fault-finding that had been descending from the stands and terraces.

Venison had received a booking that triggered an automatic ban, ramping up Durban's need for reinforcements, 'It is more essential than ever that we bring someone in.' Here was another indication that the arrival of the 'utility player' should be expected, but Durban was concerned about the impact of media hype linking him with Hodgson, 'All the inaccurate stories flying about are having an adverse effect on Rowell and West, though Gary does keep getting us out of the cart.' Durban's plan was to switch Proctor to right-back during Venison's enforced absence, 'We have already talked about it, and Mark is happy to fill in.'

Following a phone call from Arsenal, it appeared that Durban would not be bringing in any Christmas presents from the fashionable quarter of London, 'Chapman is not available for loan, and at the fee they quoted us we are not interested.' He then wearily tried to quash the repeated media speculation over Hodgson, 'I spoke to Joe Fagan three weeks ago and he promised to let me know if the situation changed. I have enough respect not to keep pestering him.' Perhaps this constituted a broad hint for reporters not to keep pestering Durban on the subject.

As well as desiring cover, the boss wished to crank up the onus on his squad, 'We have slipped up in the last couple of weeks. One or two of the players need putting under a bit of pressure. There should be pressure on them to move up the table. Having been involved in survival battles in the last couple of seasons the fact that they are out of the bottom six has led to certain players going down a gear when they should have been going up. I've been making that point to them.'

The next fixture would be the Boxing Day (Monday) trip to take on Everton but, after it emerged that Arsenal had relented on their asking-fee for Chapman, Durban had to scrap plans to fly to London to beat the 5pm deadline, 'A couple of last-minute hitches cropped up which meant that he would not be able to sign in time.' The match at Goodison would be followed by the visit of West Brom 24 hours later and, although he would have appreciated having Chapman in the squad, Durban had been irked by the introduction of a third party into negotiations, 'I made him an offer which he was happy with, then I received a call from his accountant and I am not going to negotiate with *him*.' Durban was focussed on preparing the players he did have, but two pieces of important paperwork were able to be rubber-stamped as Venison and West signed extended contracts.

## A Last Hurrah

Although James had declared himself fit, Durban did not want to risk the crucial cog in the team aggravating his hamstring. He explained, 'Leighton is unlikely to play in both the holiday matches. I particularly want him available for the visit of West Brom.' On Christmas Eve, Durban issued a message to the loyal supporters he rated so highly, 'Even though we have improved I am still not satisfied. We have got to become even stronger in 1984. I would like to thank the supporters for their patience.'

Thus it was that more than three months after being told he was being 'rested' for two or three weeks, Atkinson found himself in the starting line-up. Yet, the bruised James was forced to come on earlier than desired when Pickering failed to reappear after the interval following a nasty first-half collision with Atkins. On the hour mark, Chisholm committed a foul when he slid in on Peter Reid which prompted a gaggle of Everton players to dramatically swarm around the referee demanding further action against the already-booked defender. They got their wish, and Sunderland were reduced to ten men. Durban later delivered a withering verdict on such unseemly actions, 'It is the lowest of the low when footballers suggest that fellow professionals should be sent off. For two or three of the Everton players it was the biggest contribution they made all match.' Ouch!

West dropped back to assume emergency defensive duty as the rearguard galvanised themselves, but they were indebted to their goalkeeper for preserving a point as Turner pulled off two crucial saves in the final five minutes, stopping a Johnson header before spreading himself to deny Adrian Heath. The keeper's feats were even more laudable considering he had earlier incurred a pulled muscle. Rowell had also suffered, taking hard knocks for the team in what had proved to be an uncompromising and uncharitable Yuletide fixture.

Durban would have to wait and see who could be patched up and who needed to be rested for the following day's encounter. In charge of Sunderland for two and a half years, the manager used his programme notes to issue a general appraisal. Areas of progress highlighted were that the club had been 'stabilised financially', and the team were 'better equipped to cope with the demands of the First Division'. Although risking being stigmatised with anti-attacking inclinations, the manager justifiably pointed out a fundamental ethos, 'Our defensive strength made us a more difficult side to beat.' Durban displayed particular pride at the encouraging international recognition for the club's young players which 'augurs well for the future', before pointing out that Nick Pickering was the first player from the club to progress to the England team after starting in the juniors since Stan Anderson 21 years earlier.

The team supremo had issued a message of hope for the future and, at the tail-end of 1983, the present was a good place to be too. Just under 18,000 were in Roker Park to see James replace Atkinson in the starting line-up, but slotting into the problematic right-flank position. There was also the welcome sight of Pop Robson coming in for a battered Rowell. A patched-up Pickering made it, despite sporting a broken nose and two stitches close to his eye from the previous day's collision. He was deployed in midfield as Sunderland abandoned the sweeper system.

It was a special day. A sixth-minute James corner was headed on by West and Atkins set up a close-range chance for the evergreen Robson to rifle the ball past Paul Barron – a landmark goal. Joy was unconfined among players and fans alike. After 15 minutes, the home team found themselves in uncharted waters; a commanding early lead. Thirty-eight-year-old Robson's fine pass found relative youngster James whose vision was matched by an exquisitely paced ball into space for Bracewell to latch on to and guide a low shot from the edge of the area inside the far post. Not content to sit back, Bracewell (whose adventurousness was a prominent feature throughout) sent a 25-yard curler towards the top corner. Unfortunately, the midfielder had telegraphed his intention as he shaped up and Barron was on the move to spring across and pull off a spectacular-looking save – one for the photographers.

There were a few flutters in the second half and Regis scooped a good chance over from inside the area. Sunderland rallied, and three minutes from time the points were wrapped up with another well-worked goal. James ran on to the ball in the right-wing channel and as his marker stuck close, the Welshman outfoxed him by releasing an early cross without breaking stride. This met the well-timed run of the 'all-new' attack-minded Bracewell, who capped off a wonderful display by directing a header home like a veteran forward.

Durban was delighted but, typically, let it be known that ten out of ten had not been achieved, 'It just shows what we are capable of with the boost of an early goal. It was a very impressive performance but we went through a sticky ten-minute patch in the second half which I was not happy with.' Robson commented on his milestone strike, 'I was nervous before the game and never thought that I would get the chance to score the 300th goal of my career. It was an important game for me, but more important for the club.'

The good feeling generated by this welcome win was instantly supplemented by news of the much-awaited breakthrough in the transfer market. Lee Chapman had travelled up to Sunderland, watched the team's win, and the following day he completed a £100,000 move. On the back pages, the 24-year-old was pictured donning a Sunderland jersey while his old/new manager stood looking on. It had not escaped the attention of many that it had been less than 18 months since Arsenal had paid out £500,000 to Stoke for the big striker, who was eager to get started, 'It was a much better lifestyle in London, but this is a great chance for me. Alan Durban helped me learn my trade.'

Chapman's next observation about his new team spoke volumes, 'I was very impressed by them, and though the boss did not inherit a good team when he came here, he has some good players now. The crowd made some noise yesterday, far more than anything I heard at Arsenal, and I see no reason why we can't play like that all the time.' The articulate front-man's assessment of the improvement wrought under Durban's management was illuminating.

Durban was pleased to be reunited with a centre-forward whose capabilities he felt would upgrade the squad, 'The problems of the Everton game suddenly brought home how thin we are. He has to pick up his career again, a bit like Proctor. It also gives us alternatives at the back as West can now be described as a utility player.' The latter remark appeared to scotch hopes that the manager would still pursue his originally stated utility man target. Some fans may have blanched at West being described as such, but the player himself was comfortable with the label. As well as the previously mentioned attributes he felt he brought as an emergency central defender, West had also performed successfully in a midfield role when pitted against former England man Brian Talbot.

Another home match would end the year, and the club's newest full international, Pickering, illustrated the determination and willingness present in Durban's squad, 'I had to take Milk of Magnesia before the game to settle me down. I think the 4-2-4 system suits us better at home. I enjoyed being back in midfield but if the boss wants me to switch to left-back for away games then I will be happy to do so.'

After only one training session with his new team-mates, Durban felt confident enough to name Chapman to lead the attack against Luton. This allowed Rowell extra time for his shin injury to heal, and the manager observed, 'I am now in a position where I don't have to gamble. I just hope we can show the same commitment going forward, coupled with the same concentration at the back.'

An increased attendance of 19,482 saw Durban's hope fulfilled. Chapman replaced Robson in the number eight shirt, but Robson got to play the entire second half after James limped off. Luton's flair trio of Ricky Hill, Stein, and Walsh were kept subdued and, in the 54th minute, a raking cross launched by Bracewell saw Chisholm's header travel well wide of Sealey and inside the post. On the hour, Robson won the ball and fed Pickering who advanced confidently to hit a rasping left-foot drive into the net.

The new striker had contributed in tidy if unspectacular fashion to the 2-0 win, and Durban knew that Chapman was another who simply required a little time and patience for the club to reap rewards, 'He got goals for me at Stoke, and that was in a side which didn't score many. I don't think Arsenal have persevered with him. We now have Chapman, West, and Rowell competing for two places up front and that is a healthy situation. Pop might be our best bet for substitute.' Robson had no ambitions to bar the way of younger men, 'I thought my playing days were over, but I'm happy to play on the occasions the boss thinks I can help.'

The team had seen out the year with a solid win against fair opposition and, all in all, progress was there for all to see. There were bound to be further disappointments and unexpected setbacks in the future, but if the boardroom and the terraces kept faith and held their nerve, then Durban's 'tomorrow' vision for the club appeared to be less distant on the horizon. *If* people held their nerve.

## 1984, and Big Brother Grows Restless

It was a dreadful Bank Holiday Monday night as Sunderland continued their dismal record at Coventry. Trailing 2-0 on a waterlogged pitch, a 50th-minute goal from West proved insufficient impetus to retrieve the situation. Proctor had been pressed into defensive service in place of the suspended Venison but, in a last throw of the dice, the sweeper system was given the 'heave-ho' as Robson was thrust into the pelting pitiless conditions. An equaliser never looked likely for Durban's troops. The manager said, 'It was a complete farce. It is always hard to call a game off once the home team is in front.'

Earlier in the day, Durban had checked on the form of their FA Cup opponents as Bolton beat Millwall 2-0, 'They are a young side who played very well.' After their win, Bolton manager John McGovern, a former team-mate of Durban at Derby, had returned the compliment by travelling to watch the match at Coventry.

Amid the terrible conditions, McGovern could still observe that Sunderland were 'a really competitive side.'

Press speculation mounted that struggling Stoke were preparing to sell Chamberlain, and Durban had to spell out the same message that he had tried to convey in the Hodgson media furore, 'I have not spoken to Stoke about Chamberlain since Christmas Eve. They were adamant that the lad was not for sale. I am certain that they would let me know if the position changes.' Stoke's new manager Bill Asprey was equally bemused, 'I don't know where the national press are getting their information. It is complete fabrication.'

Another washout was the hope of boosting spending power from the sale of Hindmarch as Portsmouth manager Bobby Campbell dropped the defender. The player was soon back training at Roker, leaving Durban to comment, 'I am surprised because they are not going to get better value for the reasonable fee we quoted [£40,000].'

For the cup tie, Durban planned to include West, Rowell, and Chapman in the team despite harbouring reservations, 'A lot of other clubs have tried three strikers playing together and it has not worked.' The manager needed someone to provide them with the necessary service, however, 'Leighton's injury is a lot better, but the heavier the pitch is, the less likely he is to play.' Once again, Durban's preparation for a cup match was intense, 'It is essential that we function on all cylinders and make no mistakes – I have not considered losing.'

Durban's three-pronged approach paid dividends as the trio notched a goal each in a 3-0 win. Sunderland withstood the early enthusiasm as Bolton made use of the stiff breeze behind their backs and a raucous crowd's encouragement but, a minute before the break, a fine pass from Proctor found Pickering and his cross was rifled home by West. After 73 minutes, Chisholm put Chapman in the clear and the big striker opened his account with a slick finish. Four minutes from time, Rowell rescued the ball at the far post and found the net from an acute angle.

Durban's homework on Bolton had influenced his team talk, 'I tried to instil into our players that we were bigger, stronger, and quicker; it showed in the last half-hour.' McGovern complimented the away team and picked out a couple of key aspects, 'Atkins is a superb player. Up front, big lads West and Chapman caused us problems. Sunderland are a well-organised side.' Durban was surprised that the press had latched on to the mild rebuke he had given Chapman for sinking to his knees and back when celebrating his goal, 'It was very light-hearted. After all, nobody could catch Pop after he had scored against West Brom.' The boss 'took a bit of a gamble' on James by naming the 'gem' as substitute, and was relieved that he had not been forced into the action. It underlined the onus that Durban placed on cup success.

Chapman was delighted to get off the mark and excited by the potential of the new combination, 'I have hit it off straight away with Colin and, pound for pound, we must be the biggest twin striking partnership in the business. I had a bad year at Arsenal where I lost my confidence, but Alan Durban knew how to play me at Stoke, and I'm sure he'll do it again.'

Chapman had netted a very healthy 38 goals in 103 appearances at Stoke, and even his 18 months at Arsenal brought six goals in only 17 games. He said, 'Quite apart from rejoining a manager I rate so highly I have come into a squad of players I'm certain are going to win things.'

The manager was aware that the competition for places, while welcome, inevitably meant that some players could not be accommodated in their first-choice positions, 'A week ago I only had the bare eleven to choose from but now even the lads out through suspension might have a problem getting into the side. Any new system is not going to work straight away. I realise that Gary Rowell is not happy at playing wide on the right, but if I can accommodate an extra goalscorer, I will.'

Durban was also pleased about his keeper's growing stature, 'Chris is improving. The thing I like is his readiness to analyse his game immediately after the match. When I first came here he was a bit of a worrier.' Turner spoke about his recovery, and the mood of the camp, 'I have broken my arm, and fractured a cheekbone and skull while at Sunderland but I have still got time to pile up more matches for the club. Our team spirit is tremendous and there is a great feeling of togetherness. The boss has got a group of players who want to work for him.' Turner's former room-mate Rowell endorses his good friend's sentiment, 'Alan Durban built up an extremely good spirit among all the players.'

The fourth-round draw gave Sunderland a home tie against the winners of a Birmingham v Sheffield United replay. A match against Porterfield's team would offer an intriguing return to Roker Park for the ex-Sunderland contingent now at Sheffield. However, Birmingham were strong favourites to overcome their Second Division opponents, and although Durban was 'delighted to have been drawn at home', wounds inflicted by Birmingham were still raw in the immediate memories of Roker fans who had seen the Blues knock Sunderland out in a 1981 third-round replay, equalising in the 89th minute before winning 2-1 after extra time.

There was also the previous season's cruel turnaround in the final ten minutes when a 2-1 defeat left Sunderland staring down the barrel of another last-ditch relegation scrap.

There was an away visit to Norwich to deal with first, and Chisholm was suspended. Durban mulled his options, 'Switching West is one of those alternatives, as I want to have a look at some stage at Chapman and Rowell playing as a pair.' Bookmaker odds on Sunderland for the cup had reduced to 16-1, but at this stage Durban was reticent, 'It would be folly for me start talking about cup odds now.' Unfortunately, there was to be no sentimental return for Porterfield as two goals in the final ten minutes at St Andrew's sent Sheffield United out. The Sunderland boss had been present, 'Birmingham were physically stronger and just out-powered them.'

At Carrow Road, the defence were confronted with terrible swirling conditions and, after losing the toss, faced the howling gale first. They failed to cope; Norwich were 3-0 up after 29 minutes, and that is how things stayed. Durban had to write this one off, 'The home side are always going to adapt themselves better. When we were three down, I nearly took Elliott off to prevent him from picking up another booking. We are looking very brittle, but two defeats have been dominated by the conditions which makes it a bit difficult to assess what has gone wrong.'

## Skirmishes Before the Storm

Stan Cummins was hitting the local back page again, levelling more complaints at his former club. The forward had played only six matches for Crystal Palace who, far from being promotion contenders, were perilously skirting the drop zone. If Durban thought he had heard the last of any sniping over that mini 'soap opera' then he was mistaken as Cummins declared he had been suffering from a serious pelvic strain in March, 'Sunderland were desperate for points so they brought me in for three matches in April.

'I was told that I had only a stomach strain and was given tablets, which turned out to be only painkillers. Eventually, I went to see my own doctor, who told me that I needed rest; Sunderland cost me a year of my career.'

Cummins's 'year' timeframe must have included anticipated leave of absence with the press stating he was not expected to play again that season.

On this occasion, the Sunderland manager felt he could not ignore the accusation, 'At no time have I ever considered playing someone who was not fit, and who had stated that he did not want to play.' Durban's tone became quite acerbic as he dismissed his former player's complaints, 'I have read somewhere that Stan is not very happy. So what – nothing has changed. He is "King of the Moaners". We still have a corner in the dressing room called "Moaner's Corner". How strange Stan should write a leading article on what was to be his swansong [in May]. As usual, he got his facts wrong as he played two matches for us in April [both were lost], and two in May.'

Durban also stated that despite multiple inquiries, the highest concrete offer that any club submitted for Cummins had been £15,000. Moreover, the credibility of the player's 'lost year' claim was undermined when he returned to the Palace first-team less than six weeks after this skirmish in the sports pages.

Durban swiftly switched his attention to helping his reserve team retain their place in the Central League's top tier. Over 2,000 spectators turned up at St James' Park to see Sunderland grab a much-needed 2-1 win against Newcastle. The 42-year-old manager donned the number ten shirt and patrolled the pitch from the sweeper position, the *Echo* reporting, 'Durban coaxed and cajoled his troops as they fought a brave rearguard action against the almost non-stop attacks of the eager home side.' West had also been drafted in to beef up the attack, and he showed his First Division pedigree to score a classy second-half winner, according to the newspaper, 'The big striker chased a long ball from Cole to turn away from two Newcastle defenders before beating Carr from 15 yards with a delightful chip.'

As well as West, the line-up was packed with first-team experience, and the boss underlined why he felt it was so important to the future wellbeing of the club, 'It is essential that we stay in the First Division of the Central League. We have got to decide on a policy for the young players, at the same time retaining the highest level of football for them. I was pleased with West's display, and he appears to enjoy playing alongside Pop.'

Durban was correct in his observation, West recalling that Robson made a lot of time to work with the strikers, 'As well as advice on finishing, a good amount of time was spent working on improving sharpness.' Certain counsel given by Robson sticks in West's mind, 'Make sure you perform well at crucial points in the match; finish the half well so that the manager has the things you have contributed fresh in his mind at the break. Then, start the second half well to try and ensure it will not be you who gets substituted; and finish the game well. The manager is more likely to recall you contributing strongly which will increase the chances of retaining your place.' Quite simply, West rated his coach a particularly 'good influence', and Robson's fitness and attitude was an example to the entire squad.

The team were left kicking their heels the following weekend when the home game against QPR was postponed due to snow. Already forced to use the club's Washington indoor training facilities, Durban bemoaned the lack of practice for key players, 'I am very concerned we have lost our momentum.' As the next reserve game was also postponed, the only opportunity Durban had to give players a run-out was at the official opening of the Silksworth Sport and Recreation Centre which featured a match on their all-weather pitch. The boss included Venison, Chisholm, and James in his selection, alongside a mix of 'all-star' veterans such as Docherty, Montgomery, Bobby Kerr, Colin Suggett, and George Armstrong.

There was also snow on the pitch at St James' Park as Newcastle sought to play a rearranged home match against Leeds on Friday evening. Their manager, Arthur Cox, remarked, 'We are in a different situation to Sunderland. We have got a lot of snow, and there is no way we can put it on the terraces because they are always full.' Although possibly unintentional, there was a tacit suggestion that Sunderland could easily clear snow on to their terraces as there was no way they would be full of spectators. A pitch inspection had been planned at Roker for Friday but temperatures had risen by a few degrees, rendering it unnecessary.

## A Bitter Cup: The Beginning of the End

On the eve of the 'big game', Durban incautiously built up the significance, 'Tomorrow is a special occasion, and that calls for a special performance. I would just like to give our supporters some pleasure, for my main concern is to have a really good day out on the third Saturday in May. We have a great chance to re-establish our credibility, and I would implore our fans to come in now and not wait for the later rounds. The adrenalin has started to flow already.' Too much adrenalin was flowing in the manager's office; Durban's remarks were tempting providence.

There was not an auspicious start to the day as Cowie justifiably vented anger at the ineptitude of whoever was responsible at the BBC for Bob Wilson making an announcement that the game had fallen victim to the weather. This was the second time in less than three months that Wilson's had been the voice that misinformed a national audience concerning Sunderland. The game had never been in doubt since Thursday. The 21,000 who did turn up were in expectant mood.

Disastrously, in a match-changing (and possibly history-defining) incident, Atkins became the latest victim of a clash with Harford. The captain's broken cheekbone and black eye meant he had to come off; a bitter blow. Hopes were lifted as substitute West forced a header past Coton in the 41st minute, and this lead was held until, yet again against this bogey team, the dying minutes. Elliott survived an 83rd-minute penalty appeal after tripping Howard Gayle, but that is where Sunderland's luck evaporated. Two minutes later, Martin Kuhl fired through a ruck to equalise, and with an already-disappointed home crowd reconciling themselves to the prospect of a replay, their dark brooding nemesis, Harford, got in a header which Turner could not prevent from creeping in. This was one dramatic development too far for many of the fans. They voiced disgust, and a post-mortem *Echo* editorial declared it 'another sad chapter in the club's cup history'.

The vultures started to circle, and the new week's headline was 'Durban Dismisses Job Speculation'. But the man himself said, 'I have enough problems getting people back on song for next Saturday's match with Liverpool without worrying about my personal situation. All of us here have to get on with the job we started. At the beginning of the season we were looking to finish in the top half of the table, and if we can work to that, all well and good. We have got to learn to close games down when we are one up. Five disastrous minutes have turned our season upside down, but football is a seven-day wonder of contrasting weeks of heaven and hell.'

Superficially, Cowie adopted a measured tone, 'Now isn't the time for passion. We have to try to keep cool and get on with the job. I feel sorry for our supporters as this always seems to happen to us.' Defeat was not the only thing that grated; he was not going to let the BBC 'postponement' matter rest, 'How anyone can make such an announcement without being absolutely sure of the facts I find inexcusable. We were very disappointed with our attendance. For such an important match we expected at least 30,000. A solicitor's letter will be on the way and we shall seek compensation.'

But, on recent evidence, such cup ties had failed to excite public interest to anywhere near that mark. The chairman's exasperation was justified but the damage had been done, and any hope of monetary compensation was a forlorn one.

## Dragged Off the Canvas

As bitter a blow as the cup defeat had been, Durban had to re-energise both himself and his devastated squad. In his eyes, the promise of his 'tomorrow' team was still very much on track, and there was one young talent for whom he was keen to make a renewed move. Nineteen-year-old Michael Laudrup had been loaned out by Juventus to Lazio but had struggled to find any form, and Durban remarked, 'We have been alerted by the fact that Laudrup is unsettled in Italy where it is difficult to break through at such a tender age.'

But, the immediate task facing the Sunderland manager as he attempted to lift his team was a daunting one – the visit of Liverpool. Although it provided little consolation, the dominant reds had also disappointed in their weekend FA Cup tie, going down 2-0 at Second Division Brighton. A black cloud still hung over Roker Park from the previous weekend, but rather than retreating into a shell, the boss issued a rallying cry, 'We were very close to them last year and, having beaten them away this season, have no fear.' The reigning champions had just moved five points clear at the top of the table after a convincing 3-0 win over Watford, a game watched by Durban, 'We can't let Johnston run free. I have seen two clubs do it and that is the main thing to concentrate on. Watford were tactically suicidal. Liverpool changed the shape of their side but the goals just kept coming.'

Thankfully, Atkins was fit to retain his place in the line-up. Already a crucial presence in the team, the form of Liverpool's prolific striker meant that the captain would be needed more than ever. In their previous away fixture, the Friday-night BBC live match at Aston Villa, Ian Rush had netted a delectable hat-trick including a sweetly struck volley, and a subtle dink over Spink. The consummate nature of that display was appreciated by fellow-countryman Durban, 'Rush will develop into one of the greatest goalscorers of all time. He shows incredible patience in the box and it is amazing the variety and type of goals he gets. I am not going to help Liverpool on how we are preparing for the game; we do not mark players out of the game – that is not the right way to do it. But, we have to stop Rush.'

Overall, Durban's message was one of quiet confidence, 'I would rather have a big match any time as we play better against the better teams. We are the underdogs tomorrow and that suits us. We are far more relaxed and tend to produce our best in these situations. The players realise the importance.' As brilliant as the away win of the season had been in October, the manager acknowledged that the improvement curve had to be sustained, 'We can't live off the Anfield result, but if we complete the double it will go a little way to repair the damage of last week.'

A crowd of well over 26,000 filed in to Roker Park, principally owing to the stature of the opposition. Turner sustained a head wound after being caught by a clumsy Robinson boot, and Alan Kennedy clipped Bracewell in the face causing the midfield dynamo to soldier on clutching a sponge to stem the blood. A falling Sammy Lee managed to kick Rowell's scuffed close-range effort off the line, and Grobbelaar spectacularly pushed a clever James lob over the bar. At the other end, Rush was kept subdued but Johnston was disappointed to see an effort ruled out by an offside flag. At the close, both teams had to be satisfied with a point.

Earlier in the season, Durban had made his second attempt in three seasons to bring Johnston to Sunderland. The player was undoubtedly one of the 'specials' on the Roker boss's transfer menu, 'He is looking more like Keegan every time I see him play. He was magnificent.' After holding the champions, and restoring a modicum of pride, Durban revealed that the sweeper system would be resumed for the two tough upcoming away fixtures at Tottenham and Southampton, 'Our recent away record is not too impressive, so it is time we got the blanket out again.'

Robson assessed the treatment room situation, 'Bracewell broke a bone on the bridge of his nose, and though he had a closed eye still managed to do some training.' There was also further evidence of the extent of Turner's bravery and dedication, 'He had six stitches in the top of his head at half-time. The doctor had not finished with him when the bell sounded and, with the rest of the lads waiting, he just jumped off the table, pulled his gloves on and went out.' Finally, the coach lauded the team's efforts, 'To take four points and keep two clean sheets; it takes some doing to stop Liverpool. The lads are just pleased to get it out of their system. They had all week to wait to put it right and then go out and do it against one of the best teams.'

## Group of Death

February had kicked off with an encounter against the reigning champions and current league leaders. The remainder of the month held visits to high-flying Tottenham, Southampton, and Manchester United, with the one other home match offering little respite against Clough's Forest. The close grouping of such a rash of daunting fixtures was far from timely, and would ultimately lead to certain uncomprehending members of the club's executive hierarchy pursuing a spiritless course.

The news that Hoddle would return to the Tottenham team after recovering from a calf injury did nothing to ease trepidation. Moreover, the player who had succeeded in subduing Spurs's creative pivot in the past, Chisholm, was struggling with a groin strain, 'I will do some running and have a fitness test in London.' Up front, Rowell was going through a barren patch as he neared the club goalscoring record held by Len Shackleton of 100 first-class goals. Pop Robson (who would surely have doubled that tally if he had spent his whole career with Sunderland) offered his thoughts on Rowell, 'He has got 11 in total this season, which is not bad, but I said to Gary that he should be aiming at 20 league goals a season and that anything above that is a bonus. A lot of it is instinct. You can't teach Rush or Rowell where the ball is going to drop in the penalty area.'

Unfortunately, there was another striker on duty at White Hart Lane possessing the decisive know-how in front of goal. After Rush, the second-highest scorer in the league was Steve Archibald, and the Scot scored the first two goals before contributing to the chance that fell to Steve Perryman to put the home side in an unassailable position by the 53rd minute. Although Chapman donned the vacant number five jersey, it was West who operated as a central defender. There was no one to match Archibald's finishing instinct, leaving Durban to lament, 'We created four good chances and, for an away team, had a lot of the ball. We could have played Chisholm but it was not worth the risk of making the injury a long-term one. I have no regrets about using West at the back. He did okay and I will use him there again in an emergency.'

The fact that Durban preferred to redeploy his centre-forward rather than blood the youth team's callow David Corner underscored the thinness of the squad, and regret at not being given the funds to sign Jack Ashurst for a modest fee.

Durban held no misconceptions about the series of fixtures that the Football League's computer had dealt his team, but accepted it was a situation that must be confronted, 'I knew we were in for a difficult period, but we have to keep the team spirit going. I must make sure there are no dramatic team changes, but I am not concerned so much at the goals we are conceding as the ones we are not scoring. We missed two glorious chances against Liverpool and four better ones on Wednesday. I feel that we need West back up front as his goals have got us out of trouble in the past.'

Durban retained the same starting line-up for the trip to Southampton, but West pushed forward as Sunderland adopted a conventional back four. Another forward having a productive season, Steve Moran, bagged his third goal against Sunderland that term as he tucked away a 35th-minute penalty, conceded when Elliott brought down Danny Wallace. Only a combination of assured handling by Turner and sterling defensive work by his back four (Atkins superbly clearing a Worthington header off the line) prevented the home team opening up the sort of commanding lead enjoyed by Tottenham in midweek.

With prospects looking far from hopeful, Sunderland nabbed the all-important equaliser in the 81st minute. A swift throw-in from West was hoisted to the far post by Bracewell, where Chapman's looped header beat Peter Shilton to record his first league goal for the club. The manager conceded that his team had been slightly fortunate, but that vital commodity had been earned, 'We did better at Spurs on Wednesday, but we got our rewards out of this match for what we put in then. I must admit though, at 4.30 a draw was the most unlikely result ever.' Durban looked forward to the return of Chisholm after erring on the side of caution at The Dell, 'Chis wanted to play, but unless groin and muscle are 100 per cent you don't, especially when it is heavy.'

Ominously, the following Saturday's visitors to Roker, Nottingham Forest, were in a rich vein of form and were hard on the heels of Liverpool at the summit. They had just recorded their fifth successive away win, but Durban was upbeat, 'People sense we are not that far off making strides. There are no passengers in the side, and I feel that winning one of these big ones would remove inhibitions.'

The manager admitted that the cup nightmare had briefly 'knocked the stuffing out' of some players, but the clumping of daunting fixtures meant there were undeniable extenuating circumstances for temporary stagnation in the league, 'We knew we were in for a tough couple of months, but it is worrying that we have not scored twice in a [league] game since New Year's Eve.' Sunderland had a manager who would not flinch in addressing any identified shortcomings, but it was not a quick-fix job.

Atkins and Elliott were both one booking away from generating an automatic ban but Durban never liked to see any of his players shy out of tackles, preaching controlled aggression, 'There have been no bookings for dissent and I have never been in front of the disciplinary committee in ten years in management.' Durban was hoping to name Robson substitute if he got through a reserve outing, but the player-coach did not even get that far as he suffered a hamstring reaction in training. Further bad news followed when Venison was sent home and prescribed penicillin for suspected tonsillitis.

Despite flying in the league, Clough had brought his Forest players in for Wednesday training, cancelling their usual day off, and he said, 'I won't stand for anything less than hard graft.' Durban was not surprised, 'Clough's record speaks for itself. His sides have not changed from the early 70s. They counter-attack very quickly, and we have got to be organised and not lose concentration.' He also reminded everyone about one advantage enjoyed by his former boss, 'Two centre-forwards in their side who changed hands at over £1m each.'

On the Friday evening, a fifth-round FA Cup tie at Blackburn had been screened live and, despite coming away with a 1-0 win, Southampton boss McMenemy hit out at the way TV companies dictated the timing, 'There's a big danger that we are selling our souls. This game would have had a full house of 23,000 people if it had been played on a Saturday, and it is not sufficient to say "there's a pat on the head and £15,000" and think that everything is okay.' The sentiments in McMenemy's prescient judgement over selling the soul of the sport would gather even greater meaning in subsequent years.

On 18 February, few could have anticipated the swansong significance of the team sheet posted by Durban for that day's home match: Turner, Venison, Pickering, Atkins, Chisholm, Elliott, Bracewell, Rowell, Chapman, Proctor, James. A crowd of almost 16,000 saw Chapman cause a series of aerial problems for the Forest defence, one header from a James cross forcing Hans van Breukelen to push the ball around the post. After 74 minutes of a closely fought encounter, Bracewell won a corner and James provided variation by delivering an outswinger, picking out the run of Chisholm who planted a header into the net. Chapman soon had a massive chance to increase the lead after being played into space, but screwed his shot wide. A few minutes from time, the seemingly inevitable anticlimax descended in an unfortunate manner as a ricochet fell to Viv Anderson who prodded the ball over the line.

Clough's comment to Durban at the final whistle was, 'Well done, you deserved to win.' Although little suspecting this might be the final time he took charge of his team at Roker, Durban had an inkling that there were rumblings behind the scenes, and his post-match comments had a defensive tenor, emphasising that, despite the winless run, his team were showing resilience, 'We matched Liverpool and were more than a match for Forest; Chapman ensured enough balls dropped for us to have scored half a dozen.' The problems Chapman caused had been logged in Clough's memory bank, and he would sign the centre-forward later in his career.

Venison had played shortly after undergoing precautionary blood tests for glandular fever and the player's commitment earned his manager's praise, 'I did not feel that it could be glandular as he had so much strength. His determination to play was a fine example of the spirit which exists in the dressing room.' The boss later claimed, 'That was our best performance of the season.' Many supporters would have cited the magnificent wins over Liverpool, Arsenal, Watford, and West Brom as outshining this latest display, but Durban may have been taking into account the resolve required against such a robust and taxing outfit as Clough's well-drilled team.

There was no sense of irony intended when Durban exclaimed, 'Manchester United is another lovely game to get this week.' He was genuinely relishing the prospect of the next exacting leg in this arduous run of fixtures. The rearguard had looked relatively tight in the last couple of matches, but the team had again failed to find a killer touch, 'The four midfield players are entitled to be getting more chances inside the box. People should be gambling ten yards farther forward; they are just going for balls they know they have a chance of getting. Goalscorers are natural gamblers.'

Durban had not been backed with serious cash to buy an intrepid forager such as Wark or Johnston to deliver his prescribed formula.

## Is There Something I Should Know?

Durban's contract would expire at the end of the season and, technically, he had been offered a new one. However, the modest one-year deal put forward by Cowie gave the whole proposal a feeling that the chairman was 'going through the motions', almost inviting his manager to bridle at the niggardly parchment. The offer hardly constituted a gesture of long-term confidence, and Durban had refrained from putting pen to paper as yet. Relations with Cowie had become strained, and the contract hesitation was far from being the sole splinter between the two men as the chairman was rumoured to be stewing over a private non-football issue that had festered to the point of it becoming a convenient tool to help lever Durban out.

Realising his position was in jeopardy, and that only swift on-field success would ward off the circling vultures, Durban had reconsidered his policy on playing Pop Robson only in an 'emergency' scenario. Unfortunately, the veteran goal-getter was suffering from a troublesome groin injury, 'I really wanted him fit for the two home games early next month. In fact, I have been looking to play him more often. Despite controlling matches we have fallen behind last season's goals tally.'

It was probably a relief for Durban to travel to Glasgow in midweek to watch a Rangers team that included Nicholl and McCoist beat Dundee United to progress to the Scottish League Cup Final. Like a beleaguered under-pressure politician fighting for survival, the Roker premier had been spelling out the onerous nature of recent obstacles, and highlighting that 'damage limitation' had been achieved. Durban's repeated stress on the fact that two quick-fire, eminently winnable, home matches (against Arsenal and QPR) were in the offing betrayed the air of a man who suspected the long knives were being sharpened.

Durban was determined to keep faith in Rowell and name an unchanged line-up, 'To leave Gary out would have been the easy answer; it is only a matter of time before he starts scoring again. I was pleased overall with the shape of the team last week. Tomorrow looks the hardest fixture of the season left on paper.'

In what was arguably a last-ditch reminder to the boardroom, the boss underscored that the fixtures coming up in the final third of the season offered the opportunity to increase the points tally significantly. As Durban's squad travelled to Manchester, Len

Ashurst arrived in the north-east. A week after they had been trounced 4-0 at home by Fulham, Ashurst's Cardiff team would lose at Newcastle too, leaving them fifth from bottom of the Second Division. Despite the Welsh club's travails, the fact that Durban's fraught working relationship with Cowie had deteriorated meant that there was danger in the air.

And so it transpired that the Old Trafford cauldron hosted Durban's final match at Sunderland's helm. Amid the roars of more than 40,000, Durban's men were pinned in their own half for much of the game. It was a shock when they took a 16th-minute lead as Elliott's finely judged pass put Chapman away and, unlike the previous week, the striker found a composed finish as he slipped the ball past the onrushing Bailey to delight the 5,000 travelling supporters.

Unfortunately, the crucial combination of resilience and fortune that had earned the Sunderland rearguard shutouts at Old Trafford the previous two seasons proved an elusive commodity, and they succumbed to goals from corners either side of half-time; Muhren and Wilkins delivered the ammunition, with Moran's head twice applying the finish. The cause was not helped when a strain forced James to leave the action shortly before United levelled. Despite admitting that his team had been overwhelmed at times, Durban flagged the injustice of the decision preceding United's equaliser, 'We didn't have a problem until Whiteside tried to kick Bracewell out of the ground, yet the referee gave them a corner when we should have had a free kick. But, we were well beaten. They had so much possession and we weren't positive enough after we had scored.'

The following week saw a batch of international fixtures, England playing a friendly in Paris, while Bracewell and Pickering were on duty as the under-21s met their French counterparts at Hillsborough. The season had reached the two-thirds completed mark, and Durban offered an assessment, 'Anyone looking at our fixtures over February would realise that we were in for a really tough time but I think we did not get our rewards in terms of points, especially in the home games. It will depend on whether our preparations have been right but I am expecting to have a good last third.'

Sensing there was something happening behind the scenes, the manager may have been fighting his corner but the facts were undeniable. His team had just completed a month of five fixtures against the teams lying first, second, third, sixth, and seventh. Sunderland now lay 16th on 33 points, and were nine points clear of third-bottom Stoke with a game in hand. No cause for panic.

## Countdown to Kamikaze Cowardice

'Boardroom Shuffle' announced Tuesday's *Sunderland Echo*, reporting that wealthy Berwick farmer Iain Fraser had been appointed vice-chairman and Batey had superseded him as finance director. Meanwhile, Durban contemplated the best way to rejuvenate his team, 'I don't want to be looking too deeply into the problem after an insipid performance from half the team. Seven days earlier they controlled the game against Forest. You can create more problems by overreacting.' That lesson had been underscored when Durban had retained faith after previous years' drubbings at Coventry, Watford, and Notts County, and seen his team quickly redeem themselves.

Thursday was St David's Day, and Welshman Durban had his team motivated for the visit of Arsenal. Chapman had been a little too revved up, launching some verbal broadsides over his London stint. But, with the striker set to face his former team, his manager was eager to channel any frustration into positive energy on the pitch, not in the newspaper column, 'If Lee has any sense he will keep quiet. He can say it after the game. In the last couple of weeks I have seen some semblance of his play of two years ago. The lad has lost a lot of confidence, but he has always been a one-in-three goals-per-game player – all of them in the First Division.'

Durban received a boost when worries over the influential James's hamstring receded but his vital component in the engine-room, Bracewell, missed training. Once again, the combative midfielder had returned from an England shift 'badly battered and bruised.' Durban had been at Hillsborough to see his players in action, 'Bracewell was magnificent and Pickering had a super second half. We were the only club to provide two eligible players.' Durban's sincere pride in seeing two of his players, two *Sunderland* players, on international duty was heart-warming. His aim was to have a Sunderland team brimming over with full-international players – the tomorrow team.

Friday, 2 March dawned; the day before Sunderland would meet Arsenal at Roker Park with the aim of consolidating a mid-table position. Durban had a near full-strength squad to select from, and the prospect of two consecutive home matches. To the impartial observer, the situation seemed set fair.

On this morning, however, Durban's drive into work took a detour. He was summoned to Cowie's Millfield business offices for 9.30am; the conversation was terse, and Durban arrived at Roker Park less than half an hour later. The congregated press representatives, ready for the usual morning briefing, were not expecting anything dramatic; a general discussion on the following day's match, and injury update. It was left to the man himself to break the horrid news that he had just been dismissed. The *Echo* front-page headline was straightforward enough, 'DURBAN SACKED', but there was little insight offered for the reasoning behind the decision. Apart from anything else, the timing appeared ludicrous (in terms of the team's position, and on the eve of an important fixture).

At this stage, Cowie merely stated that Robson would be acting as caretaker. The editorial proposed one contributory factor, 'The board has become increasingly restive at the failure to attract crowds to Roker Park.' In an unfair comparison, the average attendance for the 1979/80 promotion season of approximately 27,000 was quoted, followed by the latest figure of around 17,000, which surely also reflected the state of the sport nationally, not just at Sunderland. Furthermore, no matter the chairman's claims to the contrary, if the board had displayed the ambition to push in for Keegan, or a player of renowned stature, the 'punters' would have flocked in.

For now, it was left to Durban to brief the press on the chairman's ostensible bone of contention, 'I was offered a year's extension of my contract five weeks ago and the chairman says I have taken too long in making a decision.' The miserly nature of a mere one-year deal, coupled with no increase in salary, indicated that the offer was a cosmetic exercise. Durban unequivocally offered the logical theory that Cowie had hoped the contract would prove unappealing and unflattering, 'I like to think that I am fairly principled. The offer was made and I think the chairman was reasonably happy that I did not accept it. I have not had a working relationship with him for months, so the decision to sack me has not come as a surprise.'

The now former manager proceeded to summarise what he saw as the advancements that had been achieved under often trying conditions, 'When I took the job, I knew the chances of success in the First Division are stacked against you – especially in view of the record here over the last 30 years. We embarked on a long-term policy with little chance of immediate success. All I know is that when I arrived here the club had a lot of liabilities, but there are now assets who have won youth and under-21 honours to justify the policy.'

Durban couched a parting salvo in veiled terms, 'When Jimmy Adamson left a few years ago he mentioned a certain bad influence at the club. Most people assumed that he was talking about a player. But, he wasn't. He was referring to someone who is still with the club. There are factions which hinder its progress rather than help it. My sacking will make this a very happy day for someone in a senior position in this club.'

The *Echo* report, while acknowledging the hard-edged nature of the football 'business', ridiculed the judgement of those in charge, 'It is lack of success which costs all football managers their jobs. But, on the eve of two successive home games which could make all the difference to Sunderland's league position, the board of directors never cease to amaze with their timing of dismissing the man in charge of team affairs.'

The following day, the position of manager again dominated their front page.

'Ashurst Set for Job at Roker' ran the headline, notifying readers that Len Ashurst, the club's former left-back, was the man lined up by Cowie as a replacement. Clough had been a team-mate of Ashurst, but the plain-speaking Forest boss believed this managerial switch was fundamentally misguided. Clough had experienced the fateful 'down-turned thumb' from the 'knowledgeable' Sunderland board years before when he was dismissed as youth-team coach, and was typically unequivocal in his condemnation, 'I hope they lose against Arsenal. Their timing was diabolical; to give the lad the sack now. *I can't believe they have done this to him.*'

## This One's for the Boss

Leighton James vividly recalls Durban walking in and saying to Robson and himself, 'It's down to you now; I've been sacked.'

367

The two player-coaches were staggered, and Colin West recalls the general mood of bafflement in the dressing room following Durban's exit – that, together, they had been on the right lines to achieving success, 'Alan Durban was a decent bloke. We could see something was developing, and I think the supporters felt that too.' Fellow striker Gary Rowell corroborates that the players were 'shocked', and believes Durban was a 'good manager who had built up a good team.' Rowell concedes that Durban's reign 'did not look spectacular', but 'he was dismissed before he had time to finish the job.'

The matchday programme against Arsenal still had Durban listed as 'Manager'. Bracewell's battered body had failed to recover, and Robson decided to start West, with Rowell on the bench. Cowie was booed by many in the crowd which then got behind the team, Durban's team, who gave a spirited performance but, as injury time approached, found themselves trailing 2-1. In one final desperate attack, Chapman was hauled to the ground by Caton. The defender refused to shake hands at the end, believing Chapman had gone down too easily, but a last-gasp penalty it was. By this stage, spot-kick specialist Rowell was on the pitch and his firmly struck shot was good enough to beat Jennings's outstretched hand to notch his 99th goal for the club. More importantly, a precious point had been salvaged.

Robson praised his men's efforts and 'the boss', 'The way the team played was a tribute to Alan Durban. I would like to thank the players for giving everything, but I am sure what they did was not only for themselves but for Alan Durban as they have a lot of respect for what he has done.' In the aftermath of the manager's exit, few supporters could have imagined that the point-saving penalty would mark goalscoring legend Rowell's final goal at Roker.

## Dreams of a Golden Harvest Replaced by Watery Coffee

Three days after Durban's exit, Len Ashurst was appointed manager. Supporters were unsurprised and unimpressed by the choice. The new incumbent stated, 'I am not coming here to talk about potential and sleeping giants. Those words are not in my vocabulary. The supporters want instant coffee.' Did they indeed? The sweeping statement showed a lack of perception; the silent majority wished for something more durable than an insubstantial frothy stimulant.

Following the official press conference, the *Echo* stated that the millionaire chairman was under heavy fire from the team's disgruntled fans, before quoting a selection from those interviewed, 'He never gave Alan Durban the support a manager needs, and I can't really see Len Ashurst setting the club alight'; 'He's lost touch with supporters and wasn't any help to Alan Durban'; 'Cowie should go as well. I was never an Alan Durban fan but he should have got better backing.' It is noteworthy that, when it came to the crunch, someone professing not to be an advocate of Durban still recognised the lack of support the man had suffered.

In an unconvincing alliance, Cowie and Batey were apparently working in tandem and had impressed upon Ashurst there was very limited transfer cash available. Somewhat idealistically (or laughably) Cowie declared, 'It is a good training ground for managers to be brought up without funds.' After inadvertently labelling the welfare of Sunderland Football Club as something that could be left to the vagaries of an experimental 'training ground', the chairman cited the man he saw as the ultimate managerial role model, 'Bobby Robson built one of the most successful sides in the country. It is all about one man – look at what has happened to Ipswich since he left. One man can make or break a club.'

Cowie's 'one man' theory would have dire ramifications in the future and, crucially, he failed to acknowledge that Robson, unlike Durban, had been permitted over ten years to steer his team's development through to maturity.

It was not long before Durban received a number of letters from well-wishers and he took the time to send written replies, saying that the number of people expressing their sorrow at his departure had 'helped to soften the blow.' While not indulging in any diatribes against his former employers, Durban noted that the aspect he found particularly difficult to accept was the 'cowardice' of sacking him 'prior to two home matches.' It appeared obvious that the club's executives were not prepared to take the risk that the manager might strengthen his position with a couple of good results. Durban stated to his correspondents that the faint-hearted timing of his dismissal simply illustrated the suspect nature of 'the type of people I was working with', and his 'only hope' was that 'the current team would be allowed to mature.' In the months to come, it became evident that his hope would not be realised.

In the local *Football Echo*, Durban eagerly accepted the platform to pay a final homage to the club's followers, 'During my departure last weekend, I paid tribute to the loyalty and knowledge of the Sunderland supporters. I thank you for your support, loyalty, and fair-mindedness.

'Those who have appreciated the policy and can foresee the future will understand how I feel. The future hopefully will change the attitude of those not so convinced. I leave with no bitterness, just disappointment. I wish you all well.'

Durban's valedictory message was devoid of malice, rather expressing a genuine fear that the supporters would face frustration and heartache in the future as a result of short-sighted decisions. He was not mistaken.

There was an early warning from the new man in the hot
-seat for fans hoping to see a 'name' player arriving prior to the
transfer deadline, 'There will be no six-figure buys.' The 'instant
coffee' Ashurst had promised was obviously not going to be a
premium blend. In fairness to the new manager, a phone call
tipped him off that former club Newport needed to sell their prize
asset, 25-year-old forward John Aldridge, and a fee of £75,000
had been agreed with Third Division Oxford United. There
was one factor (besides their top-flight status) that should have
resulted in Aldridge moving to Sunderland; the player favoured
being reunited with Ashurst. However, Oxford's chairman Robert
Maxwell was prepared to bankroll the deal while the Roker
board not only queried the modest asking price but insisted on
instalments. Supporters were not aware of such wrangling as
Sunderland missed out on a striker who developed into one of
the most potent goalscorers in the country.

It was clear that Ashurst had been dealt an embarrassingly
weak hand by Cowie and Batey, 'I am disappointed the board
could not come up with the cash Newport wanted. Clubs are
reluctant to let players go on loan unless they know there is a
good chance of the move becoming permanent, and I can't kid
anyone that I have £150,000 to spend.' The *Echo* reporter rated
the Aldridge bid a fiasco, stating, 'Even Fourth Division Doncaster
topped Sunderland's offer.' If reading this latest despatch, Durban
may have given a wry, knowing smile.

Deadline day was more notable for a departure. It was
revealed that the directors had been far from unanimous in the
decision to dismiss Durban; it had been an agonising split vote
and another power struggle had since erupted. One shareholder
revealed, 'There is so much squabbling at the club. A week ago I
was offered £160 per share; they came back and offered £200.'
Amid the unseemly wreckage of the sacking and shares changing

hands for obscene amounts, recently appointed vice-chairman Iain Fraser took a principled stand and resigned from the board. He had admired the work and vision of Durban but had been outvoted when attempting to save the man who had represented progress, 'I don't like the direction the club is heading. If I had stayed on then I would have been condoning what is happening.'

From a farming background, Fraser employed an enlightened analogy to convey the rewards that might have been yielded if the board had possessed the required nerve and scruples, 'In my opinion it takes a lot of time for a team to mature. It's like growing a crop of wheat – it doesn't happen overnight.'

The month ended with another high-profile managerial departure as Malcolm Allison was sacked by Middlesbrough 'for refusing to sell players to ease their financial crisis'. Days before his dismissal, Allison expressed his frustration at the position into which he had been cornered, 'Whichever way you look at it, I am in a dilemma. I am on an each-way loser.' Durban was one man who could identify with his former north-east counterpart's sense of helpless frustration.

## Disintegration as Tomorrow Dies

At the end of April, Leighton James converted two penalties in a vital 2-1 home win against relegation rivals Birmingham, and said he was prepared to commit himself to the club, 'I do not class myself as old. I would like the opportunity to continue playing in the First Division.' Two weeks later, he was omitted from the crucial final match at Leicester (won 2-0 with goals from Chapman and Robson), 'I wanted to play but the manager was frightened I turned in a match-winning performance and he had to offer me a new contract. There is no way I will play for him again.'

Inevitably, James was released, but fans were shocked when the same fate was doled out to Rowell. The forward had notched his 100th goal for the club in March, and the *Echo* reporter voiced the feelings of many, 'I find it staggering that hard-up Sunderland can afford to release a player that they turned down £500,000 for five years ago, and who has finished leading goalscorer in six of the last seven seasons.' One cynical theory was that the board had calculated that the club would be obliged to offer Seaham-born Rowell a testimonial if he stayed another year. So much for Cowie's previous claim that 'we want as many local lads as we can get in the team'.

Reflecting on his release, Rowell is philosophical, accepting that clear-outs instigated by incoming managers were an 'inevitable part of a footballer's life'. He adds, 'I felt that I wasn't ready to leave but, early in my career, Bob Stokoe had told me it was no good coming into football if you had a thin skin.'

Ashurst sensed that some players were still upset at the departure of Durban, 'I feel that there are two or three dissidents in the camp.' One of the main men he was wary of was undoubtedly the outspoken James. Under his guidance, the youngsters had again made progress in the FA Youth Cup, including a 2-0 victory over Liverpool, the Welsh international remarking, 'We must have been doing something right.' Ashurst later recorded that he had been told that the player had been promoting his own claims (with one of the directors) to be offered the managerial post. However, James's view differs, 'They should have given the job to Pop straight away.' Friction with the experienced James came as no surprise but, within a couple of days, supporters were dismayed to be informed that Ashurst was discussing the sale of Bracewell, a player Durban had envisaged building the team around.

With safety secured, Cowie saw fit to disgorge some flawed claims, 'We were on course for certain relegation.' Like a corporate accountant trying to justify a business decision, the chairman proceeded to state that the team had gleaned '32 points from 28 matches' under Durban, an error compounded when he amazingly quoted the statistics for Ashurst's small portion of the season which had seen a less daunting list of opponents.

When asked about the outburst, Durban felt compelled to respond, 'Cowie's comments are insulting and, as usual, his facts are wrong. Last year he insulted all Sunderland supporters with his statement about Newcastle fans.

'I am left extremely sad when he has come out with this after I had been so pleased for the supporters and players when I heard the result at Leicester.' That was not the only thing that Durban was approached to comment on. Bracewell had been allowed to join Everton for £250,000, and the former boss expressed sadness that a player he had hoped would serve the club for ten years had been sold after one. Overall, it would have been little surprise if Durban's feelings had prompted him to repeat his pithily understated remark of two years earlier, 'I cannot say what I want to say. I feel like using adjectives which are uncomplimentary.'

Ashurst spoke to Chapman and Atkins on the telephone and reported that he had not liked much of what Atkins had said back. A pertinent question might have been why had the players' level of future commitment not been thrashed out face to face before they had gone off for the summer break? There had been minor squad rumblings over the lack of evening meal prior to their penultimate away fixture at Ipswich, as well as a decision to replace baths with showers at the training facilities.

An unimpressed Chapman did not need much persuading to sign for Howard Wilkinson at Sheffield Wednesday. The striker made a big impact there, as well as at Clough's Forest, before linking up again with Wilkinson at Leeds and finishing league top scorer as the Yorkshire club were crowned champions in 1992. Chapman was another who Sunderland did not have the patience to persevere with as he matured into the finished article. Leighton James muses on the qualities he observed in the 24-year-old that promised further improvement, 'At that time, Chappy did not *look* the best, but you could not question his commitment, and desire.'

Regarding Atkins's candid remarks to his new manager, a disillusioned captain later elaborated on where he felt things were fundamentally going off the rails, 'The club is selling its best players. I want some indication that the club is going to *do* something. It has been second-rate for years, but it's now heading for the third-rate if this goes on. *The fans have been cheated*. It is so tragic because they could double the gates here. I'm ambitious, but I have to ask whether the club is ambitious.' Atkins's doom-laden prophecy would be fulfilled.

Having moved on Bracewell, James, Robson, Rowell, and Chapman before the start of the 1984/85 season, there was a distinct failure to recruit adequate replacements, yet financial director Batey claimed the squad were 'not that far away from being up there'. As the opening match neared, it was reported that Atkins was struggling with an ankle injury, 'I don't want to let the team down, and I am still not 100 per cent.'

But, since when had Atkins needed to be completely fit in order to turn out? Although the player's statement exhibited common sense, it was uncharacteristic for someone who had always been biting at the bit to put his body on the line for the cause. The player was obviously unhappy at the way the club was being run and, in early November, was sold to Everton for a mere £70,000. Ashurst cited that he already had Elliott, Chisholm, and Gary Bennett competing for the central defensive positions, conveniently neglecting the fact that Atkins was a fine utility player.

In the same week as Ashurst sold one of the club's most dependable and influential players, almost unbelievably, it was announced that the club had re-signed Stan Cummins who had not found the grass greener down south. On his return, both player and manager laboured on the financial theme, 'I left for nothing and I am coming back for nothing, and as far as I'm concerned the slate is wiped clean. I am not embarrassed. Steve Coppell suggested that I find another club. I have been told the directors are delighted to have me back.'

The directors delighted? The manager's view was surely more relevant, but the comment 'he will not cost us a penny and is coming for wages only' provided no shards of tactical insight about the player's envisaged role. Coppell had been keen to offload one of Palace's highest wage earners, and the 'free' nature of the business suggested that frugality was holding sway over ambition in the Roker corridors of power. One can only speculate over how events may have panned out had Ashurst been given the green light to sign Aldridge.

In a thinly veiled swipe at Durban's squad compared to the 'bargain' one now assembled, Cummins said, 'There's extra flair and this team will score a lot of goals.' In his estimation, Ashurst's team had the 'flair' that Cowie had wanted Durban to acquire for negligible outlay, but by the season's end those words appeared risible as Sunderland languished second bottom with 40 points and a mere 40 goals (even being outscored at Roker: for 20, against 26).

The disciplinary record was lamentable and an alarming number of suspensions were accrued. Two new signings, Bennett and Howard Gayle, were sent off at St James' Park and, incredibly, three players were dismissed in a so-called friendly in Sweden. By contrast, as the disaster story played out, two departed Durban recruits (Bracewell and Atkins) were picking up championship medals with Everton.

Leighton James offers a forthright view on Durban's sacking and the appointment of Ashurst, 'Alan Durban suffered because of the mentality that existed at the club. Certain people had an agenda and Len Ashurst got the job because of his past association with the club, but Sunderland was too big a job for him. He had no definitive style of play. Nondescript is the only word with which I can sum him up.'

## Aftershock Continued: All that Glitters is Not Gold

Ironically, that dispiriting Ashurst-led season brought the one thing that had eluded Durban – a cup run. A Wembley Milk Cup Final was reached and, yes, there was a temporary upturn in attendances. However, that increase was partly due to the enticement of obtaining vouchers, issued when passing through turnstiles, which the club stated would gain the holders priority in the subsequent scramble for Wembley tickets. Once this transient lure had disappeared, and the team's form completely evaporated after the 'day out' in London, so did the 'fair weather' hordes.

The build-up to the final against Norwich was riddled with internal squabbles over allocation of tickets, cup bonuses, and boot sponsorship. The day itself was a disaster. An abject display culminated in a sloppily conceded, deflected winner and a missed penalty. There was bitterness, and the striker who had scored three goals in the two-legged semi-final win over Chelsea, West, had been controversially dropped for the Wembley game before swiftly being sold to Watford.

Overall, some supporters would gladly have had the 1985 Milk Cup Final expunged from their memories, and the misery was compounded as, without on-field leaders of the calibre of Atkins, Bracewell, and James to galvanise them, Ashurst's deflated squad inexorably groaned to their relegation fate like a car crash in slow motion. But, a cup run is what most directors, and many fans, had hankered after, and the lack of one had been a factor that expedited Durban's dismissal. Many had been hypnotised by the intoxicating mirage of Wembley, and failed to see that the team was on a downward spiral. The foundations built by Durban had been dismantled, and dreams had turned to ashes. It may be appropriate to quote the 'be careful what you wish for' maxim.

The cup run *had* generated extra funds and, in the summer of 1985, much of it was spent by the chairman as he pursued his Bobby Robson-inspired theory – 'It is all about one man … One man can make or break a club.' There were three managers who seemed to fit the bill. Clough and Robson were not available, but McMenemy had just resigned at Southampton. Cowie dismissed Ashurst and persuaded 48-year-old McMenemy to come to Roker. Thus, the Sunderland fans were presented with the 'big-name' manager they craved.

There was a catch. Cowie declared 'Lawrie is a handsome man being paid a handsome salary', and it became clear that much of the cup income would be tied up in the new man's lucrative contract. The chairman would, yet again, place the onus for generating transfer funds on supporters, 'If our fans support us, we will have the cash to support him.' Cowie was asked about what he thought had been one of the prime reasons for such a high-profile manager agreeing to move to Roker, and the chairman replied, 'Without wishing to seem immodest – me.' Among further bravura statements, Cowie declared, 'I expect this is the start of something big. We must think and act big. I now expect us to go from strength to strength with promotion and Europe together our aim.'

The misplaced confidence, and eagerness to claim credit for the perceived coup, would pall within a year. Pickering and Venison were two young treasures that Durban had argued no club would be able to prise away because 'no manager having his head screwed on would consider selling his best assets' but, as the pair entered their prime, they were sold to Coventry and Liverpool respectively. Turner joined Manchester United, and the club went through a string of keepers trying to find a competent replacement. McMenemy finally stepped off the sinking ship as Sunderland descended to the Third Division for the first time in their illustrious history.

Cowie's departure had preceded that of the managerial flop. Bewildered that the man he had touted as the club's 'saviour' appeared to be overseeing general decay, and unwilling to provide further transfer funds, Cowie had allowed Bob Murray to take over the chairmanship months before McMenemy's exit. As easy as it was to denigrate Cowie, he was not alone in his thinking on McMenemy; a huge majority of supporters believed it to be a marvellous appointment, one that promised success. But, if working amid the small-minded bickering and inherently faint-hearted attitude that seemed to pervade the Roker Park boardroom in the early 1980s, such names as Clough, Robson, Cruyff (and many more top-rated managers) may have struggled to bring any tangible success to Sunderland.

Much animosity and blame was directed towards Cowie although it should be recognised that, during the national economic downturn, the club never found themselves in the dire position of some clubs who had to fight for their very existence. Cowie's legacy included a charitable trust assisting good causes, as well as funding the building of various local educational facilities.

However, he acknowledged football chairmanship as his 'greatest single failure' and, with the benefit of hindsight, may have realised that it need not have been that way if he had retained faith in Durban, and the board had backed their manager's transfer judgement to the hilt. The men Durban did recruit on a permanent basis were sound investments, and the classy priority players he earmarked (only to be denied realistic funds) would not have jeopardised the club's financial stability as they all possessed healthy resale values in the unlikely event of not settling at Roker Park.

## When We Were Young: Lost Chance for a Golden Era

In May 1987, following the club's relegation to the third tier, journalist Paul Hetherington wrote an incisive piece in the *Sunday Express*, highlighting what many were now beginning to realise, 'The irony of Sunderland's decline from a First Division team of promise to a club now humiliated by Third Division status is that it can all be traced back to the head of one of their supporters. Wearsider Mick Harford headed the goal which knocked Sunderland out of the FA Cup in January 1984.

'That Roker Park defeat was the beginning of the end for Alan Durban as manager of Sunderland and he was sacked five matches later. That decision by Tom Cowie, and the directors who sheepishly supported that move, has cost the club dearly.

'Cowie's subsequent appointment of Len Ashurst, a man with an inferior record to Durban's, was illogical. Ashurst took Sunderland to Wembley, but he also took them into the Second Division and jettisoned half the team Durban had built for the future. Only the blind couldn't see that he represented Sunderland's best chance. Subsequent events have improved some people's eyesight.'

Belatedly, there was a growing appreciation of the fundamental metamorphosis being wrought by Durban at Sunderland.

Not only had Durban been attempting to remodel the playing policy, with an emphasis on capturing and nurturing emerging local talent, he had sought to connect with the local community, and massive fan base, encouraging players and staff to attend public social engagements. The goal was for the club and supporters to be pulling in the same direction. This was another reason why the Welshman insisted his older signings committed themselves fully by moving to the north-east. The young players had grown up with the supporters, and if the more experienced newcomers also lived and breathed the raw heart of the area then a crucial emotional connection could be established.

Although operating in a different era, it is perhaps worth noting that one of the most successful managers in Sunderland's history, John Cochrane, built and guided a team to glory with very much the philosophy espoused by Durban. Arriving in 1928 from St Mirren, the crafty Cochrane set to work finding young players to 'train on'. Promising lads were brought down from Scotland and, crucially, the gestation period for the team, and the manager's long-term vision, to mature was allowed sufficient time. Spanning 1935–37, Sunderland finished runners-up before becoming league champions and FA Cup winners in successive seasons. Cochrane's astuteness led to him being dubbed 'the Napoleon of football', but none of this success would have come to pass if the then directors had not exercised patience and cooperation.

Durban had already assembled a promising mixture of young prospects and experienced quality. There was an integrity and camaraderie in his honest squad, and the jigsaw pieces to complete the 'tomorrow team' were being added slowly (despite limited funds). His players were operating in an enlightened ethos that, years later, some have labelled 'progressive'. They were prepared to give their all while battling for a manager who commanded respect and commitment, as well as developing faith in the long-term objectives he preached; to 'join the revolution' as Leighton James phrases it amid his own tribute to 'the best man-manager I've had in my life – by far'! The Durban blend was not of the 'instant' variety; it was for those who appreciated organisation and sustained quality.

Essentially, unrealistic expectations for dramatic, rapid change were what undermined Durban's term as Sunderland manager. When Everton slipped to a perilous 18th position in January 1984, an under-fire Howard Kendall was given time to achieve his goals; less than 18 months later, the FA Cup, First Division championship, and European Cup Winners' Cup were nestling in the Goodison Park trophy cabinet. A similarly under-pressure Alex Ferguson was afforded patience in early 1990, and FA Cup success bought him the time needed to restore the club's winning mentality. As well as patience, these managers also enjoyed reassuring backing in the transfer market. Sadly, as they prospered, Durban inherited the thankless task of trying to arrest the slide of an impoverished Cardiff City.

A decade later, Durban found himself back at Sunderland where he undertook scouting missions for Peter Reid. Although only serving a short stint, it was sufficient time for his judgement to be vindicated after recommending Watford's Kevin Phillips. The unheralded time and effort he devoted to assessing Phillips's goalscoring potential was particularly pleasing for Durban who recalled that the striker used to miss a fair number of openings that came his way, but his relentless ability to find those scoring positions convinced the former Roker boss that he was a player that Reid should invest in.

Amid the volatile atmosphere and poisonous infighting that often dominated the club's boardroom in the early 1980s, Sunderland, despite Cowie's claims, rarely looked capable or willing to 'think big'. Durban's long-term vision to build an honest and exciting team, brimming over with a quality blend of youth and 'know-how', was never likely to be allowed the necessary time to flourish.

The majority on the Sunderland board possessed neither the insight nor foresight to see the big picture and support Durban's plans to 'upmarket' the club. When courage and loyalty were required, they blinked, and a generation of Sunderland supporters missed out on the glories that might have been. Leighton James offers this analysis, 'Sunderland Football Club lost its way when Alan Durban was sacked, and almost 35 years later, with the exception of a few decent seasons, they are still suffering for it.'

Ultimately, Alan Durban's dream was doomed even as it burst into life on a sunny hope-filled day in June 1981. As he slowly worked his grand alchemy, too few had the patience to wait for tomorrow.

# Bibliography

Appleton, A., *Sunderland 1982 Soccer Annual* (Sunderland: Inkerman Publications).

*Roker Review* (Sunderland: Inkerman Publications, 1981–82).

*Roker Review* (Gateshead: Knight-Fletcher Print, 1982–84).

*Sunderland Echo* (1981–84).

*Sunderland Football Echo* (1981–84).